The Struggle over Democracy in the Middle East

Many residents of the Middle East—and more recently, Western powers—have placed great hope in democratization in the region. Yet authoritarianism remains the norm, and movement toward democracy is both slow and uneven.

Written primarily by experts from the region, *The Struggle over Democracy in the Middle East* examines democracy and democratization in the light of regional realities rather than the wishful thinking of outsiders. Specialists from the Middle East analyze democratic prospects in the region, while accomplished scholars from the United States and the United Kingdom analyze Western policy, providing a wide-ranging survey of the efforts of individual countries and the effect of external influences. Addressing themes including sectarianism, culture, religion, security, and the promotion of democracy, the book examines the experiences of activists, political parties, religious groups, and governments and highlights the difficulties involved in bringing democracy to the Middle East. Providing a multifaceted approach to the issue of democratization, this book will be a valuable reference for courses on Middle Eastern politics, political science, and democracy.

Nathan J. Brown is a professor of political science and international affairs at the George Washington University, where he is the director of the Institute for Middle East Studies. He also serves as a non-resident senior associate at the Carnegie Endowment for International Peace.

Emad El-Din Shahin is the Luce Professor of Religion, Conflict and Peace-building at the Kroc Institute for International Peace Studies at Notre Dame University. He was a visiting associate professor at the department of government at Harvard University (2006-2009), and associate professor in the political science department at the American University in Cairo. He specializes in Islam and politics, Arab and Muslim political thought, and political reform in the Middle East.

UCLA Center for Middle East Development (CMED) series

Series editors: Steven Spiegel, *UCLA* and Elizabeth Matthews, *California State University, San Marcos*

The UCLA Center for Middle East Development (CMED) series on Middle East security and cooperation is designed to present a variety of perspectives on a specific topic, such as democracy in the Middle East, dynamics of Israeli–Palestinian relations, Gulf security, and the gender factor in the Middle East. The uniqueness of the series is that the authors write from the viewpoint of a variety of countries so that, no matter what the issue, articles appear from many different states, both within and beyond the region. No existing series provides a comparable, multinational collection of authors in each volume. Thus, the series presents a combination of writers from different countries who, for political reasons, do not always publish in the same volume. The series features a number of subthemes under a single heading, covering security, social, political, and economic factors affecting the Middle East.

The Struggle over Democracy in the Middle East

Regional politics and external policies

**Edited By
Nathan J. Brown and Emad El-Din Shahin**

Routledge
Taylor & Francis Group

LONDON AND NEW YORK

First published 2010
by Routledge
2 Park Square, Milton Park, Abingdon, Oxon OX14 4RN

Simultaneously published in the USA and Canada
by Routledge
270 Madison Ave, New York, NY 10016

Routledge is an imprint of the Taylor & Francis Group, an informa business

© 2010 Editorial selection and matter Nathan J. Brown and Emad El-Din Shahin; individual chapters the contributors

Typeset in Times New Roman by
Taylor & Francis Books
Printed and bound in Great Britain by
CPI Antony Rowe, Chippenham, Wiltshire

British Library Cataloguing in Publication Data
A catalogue record for this book is available from the British Library

Library of Congress Cataloging in Publication Data
    The struggle over democracy in the Middle East : regional politics and external policies / [edited by] Nathan J. Brown and Emad El-Din Shahin.
        p. cm. – (UCLA Center for Middle East Development (CMED) series ; 1)
    Includes bibliographical references and index.
    1. Democratization–Arab countries. 2. Democratization–Middle East. 3. Democracy–Arab countries. 4. Democracy–Middle East. 5. Arab countries–Politics and government–1945-6. Middle East–Politics and government–1979- I. Brown, Nathan J. II. Shahin, Emad El-Din
    JQ1850.A91S77 2009
    320.956–dc22
                                2009012469

ISBN 978-0-415-77379-9 (hbk)
ISBN 978-0-415-77380-5 (pbk)
ISBN 978-0-203-86987-1 (ebk)

Contents

Illustrations

Tables

Figures

Contributors

Shlomo Avineri is professor of political science at the Hebrew University of Jerusalem. He served as director general of Israel's Ministry of Foreign Affairs in the first cabinet of Prime Minister Yitzhak Rabin, and has been involved in democracy-enhancement projects in post-communist countries in Eastern Europe.

Nathan J. Brown is professor of political science and international affairs at the George Washington University where he directs its Institute for Middle East Studies; he also serves as non-resident senior associate at the Carnegie Endowment for International Peace.

Shadi Hamid is vice chair of the Washington-based Project on Middle East Democracy (POMED), and was formerly the organization's director of research. He has also served as a program specialist on public diplomacy at the US Department of State and as a legislative fellow at the Office of US Senator Dianne Feinstein.

Amy Hawthorne is the founding director of the Hollings Center for International Dialogue and a former associate at the Carnegie Endowment.

Ersin Kalaycioglu is a full professor at Sabanci University, Istanbul, Turkey, and a student of comparative and Turkish politics.

Azza Karam is a senior advisor at the United Nations Population Fund in New York. Her areas of specialization are political Islam, international religious–cultural dynamics, transitional conflict, gender and human rights.

Walid Kazziha is chairman of the department of political science at the American University in Cairo. He gained his PhD from the London School of Oriental and African Studies. His main field of specialization is Middle East affairs, and his more recent publications have been in the area of political representation and democratization in the Arab world.

Bassel F. Salloukh is assistant professor of political science in the social sciences department at the Lebanese American University (LAU) in Beirut, Lebanon. He is also a non-resident senior researcher at the Interuniversity

Consortium for Arab and Middle East Studies, Montréal, Canada. His research interests include post-war state building and democratization in Lebanon, electoral engineering in divided societies, and changing regional alignments in the Middle East.

Emad El-Din Shahin is the Luce Professor of Religion, Conflict and Peace-building at the Kroc Institute for International Peace Studies at Notre Dame University. He was a visiting associate professor at the department of government at Harvard University (2006-2009), and associate professor in the political science department at the American University in Cairo. He specializes in Islam and politics, Arab and Muslim political thought, and political reform in the Middle East.

Richard Youngs is associate professor in the department of politics and international studies at the University of Warwick, UK, and director of the democratization programme at FRIDE in Madrid. He is the author of four books and the editor of nine volumes on different aspects of European foreign policy and international democratization.

Preface

The Center for Middle East Development of the International Institute at UCLA (CMED) is pleased to present the first installment in our book series on Middle East security and cooperation. The series is designed to offer discussions on the current problems in the Middle East with volumes that are unique because the participating authors are from a variety of countries and provide a range of perspectives on a specific topic. We envision that this diversity will contribute directly to the global discourse on the ongoing developments in the region.

The Editors want to extend our deepest gratitude to James Whiting, Acquisitions Editor for Middle Eastern & Islamic Studies, of Routledge, Taylor and Francis Group, who has served as such a critical asset to us in the complex preparation of these exciting, but complicated to prepare, volumes. We greatly appreciate the patience and dedication of Suzanne Richardson, Editorial Assistant, Middle East and Asian Studies for Routledge, Taylor & Francis Group, who assisted us so admirably in preparing this manuscript. We also want to extend our thanks to Professor David Newman, who first conceived of the exercise and placed us in contact with Routledge. And we deeply appreciate the work and gargantuan efforts that are being pursued by the editors and authors responsible for each volume, and of course our International Advisory Board. We also which to recognize the support to this project and CMED provided by the Institute on Global Conflict and Cooperation (IGCC) of the University of California based at UC San Diego.

UCLA's Center for Middle East Development (CMED) conducts research and provides educational programs on political, economic, and diplomatic development in the Middle East.

CMED programs approach these issues through a multi-tiered regional security program. Through reports and monographs, CMED explores key subjects on the region, including but by no means limited to democratic culture, regional business and economics, gender issues, media, technological cooperation across borders, and a full range of security and political issues including strategic challenges in cooperative and conflictual contexts and specific dynamics of regional problems such as the Arab-Israeli dispute, Iraq, and Iran. This series is a product of these studies and the promotion of intellectual interchange to which CMED is committed.

We expect that this volume and those that will follow will offer the highest possible quality to our readers so that we will be able to fulfill our goal of providing unique and stimulating discussions as the series expands. The series is four years in preparation, and we are delighted to present this first book, The Struggle over Democracy in the Middle East: Regional Politics and External Policies.

Over the past few years, the issue of democracy in the Middle East has provoked alternative waves of cynicism and irrational exuberance. Western pundits and policy makers have swung between viewing democracy as impossible or irrelevant (and maybe both) and as absolutely essential to world peace and security.

The manic Western debate over Middle East democracy has tended to obscure a more fine-grained and nuanced regional discussion. The purpose of this volume is to bring a variety of perspectives to the question; most of the contributors are from the Middle East and all have a deep familiarity with regional politics. The focus is much more on analysis than on policy prescription–though it might not be a bad idea if policy makers looked hard at an analysis of current realities before leaping into the fray of the efforts to promote political reform in the region.

The picture that emerges from the contributions to this volume is not particularly optimistic but they are not devoid of hope. When the volume's editors, Nathan J. Brown and Emad El-Din Shahin, ask themselves the question of whether democracy is occurring in the region, their answer is "In a word, no." But they hasten to add, "political developments in the region are far more interesting than the simple (if accurate) negative view suggests." What we present in this volume is that far more interesting picture of the struggle for democracy in the region.

Steven L. Spiegel, UCLA
Elizabeth G. Matthews, CSUSM

1 Introduction

Nathan J. Brown and Emad El-Din Shahin

This book is an effort to engage academics and activists interested in the Middle East with the prospects for democracy in the region. All of the contributors are familiar not only with the politics of the Middle East but also with various social science approaches to issues of democracy and democratization. The only authors not from the region itself are those who write on the policies of the United States and Europe.

A bleak landscape for democrats?

For many area experts, the state of democratic transformation in the Middle East region, particularly the Arab world, does not look promising. Most countries in the region are faced with obstinate domestic and external obstacles that make democracy seem like a distant dream. The peoples of the Middle East live under autocratic and authoritarian systems; few would question the desirability of the political systems becoming viable and functioning democracies. But paths of transition are far from obvious, and the dedication of key actors to the practical realities of democracy is questionable at best. Even the recent US and European Union (EU) drive to promote democracy has been blunted by the harsh and all too familiar press of security concerns and interests.

To many, therefore, the future of democracy in the region is bleak. Some might rightly reach this conclusion on the basis of persistent domestic structural obstacles, while it may appear to others that the future of democratic transformation (or any political change) in the region will always be predicated on the interest and security concerns of the external actors. After all, the Middle East is not Eastern Europe where Western security interests and democratic transition seemed to coincide for a decade.

When compared with countries in other regions, such as Latin America, Eastern Europe, and Africa, which had limited prior experience of democracy yet still managed to achieve some form of democratic transition, the countries of the Middle East stand out for the small and limited extent of change. Unlike those other areas, where political leaders lost their ability to manage events, autocratic regimes in the Middle East are in control of the process of political change. And most still enjoy the support and backing of the Western powers. Thus, when apparently democratizing changes occur, they deliver far less than they promise: elections are held on a regular basis but are not clean, pluralistic, or competitive; the legal and institutional structures associated with the rule of law are elaborate and often well established but restrictive and under executive domination; the scope of political and social association has been broadened but remains controlled and ineffective. Whenever the region seems to be taking a step forward toward transformation, countervailing strategies by nimble leaders and regimes seem to set the process several steps backwards.

Signs of hope?

There is thus much basis for despair, but a more thorough look at the state of the process of democratization in the region might still give some hope.

On the intellectual level, there are indications that democratic pressures are more deeply rooted than previously realized and reflect genuine local conditions more than external pressures. The debate over democracy is decades old. The Arab defeat in 1967 generated vigorous debates among Arab intellectuals about the need for democracy, citizenship rights, constitutional legitimacy, popular participation, government accountability, and the promotion of democratic values. Most of this debate remained confined to a small circle of intellectual elites and did not penetrate the grassroots levels until recently.

But that may be changing. Looking at the societal level, and bearing in mind that democratization is a gradual process, one can safely reach the conclusion that democracy is increasingly gaining roots and that the societies of the region are gradually acquiring experiences with democratic practices and institutions. That is clearly different from claiming that democracy is becoming a primary value for the people of the region. Other issues are perhaps far more important than democracy for most regional residents. This is, of course, true for those outside of the region as well, but in the Middle East, so many other issues seem especially pressing: military threats to Arab security and sovereignty; the daily struggle for social and economic survival; and the global threats to culture and identity. That might partially explain why people in the region are readily willing to protest against the Israeli and US military actions in the region and/or against cartoons defaming the prophet of Islam, while sporadically and reluctantly taking to the street to demand more freedoms. But even here, one can note a stronger social basis for democratic change: many residents of the region have come to see the battle for justice, security, survival, and identity as linked rather than opposed to the battle for democratic change.

At the level of the process, political opening and liberalization started in the region long before September 11, 2001, even before the collapse of the Berlin Wall in 1989. Egypt's political liberalization started only one year after the collapse of Franco's regime and Spain's transition to democracy. Tunisia allowed for some sort of pluralism in 1974, and moved from a single party to a multiparty system in 1981. Algeria's "perestroika" took place in 1989, the same year that marked the end of the communist regime in the Soviet Union and earlier than many East European countries. King Hussein of Jordan scrapped martial law in 1989 and legalized political parties in 1992. In 1989 and 1993, Jordan witnessed fairly free legislative elections. Contrary to the wide generalizations that view the Arab regimes as immune to changes, in fact, compared with two or three decades ago, the Arab regimes have been transforming in response to increasing pressures for political liberalization.

And it must be noted that democratic institutions and processes do exist in the Middle East, however frequently they are robbed of their vitality. Elections have been taking place in the Middle East region on a frequent and regular basis. According to Anoushiravan Ehteshami, "Elections have become a common feature of the political landscape of the Middle East and North Africa."[1] Within a decade (1989–99), eighty elections at the local, municipal, provincial, and national levels have taken place. Each year, one type of election was held in one or more countries in the region. Voter turnout has remarkably been very high ranging from 69 percent to almost 90 percent.[2] This does not necessarily mean that the region is really democratizing. In the Arab world, none of these elections produced major policy shifts or transformations of the system. (And since that period, only the Palestinian parliamentary elections of 2006 saw an incumbent party defeated.) In addition, it is difficult to characterize these elections as free and transparent. Most were carefully structured, and the election outcome was easily predicted. The elections were used to enhance the eroding legitimacy of Arab regimes and reinforce their claims of adhering to legal procedures and democratic practices. On the positive side, they may indicate in some cases that the people of the region are acquiring an experience and a culture of electoral practices that could be useful in any future democratic transformation.

While the motivations of leaders in allowing change can (and should) be questioned, the region has recently experienced some meaningful structural reforms, even in unlikely countries. In 1992, following the First Gulf War, Saudi Arabia introduced a series of reforms aimed at streamlining its system of government. It introduced the Basic Law of Government (a kind of constitution); established an *appointed* Consultative Council; and reorganized the Kingdom's provincial governance. More recently, municipal elections were held in 2005 (half the members of the local councils were directly elected). Official promises have been made to allow for Saudi women's participation in the next elections. If these promises are kept, they could certainly generate societal changes. Earlier in 2003, Saudi Arabia allowed for a structured National Dialogue to debate the prospects of reform, direct elections to an association of Saudi journalists, and the establishment of a semi-independent National Association for Human Rights in 2004. After intense debates and a long wait (since 1975), Kuwaiti women were finally granted the right to participate in the political process as voters and candidates, beginning with the

2006 parliamentary elections. For the first time in that country's history, a woman assumed a cabinet position. Over the past few years, Bahrain has embarked on a series of significant political reforms and structural changes that included the release of political prisoners, scrapping the emergency laws and state security courts, granting women the right to vote and to stand as candidates in the national elections, holding legislative elections in 2002 and again in 2006 by universal suffrage (restoring parliamentary life after a gap of nearly three decades). In 2002, six women were appointed to the Upper House, the *Shura* Council; and two years later, the first female minister joined the cabinet. In Qatar, voters voted for a constitution in 2003 that allowed for the establishment of a forty-five member parliament, two thirds of which is directly elected. The constitution also expanded the margin of political and civil rights and public freedoms as it guaranteed the freedom of association (although not the formation of political parties) and the freedom of expression. Other countries in the region with relatively long experience in liberalization, such Algeria, Egypt, and Morocco, introduced some reforms to their existing laws—electoral, press, party formation, and even constitutional amendments—to allow for some form of national reconciliation, more competitive elections, more political pluralism, and/or more freedom of expression. Across the Middle East, civil society organizations, particularly the advocacy oriented, emerged and gradually began to acquire some skills and address various reform demands.

A more realistic assessment

None of these reforms should be taken to indicate that there is a clear or linear movement toward democratization. Most of these steps are not only limited in effect but also double edged: the restoration of the Bahraini parliament, for instance, came with the creation of an appointed upper house designed to act as a check on the restored democratic body. And gerrymandering prevented the parliament from reflecting the true distribution of popularity among various political forces.

One of the most fundamental limitations of the wave of political reforms is closely related to the motivation behind them. All are top-down efforts undertaken to enhance the grip of faltering authoritarian or semi-authoritarian regimes on power. Most of these reforms are perceived to have been promoted by internal instability or external pressure. The rulers reacting to such pressures are seeking to parry off demands for future change; none have yet accepted democracy as a primary value. These reforms have been selectively designed to absorb domestic popular dissatisfaction, as well as to ease an increasing Western anxiety over their vital interests in the region. The driving force behind them is to address the need that most of these regimes feel to salvage their eroding legitimacy, prolong their authority, and continue to secure the support of outside actors. Once these regimes feel that the pressure has eased, they revert to their old repressive practices (witness the de-liberalization in

Jordan 2001, or in Egypt following the parliamentary elections in late 2005). The reforms are occurring in the absence of any clear vision of democracy as a concept and the instruments that would lead to its fulfillment. Incumbents seek a democratic transformation that falls short of the possibility of power transfer, fully accountable government, true representation, and the presence of effective political parties. Even those pressuring for reform often focus their demands on the transfer of power, without sufficiently considering the structural and institutional requisites that could make an effective democratic transformation and consolidation of democracy possible. There are growing demands for change and reform, but understanding of the mechanism to achieve them is still underdeveloped.

The seeming wave of reforms can be criticized on another basis as well: they may bring changes but, taken as a whole, they certainly do not amount to democratization and indeed barely affect the existing imbalances that continue to characterize the distribution of power among branches of the state and between state and society. There is a remarkable disparity between the powers of the executive and the legislature, which is almost controlled by the former. The heads of the executive in monarchical or republican systems alike enjoy extensive formal powers that range from vetoing their parliaments, appointing their cabinets, declaring states of emergency, suspending political life, or ruling by decree. And their informal powers—unwritten but very real rules by which they dominate the party system, the parliament, and sometimes the judiciary—augment their already formidable positions.

Thus, the legislative and monitoring powers of parliaments in the region are remarkably weak. This weakness precludes the possibility for the evolution of the necessary legal and constitutional frameworks that can effectively push the process of democratic transformation further. The existing parliaments usually succeed in passing laws that circumvent and outmaneuver the demands for reforms. Most parliaments in the region are not representative. They are often appointed rather than elected bodies. Sometimes their appointment comes in the formal sense, with some or all deputies appointed by the head of the state. More often, however, membership is formally elected but dominated by rigged electoral procedures and by a state party through a manipulated electoral system. Popular political actors are often excluded (or, in more recent years, included but marginalized), a phenomenon that adversely reflects on the effectiveness of the political life and the opposition parties.

One major consequence of this situation is that pro-reform actors remain unable to pass laws that promote a genuine democratic transformation. The continuous state of exclusion and marginalization also forces the opposition parties to atrophy and generates a state of apathy on the part of large segments of the population, often manifest by a conspicuously low voter turnout and widespread indifference to political life. In sum, the transformation that is currently taking place and the way it is being engineered should not conceal the persisting authoritarian practices, absence of adequate channels of participation, and low capacity of the opposition. Thus, the changes that have taken place have not limited the powers of the ruling elite or allowed for some form of real power sharing. At best, they open some limited political space; at worst, they merely mask the authoritarian nature of the regime and create a superficial atmosphere of change that allows for a further manipulation of the political process through cunning cooptation, containment, and/or repression.

One can still argue that, as cosmetic and manipulated these reforms may seem, they will certainly have a residual and incremental effect on the Middle Eastern society's capacity and experience with democratization. Several recent developments clearly reflect some positive signs. First, there is a growing realization on the part of the regimes that it is becoming increasingly difficult to maintain the status quo through the application of systematic violence and brutal force alone. Second, many Middle Eastern societies are increasingly willing and able to articulate public demands for reform and more political and social rights. The region has experienced an upsurge in demonstrations and public protests expressing such demands in the past few years. Third, despite the continued weakness of civil society, several pro-reform grassroots movements and groups have been formed, crystallizing at different times some form of an agreement over a list of political demands. Many have broken the fear barriers and put the regime and its leading members (the untouchable symbols) under close scrutiny. Finally, the states in the region have adopted a neoliberal economic model in an attempt to reform their economic performance. This model, which is based on liberalization and private initiative, should eventually reduce the state control and enhance the economic and political capacity of the society. Further, as the implementation of this model will produce losers, primarily the salaried middle classes and the lower classes, the regimes have to accompany the process with political openings to absorb these discontented groups.

The great challenge now for the pro-reform actors in the region lies in developing the necessary instruments to exploit the openings, limited though they are, that have occurred. And they cannot do so without casting democratic values and practices in terms that resonate with the region's particular history, culture, and socio-political realities. Such a process might be facilitated by several efforts: the development of an informal national consensus or even a more formal accord that guides present and future political practices; coalition building; preparing the necessary constitutional and legal frameworks for a transitional phase; insisting on independent monitoring of national elections; and neutralizing the external support for the authoritarian regimes in the region.

This volume

In this volume, we have asked a variety of scholars and activists in the region to examine the prospects for democracy from a variety of angles. But we have also asked external analysts to review and analyze the role of external actors who appear to have embraced the cause of Middle Eastern democratization so enthusiastically. We begin with those externally focused essays. Nathan J. Brown and Amy Hawthorne examine the evolution of American policy, emphasizing the evolutionary nature of American policy and its growing embrace of democratization. They argue that the Bush democratization agenda was less of a departure than it appeared: while it led to a brief but intense period of soaring reform rhetoric, it never found the policy tools to realize the vision and ultimately beat a retreat under intense pressures. While American support for democratization programs did not disappear, the effort reverted to the collection of modest, politically safe, and opportunistic efforts that characterized American democratization efforts in the region since their beginning in the 1990s. Richard Youngs explores European policy, focusing on the relationship between security and democratization. His frank discussion of the facile assumptions underlying the claimed coincidence of democratic values and security interests provides a sobering reminder of the quandaries faced by external actors. Youngs does not advocate a reversion to a cynical realism that abandons any claim of linkage between regional political reform and Western security interests. But he does observe that the two alternative approaches that have emerged in recent years—working for security through promoting reform and through ignoring it—rest uneasily with each other. No middle path has been found in which reform has become one of a set of tools for promoting Western security. Instead, in a sense, we have the worst of both worlds—much talk about political reform but little sustained commitment to it. The result is likely to be only deepening political cynicism among Western policy makers and regional publics. Youngs, Brown, and Hawthorne all describe external actors who base their policy on overlooking some difficult choices and unresolved contradictions.

Two scholars from the region also give a general overview of Middle East democratization efforts. Shlomo Avineri compares the Middle Eastern experience with that of other regions, with a special focus on the transitions in the former Soviet bloc. Avineri rejects a narrow cultural determinism, but his essay still points to some severe difficulties, such as lack of a usable democratic past; the weakness of civil society; and the weakness of democratic political culture. Avineri is just short of grim about regional realities, but he clearly views the challenges as enormous and believes that those who wish for reform in the region have been dealt a difficult hand indeed. He does find some kind words for external efforts but also cautions about excessive expectations. The clear conclusion is that democracy is a long and difficult historical process and much of the region is only—and at best—beginning that journey. Walid Kazziha starts from a very different point—one which rejects some of the cultural and historical claims of Avineri—but ultimately comes to similar conclusions about the outlook for democracy. He turns the focus to internal aspects of the struggle for democracy in the Arab world. While aware of external interest, Kazziha finds Western discussions strangely disconnected from those in the region. He does find that interest in democracy has a long history among intellectuals and therefore argues that the weakness of democracy is far less on the intellectual and much more on the practical level: a democratic environment will only emerge when genuine political constituencies appear on the scene and pave the way for the emergence of a vibrant political life in Arab societies. Until that time, talk about democracy will remain only talk.

In another essay focusing on the region as a whole, Azza Karam insists on questioning sharp divisions that are often taken to dominate politics in the region. She explores the main features of the debate on democracy occasioned by the rise of Islamist movements, examining Islamist stances toward democracy, the nature of their practices, and the reasons for and implications of their electoral appeal.

She shows how Islamist movements have arisen both because of the decline of secular movements and because of "blowback" from efforts by governments to suppress other forms of dissent or to use them for other purposes. Extremists in the region and in the West pursue the "clash of civilizations" and seem to wish for one, but there is far more common ground than the extremists want to see emerge.

The final section of the volume consists of a series of case studies: Egypt, Jordan, Lebanon, and Turkey. For Egypt, Emad El-Din Shahin assesses the political developments that Egypt has experienced over the past few years and the prospects for a democratic transformation. He analyzes the changes, or calculated reforms, that the regime has introduced to the system as a way to contain a growing popular discontent and outside pressure. He also investigates the impact of these changes on the political dynamics and major actors within Egyptian society. Shahin sees these changes to have produced positive political outcomes. However, they fall short of placing Egypt on a genuine democratic transformation.

Shadi Hamid turns our attention from a presidential republic to the Jordanian monarchy, testing the argument—surprisingly commonplace in recent years—that Arab monarchies are friendlier to democratization than republics. He thus examines the Jordanian experience in comparison with the republican Egyptian counterexample. He concludes that monarchies in the region have proven to be effective initiators of reform but that such efforts fall prey to clear structural and institutional limits.

In his essay, Bassel F. Salloukh poses the question of why democratic transition did not take place in Lebanon. Unlike the monarchies and the presidential republics, conditions in Lebanon would seem to be more favorable for democracy, but Salloukh demonstrates how sectarianism, regional factors, and external actors (including the US) have inhibited democratic development. Democratic structures and mechanisms have survived Lebanese confessionalism only by molding themselves completely to it.

Finally, Ersin Kalaycioglu examines the history of republican Turkey, focusing on the two poles of secularism and Islamism, or what he terms competing "positivist" and "Islamic revivalist" positions. Examining public opinion polls, he shows that the sharp dichotomy between the religious and secular dimensions at the level of the political elite seems to break down—at least in part—at the level of popular preferences and practices. In a sense, the relationship between religion and public life becomes less clear the closer one is to the ground. In some ways, Kalaycioglu is one of the volume's more sanguine authors. He is certainly not unaware of how complicated the issues are—noting at one point the odd feature of the wife of the country's current president earlier having pursued a lawsuit on a core emotional issue (women's head covering) against the government even while her husband sat as prime minister. Kalaycioglu views the struggle over Turkish culture and identity—as intractable as it seems—as increasingly amenable to democratic politics. Instead of suppressing the struggle or imposing a specific solution, the current incarnation of the Turkish republic is uneasily managing it through democratic structures and procedures. Ironically, it may be elections themselves (the very strong showing by the currently governing AKP party) that lead to an end to careful negotiation of Turkey's differences.

The essays in this volume thus examine a wide variety of experiences from a number of different perspectives. Despite this apparent cacophony, some strong areas of consensus emerge. We will turn our attention to those in the conclusion.

Notes

1 Anoushiravan Ehteshami, "Is the Middle East Democratizing?" *British Journal of Middle Eastern Studies* (1999): 199.
2 Ibid.: 204.

Part I
The view from outside
External efforts at democracy promotion

2 New wine in old bottles?

American efforts to promote democracy in the Arab world

Nathan J. Brown and Amy Hawthorne

In the years between 2002 and 2006, the United States suddenly embraced an ambitious project to promote democratization and political reform in the Arab world. The effort was startling for the rhetoric it produced and for the brashness of the vision. Yet a long-term look at American policy leaves a less revolutionary impression of the period. Prior to 2002, the US had experimented with political reform on the edges of a policy that was more centrally focused on security and economic issues. The Bush administration brought a far more robust spirit to the enterprise, but its policies in implementation never matched its rhetoric and ultimately were scaled back to resemble simply a more garrulous version of what had come before. While the Bush administration was willing to question past assumptions that had pushed democracy out to the margins of US policy, the answers it developed to those questions proved to be familiar ones.

Evolution of a policy

While the US prides itself on being one of the world's oldest democracies, promotion of democracy as a practical (and not merely rhetorical) element of US policy is little more than two decades old. It is true that the US did include defense of democracies among its war aims in World War I; after World War II, the US worked to install democratic political systems in some defeated countries. But spreading democracy was a secondary war aim in both instances; in the case of World War II, it did not become a noticeable goal until after the fighting had ceased, when the US set out to democratize Germany and Japan. And other American interventions—most notably in Latin America—hardly showed an unswerving focus on the promotion of democracy.

Indeed, during the Cold War, promotion of democracy was generally seen as a worthy but distant goal—even those who believed passionately in the universality of democratic values were easily persuaded to subordinate them to security concerns in the short term. A strong domestic consensus emerged that helped center policy on what the US was against (communism and Soviet expansionism) rather than what it was for. The US viewed with suspicion democratic transitions (such as in Portugal in 1974) and democratically elected leaders (such as Allende in Chile) when they seemed to lean away from the US in foreign policy. The American consensus began to break apart in the 1970s, however. Despite this, both left and right eventually traveled roads that wound up in a similar location: promotion of democracy.

On the left, the aftermath of the Vietnam War led many to charge that the US had greatly overstated the threat posed by the Soviet Union and forgotten its own fundamental values in the process. In 1977, President Jimmy Carter endorsed this feeling as part of an effort to push human rights to the center of American policy:

> Being confident of our own future, we are now free of that inordinate fear of communism which once led us to embrace any dictator who joined us in that fear. I'm glad that that's being changed. For too many years, we've been willing to adopt the flawed and erroneous principles and tactics of our adversaries, sometimes abandoning our own values for theirs. We've fought fire with fire, never thinking that fire is better quenched with water. This approach failed, with Vietnam the best example of its intellectual and moral poverty. But through failure we have now found our way back to our own principles and values, and we have regained our lost confidence.[1]

Carter's human rights campaign, while accompanied by strong rhetorical commitment, was implemented through tools that seem rudimentary in retrospect: reporting (a year before Carter took office, Congress had mandated that the State Department report annually on the state of human rights) and limited diplomatic pressure.

Carter's policy provoked a strong backlash from the right, which charged that it treated America's authoritarian allies more harshly than its adversaries in the totalitarian communist bloc.[2] But when Ronald Reagan succeeded Jimmy Carter, he inched toward a more ambitious form of democracy promotion than Carter had pursued. There were three motivations for Reagan's new focus on democracy. First, it highlighted the ideological nature of the contest between the US and the Soviet Union. Second, in selected locations (such as the Philippines), the US finally found what it had sought for three decades: credible anti-communist democrats. This made it less necessary to choose between advancing short-term security and long-term democratic objectives. Third, aid to such democrats provided an answer to domestic critics on the left who charged that the US had allied itself with unsavory regimes in the battle against communism.

In El Salvador, the Philippines, and South Korea, the Reagan administration (initially reluctantly but eventually with enthusiasm) supported democratic elections that replaced decades-old authoritarian regimes. Yet, like the Carter administration's approach, the Reagan administration used a collection of tools that seem crude in retrospect. First, there was a tremendous emphasis on founding or transition elections as the pinnacle of democratization, following which attention on a democratizing country often quickly faded. Second, other aspects that later came to be seen as critical to democracy promotion (such as encouragement of civil society) received virtually no attention—the intellectual and institutional tools that later seemed an essential part of democracy promotion existed in embryonic form at best and were not yet part of the democracy promotion lexicon. Third, promotion of democratic transition often consisted of support for specific, non-communist leaders—this was most notably the case in central and Eastern Europe where a small group of activists and dissidents emerged as heroes, lending the policy a very personalistic tone. As the approach spread elsewhere, building democracy often seemed more a matter of supporting individual democrats than focusing on democratic structures. Yet while the naïveté of such approaches may seem clear in retrospect, it must also be noted that it was in this period that the basic tools and structures of democracy promotion were built. Most notably, Congress established the National Endowment for Democracy (NED) in 1983. The NED, a government-funded, privately run organization, was a leading conduit for democracy aid during the Reagan administration. The National Democratic Institute and the International Republican Institute, democracy organizations informally affiliated with the two US political parties, were also created during these years and supplied with government funding.

Thus, by the end of the Cold War, both left and right had different (and somewhat vague) versions of democracy promotion moving toward the center of their foreign policy agenda. Central America was an early (and fairly contentious) proving ground, but when democratic transitions took place in the mid- to late-1980s in South America, there was little dissent about the idea that the US should enthusiastically support the process. Many American organizations (both governmental and non-governmental) accumulated their first set of practical experiences in democracy promotion in the Latin American transitions. And when the collapse of the Soviet bloc (as well as later transitions in some parts of Africa and Asia) finally removed the central point of contention between left and right, the different visions began to meld into a coherent consensus. Equally important, the collapse of the Soviet Union, the consequent diminution of overriding security concerns, and the welcoming of international assistance by formerly Soviet bloc states erased any trace (at least at a global level) of a perception that the US had to choose between its ideals and security. When transitions occurred in various parts of Asia and Africa, there was no ideological divide preventing a supportive American response. Moreover, there were some clear success stories that appealed to various parts of the American political spectrum—the fall of communist governments gave the center and right a feeling of vindication; the fall of authoritarian governments in South America and a racist government in South Africa inspired the center and the left. The world was safe for promoting democracy: democracy was both realistic and a guarantor of a more secure American future.

The emergence of the democracy industry

After 1989, therefore, the US plunged into democracy promotion with a dedication that it had lacked for decades. Underlying the new enthusiasm was a general mentality rather than a well-honed philosophy. This mentality— enunciated in countless policy statements and addresses—identified the pursuit of democracy as consistent with—and even highly supportive of—other American foreign policy goals. It emerged during the first Bush administration, and sharpened under the Clinton presidency. American officials bundled together market reforms, rule of law, respect for human rights, and democracy as if they were mutually reinforcing and sometimes even interchangeable. Capitalism and market reforms were seen as buttressing political reform and as consistent with American economic and security interests. Economic and political reform seemed virtually coterminous.

Even a more traditional security focus seemed to favor democracy promotion. The argument that democracies rarely fight wars against each other buttressed a general feeling that American security could be enhanced by the spread of democracy. More specifically, the spread of democracy would aid the incorporation of former communist states into a security order favorable to the US and its allies.

The demise of military rule in South America and of communism in Europe obscured the essentially reactive nature of the American interest (as well as the exclusion of the Arab world from a perceived global trend). But the attention to democracy was not modest: whereas in the past, there was an excessive concentration on electoral democracy (and even more specifically on the founding or transitional elections), now democratization was taken to encompass a whole host of developments from constitutional reform to the development of civil society. Most remarkable, perhaps, was the simultaneous promotion of market reform and democratization—and the effort to portray this effort as the logical successor to the Cold War. Speaking at the beginning of the Clinton administration, National Security Advisor Anthony Lake proclaimed:

> In such a world, our interests and ideals compel us not only to be engaged, but to lead. And in a real-time world of change and information, it is all the more important that our leadership be steadied around our central purpose.
>
> That purpose can be found in the underlying rationale for our engagement throughout this century. As we fought aggressors and contained communism, our engagement abroad was animated both by calculations of power and by this belief: to the extent democracy and market economics hold sway in other nations, our own nation will be more secure, prosperous and influential, while the broader world will be more humane and peaceful.
>
> The expansion of market-based economics abroad helps expand our exports and create American jobs, while it also improves living conditions

and fuels demands for political liberalization abroad. The addition of new democracies makes us more secure because democracies tend not to wage war on each other or sponsor terrorism. They are more trustworthy in diplomacy and do a better job of respecting the human rights of their people.[3]

Perhaps more significant, the US no longer relied primarily on high-level diplomacy in order to purse democratization. Alongside hortatory and diplomatic pressure, US efforts came to depend heavily on assistance. Various bureaucratic actors became involved as democracy promotion was gradually built into the American foreign policy machinery and new positions were created to oversee the large amounts of democracy aid devoted to Eastern Europe and the former Soviet Union and to follow the issue for the National Security Council and the State Department. But the most significant actor in the area of assistance (at least in terms of its budget) was the US Agency for International Development (USAID). USAID, an organization that had previously been devoted to economic growth, social development, and infrastructure, and that had striven to avoid any direct work on politics, now found itself called upon to pursue an ambitious and deeply political agenda throughout the world, including some regions where it had never operated, such as Russia. As much USAID work began to be carried out through contractors, an industry rapidly emerged as older development-oriented companies and organizations quickly added democratization to their repertoire in order to expand their work and benefit from the new stream of funding.

The US was hardly alone in the field: other donor states (most particularly but not exclusively European) also showed a striking new dedication to the promotion of democracy. Some countries pioneered in ways which the US learned to emulate—such as the German experiment with party foundations. Even the two chief international financial institutions, the World Bank and the International Monetary Fund (IMF), showed a far greater interest in "governance," although they almost always shied from using the term "democratization." Each participant brought a particular set of priorities and interests, but the general list of activities—including matters such as the promotion of elections, civil society, rule of law, constitution writing, commercial law reform— was consistent across most donors and recipients. And in some major multilateral efforts—in Bosnia, Kosovo, and East Timor, for instance—American non-governmental organizations (NGOs), private firms, and governmental agencies not only took a major role themselves but also showed a capacity to learn about other orientations and approaches to political reconstruction and democracy assistance.

The US was unusual internationally in the degree to which priorities were set not simply by the executive but also by the legislative branch, with the result that particular constituencies—such as those for labor rights and religious freedom—had an impact on the nature of US policy. Their influence was felt particularly in the arena of reporting, in which Congress directed the executive branch to report on respect for human rights in key countries.

A byproduct of this developing set of tools to promote democracy was to render it dependent on the presence of access and aid: democracy was generally promoted in those countries that accepted assistance. If access was denied or no assistance relationship prevailed, the US found it far more difficult to implement democracy aid programs. Some in the US government persevered in promoting democracy in very difficult circumstances, but even in such cases, the salience of democracy promotion in US policy often declined in the absence of a supportive political climate. There were some notable exceptions, to be sure: the US was capable of using democracy quite prominently as an ideological weapon against regimes deemed unfriendly in such countries as Burma, Cuba, and Iraq. But in many other countries, the claimed coincidence between promoting democracy and protecting US security simply did not seem to apply: in places as diverse as China, the Central Asian republics, and Pakistan, the US allowed general security concerns and economic interests to eclipse efforts to democratize in a manner that a cold warrior would quickly recognize.

Democracy promotion in the Arab world prior to September 11

The impact of the reliance on aid and the prioritization of security on US policy toward the Arab world was to form a minor element of US policy—although it was not totally ignored. The reasons for the downgrading of democracy were obvious. Many Arab leaders were close allies of the US, providing support for US political economic and security interests in the region. US officials during the George H.W. Bush and Clinton administrations also viewed authoritarian Arab regimes as bulwarks against the Islamist opposition movements that were gaining ground in the early 1990s. Even unfriendly authoritarian governments, such as Syria's, Libya's, and Iraq's, seemed preferable to Islamist alternatives. The apparent absence of any viable pro-democracy, pro-American movements in the region also gave the US a ready excuse for its lackluster support for democratization. In sum, throughout the 1990s and through the first eight months of the George W. Bush administration—that is, before the attacks of September 11, 2001—the US saw the undemocratic status quo as far preferable to the instability and anti-Western sentiment that many feared would sweep the region were authoritarian rulers to fall from power.

The US did not completely ignore the issue of democratization, however. Beginning in the early 1990s, in testimony before Congress, State Department officials (although never the most senior ones) commended the modest liberalizing steps initiated by some Arab governments, such as the controlled multiparty parliamentary elections held in Yemen, Jordan, and Morocco. (Their remarks tended to be generic, pointing to the importance of "pluralism," and avoiding any criticism of friendly Arab governments.) Some Clinton administration officials saw potential for the first Arab democracy to emerge in the West Bank and Gaza under the new Palestinian Authority, although at the highest administration echelons support for Yasser Arafat and for the development of a powerful Palestinian security apparatus always trumped concerns about democratic practice taking root.

The first Arab world democracy aid programs dated back over a decade before the attacks of September 11, 2001—they were launched during the George H.W. Bush administration. They took the form of small-scale projects that aimed to promote good governance, accountability, and the rule of law, all of which were seen to buttress the market-based economic reforms that were the US priority at the time. Middle East democracy aid expanded in the Clinton administration, reflecting Clinton's emphasis on democracy promotion as a global theme. The largest projects were implemented by USAID in Egypt and the West Bank and Gaza, drawing on funds from the massive economic aid packages the US channeled to both places. These were multi-year initiatives to build up parliament, NGOs, and the court system. In 1997, the State Department created the much smaller Middle East Democracy Fund, which allocated up to $3 million a year to support small-scale projects for elections, parliamentary development, and political party training in Algeria, Morocco, and Yemen. The motivations for such democracy aid were multiple. Many US officials believed that Arab countries' gradual moves toward political liberalization would advance economic liberalization, which was the main US reform priority for the region at the time. There was also a general sense that small doses of democracy aid would help to combat Islamist fundamentalism. Officials who championed global democratization and human rights as the hallmark of the post-Soviet era did not want the US to leave democracy off the agenda in any region, including the Middle East.

The democracy aid projects of the 1990s generally were quite cautious. Most programs were fairly unimaginative, reflecting the tendency to borrow templates from programs implemented in democratizing regions, such as Eastern and central Europe, instead of developing strategies tailored for the authoritarian, pre-democracy transition conditions of Arab countries. The US avoided controversial initiatives that would irritate friendly Arab governments or that seemed to be an intervention in local politics. And most projects were quite technical, rather than political, in nature. For example, parliamentary assistance programs aimed to improve the research capacities and efficiency of legislatures without addressing the underlying reasons for their weakness, such as domination by the executive branch. Rule of law programming tended to focus on making courts more efficient, encouraging alternative dispute resolution, and bringing commercial codes in line with prevailing international standards, rather than tackling the more serious, and more sensitive, issues of human rights abuses and corruption. Civil society strengthening tried to improve the management of Arab NGOs while sidestepping the issue of repressive laws restricting associative life. Some issues seemed off limits entirely. Democracy aid carefully avoided any initiatives that addressed the issue of political Islam too directly or that supported opposition groups. And while a few Arab governments (Morocco, Yemen, and the Palestinian

Authority) allowed international observers for their elections, most regimes staunchly refused.

Furthermore, Jordan, Tunisia, and most of the Gulf Cooperation Council (GCC) countries rejected democracy assistance altogether. The wealthy GCC countries had no need for foreign aid and the democracy aid that often accompanied it, as they had a far easier way of earning US dollars: selling oil. And the US showed little interest in imposing a democratization agenda on these allies. The sole—and quite partial—exception was Kuwait in 1991, where domestic groups pressing for a restoration of parliament after liberation from the Iraqi occupation found a sympathetic ear in the US Embassy. (And even Kuwait, the country most obviously dependent on the US in security terms, felt comfortable soon after its liberation from Iraqi occupation in banning activities sponsored by the International Republican Institute.) Even countries receiving tremendous US assistance still managed to fend off democratization programs they found noxious. For a quarter century, the largest US development assistance program in the region was in Egypt. The USAID mission there crept into issues of governance and rule of law in the 1990s, but under the terms of the aid relationship, the Egyptian government could approve or veto all democracy aid projects. This had the effect of stripping the assistance of any "political" character and of putting democracy programs under the control of Husni Mubarak's regime.

On the diplomatic level, efforts to encourage democratic change in Arab countries were sporadic and restricted to mid-level State Department officials. Public statements usually took the form of praise for Arab leaders' very modest steps toward political reform. Criticism of authoritarian practices was rare indeed if not absent, with Arab leaders typically escaping even mild censure for manipulated elections or arrests of dissidents. Most notably, neither the president nor senior administration officials ever uttered a public word about Middle East democracy during the Clinton administration. The lack of interest in the topic was clear in a 2000 speech delivered by then Secretary of State Madeleine Albright, in which she extolled the Clinton administration's global democracy promotion efforts and described the march of democracy around the world—but made no mention of the absence of democracy in the Middle East. And according to US diplomats who worked on US–Middle East relations prior to September 11, 2001, democracy and human rights issues were never included on the agendas of meetings with Arab leaders—indeed, the idea of raising the issue at the highest levels of government was simply unthinkable.

A radical new approach to democracy promotion in the Arab world?

As a result of this hesitant approach to democracy promotion in the Arab world, US policy was often denounced as hypocritical because it coupled platitudes about the importance of democracy with cozy relationships with authoritarian regimes. Why, it was asked, was the Arab world the only region of the globe excluded from American championing of human rights and freedom? After the attacks of September 11, 2001, some Bush administration officials themselves adopted the core of this critique. They believed that the magnitude of the attacks required a Middle East policy re-orientation of similar magnitude. Although discussions about using the promotion of democracy as a tool to fight Al Qaeda and to dampen anti-American sentiment in the region began both inside and outside the administration (among Washington journalists and think-tank scholars) within days of the attacks, the transformation in rhetoric and in policy was more gradual. It took a year before a leading official publicly acknowledged that US policy toward the Middle East had been operating in error and suggested a new approach. In December 2002, Richard Haass (then director of policy planning at the US Department of State) pled guilty to a gentle version of the criticism:

> At times, the United States has avoided scrutinizing the internal workings of countries in the interests of ensuring a steady flow of oil, containing Soviet, Iraqi and Iranian expansionism, addressing issues related to the Arab–Israeli conflict, resisting communism in East Asia, or securing basing rights for our military. Yet by failing to help foster gradual paths to democratization in many of our important relationships—by creating what might be called a "democratic exception"—we missed an opportunity to help these countries become more stable, more prosperous, more peaceful, and more adaptable to the stresses of a globalizing world.[4]

Haass's 2002 speech was echoed in a far gentler version by Secretary of State Colin Powell the following week; Powell announced a very modest $29 million start to the "Middle East Partnership Initiative," a new set of programs designed to place "the United States firmly on the side of change, of reform, and of a modern future for the Middle East."[5] But Powell backed off the self-criticism and reverted to the traditional US pattern of lauding positive examples by friendly regimes rather than rebuking allies. The theme was eventually picked up by President Bush himself, but not until a year later, when, in the run-up to the US invasion of Iraq, he asserted that a regime change in that country would allow democracy to take root there and that a democratic Iraq would generate a wave of democratization across the region.[6] Then, in November 2003, Bush announced a "new policy" toward the Arab world:

> Sixty years of Western nations excusing and accommodating the lack of freedom in the Middle East did nothing to make us safe—because in the long run, stability cannot be purchased at the expense of liberty. As long as the Middle East remains a place where freedom does not flourish, it will remain a place of stagnation, resentment, and violence ready for export. And with the spread of weapons that can bring catastrophic harm to our country and to our friends, it would be reckless to accept the status

quo. Therefore, the United States has adopted a new policy, a forward strategy of freedom in the Middle East.[7]

After Bush's re-election in 2004, the "freedom agenda" for the Middle East, as the administration called it, became even more central to official American rhetoric—it served as the basis for Bush's inaugural address and early in Bush's second term was reiterated often by Secretary of State Condoleezza Rice and other senior officials. This rhetoric was affirming to those longing to see the US use its global bully pulpit to push for freedom, and jarring to Arab leaders as well as to US officials skeptical of the new emphasis on democracy.

The full logic behind the shift is difficult to detail, partly because policy statements remained fairly vague even as they grew increasingly sweeping in scope, and partly because some of the most enthusiastic advocates of the policy shift were not members of the administration but influential writers, journalists, and intellectuals outside government, both affiliated with and independent from the Bush administration. (In fact, many administration officials, mainly in the Near East Bureau at the Department of State, were dubious about the new policy and pushed back against its implementation.)

But the logic of the policy, if vaguely articulated, was still clear in its general thrusts. Regimes in the Arab world were denounced as both authoritarian and unimpressive in their economic performance. Their policy failures were held to prompt deep social and political resentments to which the undemocratic systems of the region could not respond effectively, encouraging the rise of radical Islamist movements. Some of these movements sparked not only domestic unrest but also international terrorism aimed against the US and its allies. The structures and practices of democratic governance would channel political and social protest in a constructive direction, dampen the appeal of radical movements, and lead to better economic performance, enhancing the prospects for long-term stability in the region. Those within the region who denounced liberal democracy as a Western imposition would lose their audience as democracy's benefits became clear; democratization would allow Arab liberals, long suppressed by Arab regimes, to emerge as a powerful force to fight Islamist radicalism. In addition, because the long US support of authoritarian regimes had created mistrust of the US among Arab publics, it was thought that a shift in US policy to push for democratic change would help the US gain regional allies in its fight against Al Qaeda and other extremist movements.

As the US had spoken in subdued tones about democracy and liberal values in the Middle East but had never repudiated them, the rhetorical shift was not total. But it was striking. Since sustained American involvement in the region began after World War II, the US has pursued a policy fundamentally based on preserving the status quo. The watchwords for much of the period were not "transformation," "democracy," or "reform" but "stability" and "moderation." Yet many US officials came to view the status quo they protected for so long as itself deeply flawed and in need of radical revision. In one 2002 forum, one of the authors heard a mid-level official—often identified with the more radical features of Bush administration policy—say, "I think chaos in the region would be a good thing."

The Bush administration's policy featured frequent declarations by the President himself about the need for democratic change in the region as well as occasional public comments gently pressing friendly Arab leaders to democratize. When Egyptian President Husni Mubarak visited Bush's Texas ranch in 2004, for instance, Bush exhorted him to strengthen democratic institutions and expand political participation in his country. Such public comments to a close US ally were unprecedented. The need for Egypt and other friendly countries to launch political reforms was echoed regularly by the Secretary of State and other senior officials in public and private.

The administration initially pushed the new democracy policy hardest in Iraq and Palestine, where the complications seemed fewer: for reasons unrelated to democracy, the Americans wished to see leadership change. There was no need to choose between cultivating friendly leaders and promoting democratic change: in both Iraq and Palestine, the Bush administration viewed the leaders as unfriendly and wanted them ousted. Perhaps because these cases allowed the administration to avoid hard choices, Iraq and Palestine seemed to become the fulcrum of the new policy to transform the region. Democracy became a convenient—although not necessarily insincere—rubric for packaging US policy that had several different motivations. The same impulse was evident in US policy toward Syria, where the US opposed President Bashar al-Asad for a variety of reasons, not simply because of his authoritarian leadership, but often highlighted the non-democratic character of the regime. In March 2005, Secretary of State Condoleezza Rice summarized American anger at Syrian policy on Lebanon, Iraq, and terrorism by reference to democracy: "Syrian policies and Syrian behavior are barriers to a better life and a more democratic future for the people of the Middle East."[8]

The Bush administration also dramatically increased regional democracy aid, pouring tens of millions of dollars into the effort to democratize post-Saddam Iraq and creating democracy promotion initiatives for the rest of the region. Most prominent was the Middle East Partnership Initiative (MEPI), launched by the State Department in late 2002 after the speech by Secretary of State Powell mentioned earlier. MEPI funds Arab and American organizations working to promote political, educational, and economic reform and the expansion of women's rights. MEPI operates across the region, including in countries where Arab governments had previously rejected the idea of democracy assistance such as Tunisia and some Arabian Peninsula states. MEPI has received up to $88 million in annual congressional appropriations since its establishment.[9] The administration also expanded the funding and scope of Middle East democracy programs run by USAID and by the State Department's Bureau of Democracy, Human Rights, and Labor (DRL) and doubled funds for the National Endowment for Democracy's Middle East initiatives. Older bureaucratic structures—such as the State Department, the intelligence community, and USAID—were asked to restructure themselves in ways appropriate for the new emphasis on democracy promotion. American embassies in the Arab world, which often worked to smooth relations between the US and their hosts, were asked to re-orient themselves to place more emphasis on encouraging Arab governments to open up—for instance, each embassy has been required to designate an officer responsible for MEPI. And such officials moved Arab democracy—albeit in a hesitant manner—on to the multilateral agenda in 2004 by launching the "Broader Middle East and North Africa Initiative" of the G-8, which encourages reform through diplomatic dialogue, aid, and technical assistance (its offshoots include the Forum for the Future and the Foundation for the Future).[10]

Implementing the new policy or repackaging the old one?

But the problem for the US was that it had little experience and even less success in more confrontational policies supporting democracy. Success stories in the field of democracy promotion almost all come from countries already enjoying significant momentum toward democracy and enthusiasm for international support. Despite some stirrings of reform since 2001, Arab countries remained in an authoritarian mode; their governments only grudgingly allowed (and sometimes sought to water down or even block) MEPI and other assistance programs. Furthermore, the democracy industry was far more experienced in techniques associated with supporting the consolidation phase of democratization than in stimulating its initial steps—the approach that is generally called for in the Arab environment. The democracy promotion community was still grappling to formulate a strategy appropriate for the unique set of challenges presented by the Arab world. These included entrenched authoritarian systems strengthened by oil revenues, weak liberal democratic movements, and strong Islamist oppositions with an uncertain commitment to democracy and hostility to the US role in the region. The pervasive suspicion about US policy among Arab publics, which led some important Arab civil society groups and other potential reform partners to shun US assistance, represented an additional challenge that the Bush administration could not resolve.

The vision of a *pax democratica Americana* was problematic as well because of an odd feature it shared with older efforts: it assumed congruence with other US goals. The US was now claiming to fight terrorism, prevent the spread of weapons of mass destruction, promote economic liberalization, pursue Arab–Israeli peace, guarantee the free flow of oil, and spur Arab democratization—all at the same time. While the new emphasis on democracy promotion might rearrange some of the elements on this agenda, it did not disavow it, and there was no sign that the traditional US policy goals had decreased in importance. The Bush administration did not provide a systematic explanation about how to balance these interests and never developed a coherent approach, even for a single Arab country. The hope seemed to be that (at least in the long run) the goals were consistent and perhaps even mutually reinforcing. Whether or not this was true in the long term, it quickly became clear that, in the short term, some of these goals pulled the US in contradictory directions. The radical vision provided few clues on how to sort out conflicting claims on policy.

This was sometimes a problem in terms of the signals it sent to the region—leaders and activists in the Middle East strove to uncover how serious the new US determination was and what form it would take. But it was perhaps a more serious problem at home. Different parts of the machinery of the US government showed varying degrees of enthusiasm for the project. MEPI was established inside the State Department to pursue the cause, but older diplomats in the Bureau of Near Eastern Affairs worried that other US goals might be harmed by MEPI's enthusiasm. USAID regarded MEPI warily as a new actor long on political connections and short of experience. The close identification of the cause with an increasingly unpopular president weakened congressional support for the new policies, even among those sympathetic to the reform cause. In short order, the Bush administration earned a reputation for declaring goals without knowing how to pursue them.

And in practice, democracy failed to trump, or even seriously compete with, other interests. The abiding concern of many US officials that democratic change in the region would produce new governments opposed to US policy suppressed for a few years beneath President Bush's confidence about democratization, resurfaced in force after the Hamas victory in the Palestinian legislative elections of January 2006. The administration had pushed hard for the elections and seemed genuinely stunned when Hamas won; after a period of confusion, a new policy of pushing Hamas from power emerged, replacing the focus on democracy. Despite triumphalist rhetoric after elections in Lebanon and Iraq, the Bush administration seemed unsure of how to deal with the strengthening of Islamist forces and the parliamentary gridlock that followed those elections.

As the US position in Iraq deteriorated, Iran rose as a regional power and its nuclear program loomed larger in American thinking, and open warfare broke out between Israel and Hizbullah, older security concerns forced themselves on US policy makers. As they lurched from crisis to crisis, long-term political reform no longer pressed itself on their minds as urgently.

And most critically, designing policy for countries where the US maintains a closer and deeper relationship with the leadership (Egypt, Morocco, Saudi Arabia, Jordan) proved difficult. Perhaps unsurprisingly, the actual process of pursuing democracy in a region where the US has many other countervailing goals and interests—the same ones that existed prior to September 11, 2001—resembled the previous policy more than much of the strong rhetoric might seem to imply. In Egypt, for instance, the administration displayed ambivalence about how hard to push Husni Mubarak—an important ally on Israeli–Palestinian peace and the "war on terror"—to ensure that the 2005 parliamentary elections would be free and fair. It was able to muster up only slight, and belated, criticism of the deeply flawed vote, and Mubarak managed to rebuff much of the criticism. The strong showing of the Muslim Brotherhood in those elections, followed a few weeks later by the Hamas victory, made US officials suddenly nervous that too rapid political openings in Arab countries would bring forces unfriendly to US interests to power. The enthusiasm for democracy promotion quickly dissipated and the policy stalled. By mid-2006, the administration's public criticism of the Mubarak regime—once a prominent sign of the application of the freedom agenda—had receded, as had critical comments about other pro-American Arab governments. And by this time, Arab leaders, initially quite unsettled by the administration's forceful democracy rhetoric, began to regain their footing and to feel more comfortable mollifying the US with cosmetic reforms or, as time went on, ignoring US entreaties altogether. In his May 2008 address at the World Economic Forum in Sharm El Sheikh, Egypt, President Bush gently prodded Mubarak to expand political reforms, but the Egyptian leader did not even bother to attend the speech.

Concerning democracy aid, the basic template for most programs remained similar to those that were implemented in the 1990s—projects were still relatively cautious and lacked a strategic approach. Although MEPI supported some valuable initiatives, many of its programs recreated those earlier efforts (working with established civil society groups, training judges, supporting civic education with a very technical approach) and generally avoided the most sensitive areas and direct challenges to existing regimes. As it did prior to September 11, the US quietly included mainstream Islamist parties in its modest training in Algeria, Yemen, and Morocco (as part of a broader effort to strengthen political parties in the region). Yet the administration never developed a coherent aid strategy toward political Islam: was the underlying strategy to promote "moderate" Islamist movements through engagement and democracy aid, or was it to build up pro-US alternatives to Islamists and ruling regimes? Sometimes American NGOs associated with the US democratization project (such as the National Democratic Institute) pursued projects that were a little bolder in intention and design (making even supportive US officials a little nervous). Far more often, however, the basic thrust was to encourage friendly authoritarian regimes to reform by gradually transforming themselves. Unfriendly regimes such as Syria's, of course, received quite different treatment, but this was nothing new—US officials never had any difficulty criticizing the governance practices of regimes they disliked. The main change in such instances was simply a sharpening of the rhetoric and a greater enthusiasm for meeting with dissidents.

Initially, Iraq stood out as the most complete departure possible from past efforts at democratization; military invasion was not part of the standard democratization tool kit in the 1980s and 1990s. The US effort to build democracy in Iraq was quite unusual and therefore served as the centerpiece of the new policy. For several years after the invasion, the administration continued to champion the goal of democratizing the region through democratizing

Iraq. In late 2005, National Security Advisor Stephen Hadley proclaimed, "A democratic Iraq will serve as a beacon of liberty, inspiring democratic reformers throughout the Middle East. As freedom and democracy spread, it will ultimately lead to a Middle East that is more peaceful, more stable, and more inhospitable to terrorists and their supporters."[11]

By having given central place to Iraq, the US government may have created not a keystone but an albatross for regional democratization efforts. Within the administration and in Congress, Iraq dominated US policy, sucking up resources and attention. By 2005, as conditions in Iraq worsened, violence surged, and pro-Iranian parties gained influence, democracy promotion faded as a priority in rhetoric and action; some US officials (and some Iraqis) expressed doubts that Iraq could ever become a functioning democracy. And not only did US policy in Iraq frighten away possible partners for the US project in the region by connecting democracy promotion with regime overthrow and by presenting a terrifying vision of what could follow when authoritarian governments actually fell, it also tended to dominate the bilateral agenda with many countries, edging democracy aside. In Jordan and many of the Gulf states, for instance, the US probably pushed reform and democracy far more gently because of those countries' helpful role in the US military effort in Iraq. And in the longer term, growing uneasiness at home about the war in Iraq (and its aftermath) began to cut away at domestic support for the Bush administration's policy of trying to transform the region.

Conclusion: forward to the past

The US invasion and occupation of Iraq was accompanied by a stunning change in US rhetoric toward democracy in the Arab world. Previously, the US had rarely acted in favor of democratic change in the region; the occasional statements of US officials were subdued in tone and content and often went justifiably unnoticed. A variety of fairly gentle policy tools that appeared to constitute an afterthought to the main thrust of US policy were deployed in support of a low-key effort to encourage democracy. But in 2002, the US rhetorical and aid commitment to Middle East democracy increased dramatically. At the level of declaratory policy, democracy promotion was suddenly transformed from a bromide to a centerpiece; over the subsequent five years, democracy assistance was increased by several hundred million dollars. But the new rhetoric did not result in anything approaching the dramatic shift implied; nor was it accompanied by the development of viable tools to realize the ambitious vision of transforming the region on liberal and democratic lines. After 2006, the policy faltered badly after the US encountered severe disappointments in Iraq and unexpectedly unfavorable developments in Palestine, Egypt, and elsewhere.

In short, during the George W. Bush presidency, the new US policy of democracy promotion was dramatically different in rhetoric from the approach of earlier administrations. It sketched a clear vision of transforming the region and involved a significant expansion of democracy assistance. But in practice, it amounted to a combination of more muscular and assertive versions of older programs along with an invasion and occupation of one country that colored the way the project was perceived without resolving any of the tensions and ambiguities that bold policy statements could not obscure.

Notes

1 J. Carter (1977) *Address at commencement exercises of the University of Notre Dame*, Human Rights Document. Online. Available: www.thirdworldtraveler.com/Human%20Rights%20Documents/Carter_HumaneFP.html (accessed October 1, 2007).
2 J. Kirkpatrick (1982) *Dictatorships and Double Standards: Rationalism and Reason in Politics*. New York: Simon and Schuster.
3 A. Lake (1993) *From Containment to Enlargement*. Washington, DC. Online. Available www.mtholyoke.edu/acad/intrel/lakedoc.html (accessed October 1, 2007).
4 R. Haass (2002) *Towards Greater Democracy in the Muslim World*. Washington, DC. Online. Available www.cfr.org/publication/5283/towards_greater_democracy_in_the_muslim_world.html (accessed May 6, 2009).
5 C. Powell (2002) *The Middle East Partnership Initiative*. Washington, DC: The Heritage Foundation. Online. Available www.heritage.org/research/middleeast/WM180.cfm (accessed November 23, 2008).
6 G. Bush (2003) *President Discusses the Future of Iraq*. Washington, DC: American Enterprise Institute. Online. Available http://georgewbush-whitehouse.archives.gov/news/releases/2003/02/20030226-11.html (accessed May 6, 2009).
7 G. Bush (2003) *President Bush Discusses Freedom in Iraq and Middle East*. Remarks by the President at the 20th Anniversary of the National Endowment for Democracy. Washington, DC: United States Chamber of Commerce. Online. Available http://georgewbush-whitehouse.archives.gov/news/releases/2003/11/20031106-2.html (accessed May 6, 2009).
8 C. Rice (2005) *Interview with Sir Trevor McDonald of ITV*. London: US Department of State. Online. Available http://merln.ndu.edu/archivepdf/iran/State/42881.pdf (accessed May 6, 2009).
9 Middle East Partnership Initiative (2006) "Fact Sheet: US Actors Promoting Democracy in the Middle East." Carnegie Endowment for International Peace. Online. Available www.carnegieendowment.org/files/democracy_fs.doc (accessed October 1, 2007).
10 The Forum for the Future convenes government officials from the broader Middle East and their G-8 counterparts and regional representatives of business and civil society to discuss reform. The Foundation for the Future makes grants to Arab civil society groups across the region.
11 S. Hadley (2005) *Remarks*. Washington, DC: Center for Strategic and International Studies. Online. Available http://merln.ndu.edu/archivepdf/iraq/WH/20051220-4.pdf (accessed May 6, 2009).

3 Democracy and security in the Middle East

Richard Youngs

International perspectives on the Middle East have been dominated since the terrorist attacks of September 11, 2001 by a reinvigorated debate over the relationship between the region's internal politics, on the one hand, and its generation of security challenges, on the other hand. This debate has polarized between two competing positions. At one extreme, pressure for democratic reform in the Middle East has been presented by some as the primary, fail-safe means of enhancing Western security countering international terrorism. At the other extreme, skeptics of this new focus on democracy promotion in the Middle East have warned that political liberalization would at best have negligible impact on the incidence of terrorism, and at worst actually facilitate the further flourishing of violence and anti-Western sentiment. Since 9/11, Western policies have fluctuated between these two poles, as a reinforced commitment to support democracy has given way to a return to traditional realism. This chapter argues that both positions are unsatisfactory and appeals for a more nuanced view that neither reifies nor discounts the potential strategic benefit that would flow from political change in the Middle East.

Democracy's virtue

An extensive body of academic work has catalogued a well-established range of reasons why it might be reasonable to expect political pluralism to enhance peace and stability. A vast number of standard "democratic peace" studies profess to demonstrate that democracies are less prone to engage in international conflict. Democracy is held to be predicated upon the principles of tolerance and compromise, and to provide opportunities for the peaceful articulation of social and economic grievances. Democracy's advocates assert that anti-Westernism expressed democratically is less likely to assume violent form, while political repression by necessity drives discontent into illegal and radical forms. Cross-cutting patterns of associative activity are routinely held to be integral to the moderation of individual actions and values. Authoritarianism, it is argued, can only hope to suppress grievances, in increasingly costly and precarious fashion. Freedom of information also ensures scrutiny of political actions that risk stoking harmful and costly conflict. Moreover, the same norms of mutual compromise that underpin democracy internally are, it is claimed, invariably also reflected in democracies' external behavior. It is argued that democratic leaders will be constrained by public opinion from military adventurism and immoderation in their external comportment. The fragility of many new democracies may even act as an added disincentive for governments to neglect urgent domestic demands to press external interests. It is frequently argued that governments operating in a democratic context tend to be more predictable in their foreign policy, an advantage compounded by the transparency of political debate to international scrutiny.

Analysts have also suggested that democracies tend to be more embedded in mutually constraining economic interdependencies. A "triangle" of mutually reinforcing relations is seen as having emerged between democracy, trade, and membership of international organizations. In short, for a variety of structural, political, and economic reasons, the reshaping of domestic political structures is presented by many as essential for international security and a far firmer basis for stability than strategies predicated on containment and deterrence.[1]

Much of this general conceptual logic has increasingly been judged to have particular pertinence to the West's relations with the Middle East. Pages could be filled with excerpts from the post-9/11 speeches of US and European ministers and representatives of international institutions attesting to a declared recognition that achieving sustainable security requires promoting democracy in the Middle East. Citations known to American observers from a series of President Bush speeches have been echoed, often with greater depth, in the pronouncements and policy statements of European governments. Such commitments have molded themselves into what is presented as a new Western approach to security in the Middle East, supposedly focused on attacking the roots of international terrorism, as opposed merely to containing its symptoms.

Both official and academic arguments have emphasized democracy's largely indirect and long-term utility. The argument has not primarily been that Middle East democratization would usher in governments either overtly more favorable to the West or more effective in any direct sense in containing terrorism. Rather, encouragement of pluralism has been advocated as a means of "draining the swamp," or drying up the "pool of discontent" seen as having been nourished by autocratic repression in the only region of the world still to lack a fully fledged democracy. The seminal 2002 Arab Human Development Report itself concurred with—and did much to disseminate and legitimize in the Middle East—the contention that democracy's absence has been a root cause of economic deprivation, which in turn has bred such pervasive popular frustration.[2] In relation to Egypt, it has been argued that the regime's prohibition of Islamist political parties is what has driven Islamism into a highly conservative form of influence through the religious establishment.[3]

It has, of course, been increasingly asserted that Middle Eastern resentment against the West can be traced to Western support for the region's repressive authoritarian regimes. If Middle East authoritarianism was initially welcomed by the West as a bulwark against resurgent Islam, its limited success in fulfilling this function has become increasingly patent. Across the region, nominally pro-Western autocrats have stoked up anti-Western feeling and played to Islamist opinion in order to shore up the precarious legitimacy of their own rule. This was a particularly notable trend during the late 1990s in Egypt and Jordan, and has inter alia compromised regimes' containment of opposition to the Middle East peace process. By the end of the 1990s, the West's "client" regimes appeared often to be acting in a manner more antithetical than helpful to Western strategic interests.[4] Middle Eastern regimes have in practice been neither cocooned from domestic pressures nor provided the material basis and incentive for their populations' moderation.

If the West's fear had long been that democracy would bring to power Islamist-oriented governments, in the post-9/11 environment greater faith appeared to be invested in the moderating impact that the democratic process would itself be likely to have on groups currently espousing radical positions. Many analysts suggest that, if democracy enabled Islamists to assume power, the latter's mystic appeal would soon dissolve and their so far vague recipes for tackling economic and social imperatives would take firmer and more realistic shape. Arab regimes were increasingly perceived to have exaggerated the Islamist "threat" in an attempt to purchase the indulgence of Western governments for their—regimes'—refusal to implement political reforms. Arab regimes were seen to have played a self-serving game: the more instability that autocracy bred, the easier it had been for regimes to convince the West that this very authoritarianism had to be tightened. Democracy would, it was argued, help break this Gordian knot.

Indeed, if there has been a defining feature of post-9/11 intellectual debates, it has resided in the ubiquitous warnings against "Islam" being seen as a "threat" to the West. Increasingly, broader recognition has emerged of the extent to which contemporary trends in Islam have been determined by prevailing political contexts. The vast majority of analysts and policy makers alike have repeatedly rejected the notion that Islam should be conceived as a monolithic assault against Western values. It has been broadly acknowledged that the most resonant "clash" exists between different constituencies *within* the Muslim world, rather than across civilizational fault-lines. While some die-hard Orientalists of course remain, to most observers, the fluidity and variety of Islamist political ideology has become more striking, with much ostensibly Islamist discourse in fact replaying many secular and material dimensions of the third world populism witnessed in other regions. The perennially raised question of whether Islam and democracy are compatible over the long term has for most analysts become a non-debate. Organizations such as the Moroccan Party of Justice and Development, the Egyptian Muslim Brotherhood, and the Jordanian Islamic Action Front have issued increasingly unqualified pronouncements in favor of multiparty democracy. Such change in both the self-definition and external intellectual perceptions of political Islam has had bearing upon the judgments made about the likely impact of democratization in the Middle East. Crucial to the pro-democracy argument is an optimism that support for democratization appears increasingly to be going with the grain of ideological evolution in the Middle East. In this context, democracy promotion is more of a hedged bet on the future than an open invitation to the West's declared "enemies."

In sum, it is the entwining of new strategic thinking and (apparently) less "essentialist" readings of Islam that has for many observers and policy makers made the case for democracy so much more potent. This is the context that has made the promotion of democracy such a prominent concern, and one central to study of the changing dynamics of Middle Eastern politics.

The case against

As firmly as democracy has been advocated as an essential strand of Western security strategies in the wake of 9/11, so has its value to efforts to mitigate international terrorism been questioned. Western governments have been criticized for mistakenly moving from a strategic policy based on containment to an unfounded assumption that efforts to democratize the Middle East can provide an antidote to terrorism. Critics charge that the pendulum has swung too far from a prioritization of alliance building to a simplistic formulation of democracy as strategic panacea.

The doubts raised against democracy can be broken down into a number of different concerns. The warning most commonly forwarded is that, in bringing to power anti-Western Islamists, democratization in the Middle East would be inimical to security interests.[5] Recent trends in the Middle East certainly suggest that Islamists stand well positioned to reap the benefits of more open and genuinely competitive elections. While press attention focused primarily on the rise of Hamas, Islamist opposition groups have also made strong showings in Morocco, Algeria, Egypt, and Kuwait, and in Saudi Arabia's 2005 municipal elections.

On this, democracy's advocates would mostly not demur. Crucially, however, skeptics question the optimistic assumption that participation in democratic politics and, probably, in government would be likely to seduce Islamists into moderation. Opinion polls indeed suggest there is little correlation between relative degrees of political repression in the Middle East and "radicalism." Some of the most virulently anti-Western views have been registered in Jordan and Morocco—countries enjoying, of course, some of the most generous political rights in the Arab world and whose political systems have allowed increased representation of Islamist parties. Questioning the empirical evidence offered to substantiate the democracy–security link, it has been pointed out that many authoritarian regimes have not bred radicalism, while the latter has risen in many established democracies.[6] In light of this, two experts draw attention to the uncomfortable fact that the most successful control of radical Islamist groups has been secured through repressive measures in states such as Tunisia, Algeria, and Egypt, thus rebutting the "wishful thinking" that democracy is a "cure-all for terrorism."[7] After performing strongly in Egypt's parliamentary elections at the end of 2005, several members of the Muslim Brotherhood leadership dismissed suggestions that greater political participation would involve the group being more willing to recognize Israel.[8]

Conceptually, many of the arguments relating to democracy's supposed virtues have emerged from work either on the "democratic peace" or on conflict resolution. Arguably, the conclusions of such work have been extrapolated too readily to the issue of Middle Eastern instability and Islamist-linked international terrorism when it in fact speaks to a quite different set of issues. Democratic peace theorists might have observed that wealthy, Western democracies have not gone to war with each other, but it would be wrong to suppose from this that poorer, more turbulent societies become more peaceable through democratization, given their more acute economic difficulties and challenging regional environment. In this sense, it is contended that democracy is likely to be harmful and destabilizing without a number of preconditions having been met, in particular the existence of national consensus and strong state institutions.[9] It is argued, moreover, that recent evidence casts doubt on the contention that non-democracies are more reluctant to embed themselves in networks of mutual interdependencies, thus questioning one of the central tenets of the democratic peace thesis.[10] It has similarly been suggested that democracy's value is heavily conditioned by the broader regional context, and may often have more to do with the existence of cooperative ventures between groups of neighboring states that happen to be democratic than the intrinsic virtues of democracy per se.[11]

In addition, danger lies in extending evidence of democracy's virtue in managing context-specific, low-level societal tension, in particular in Africa's "failed states," to a conviction that governance reform is pertinent to combating the qualitatively distinct threat of Al Qaeda. Crucially, most work on democracy and security has focused on either full-scale war between states or internal ethnic conflict; it has related less directly to soft security challenges involving substate actors and low-level social and ideational tensions. Democracy's presumed relevance to such concerns is so far based more on intuitive reasoning than detailed empirical study.

In short, the proposition that internal democratic accountability engenders moderation in external behavior is widely questioned, especially when applied in the context of the Middle East. Indeed, it might be argued that democratic leaders may actually have greater incentive to harden external positions to divert attention from their domestic constraints. Far from being a moderating effect, liberated electorates might push democratic governments in a more radical direction, with democracy threatening to be a spark igniting the tinderbox of Middle Eastern resentment. Moreover, the most hard-edged realist might caution that democracies tend to make the stronger, more technologically advanced strategic rivals and that encouraging such advancement in the

Middle East would, contrary to all "democratic peace" rhetoric suggesting otherwise, not ultimately sit easily with a correct reading of realpolitik's exigencies.

A different critique has focused not on democracy per se, but the inadvisability of Western governments championing and actively promoting political liberalization. Even if democracy were to be beneficial, one standard argument is that it would be counterproductive for the West to seek to be its midwife. Critics have contended that, with democracy promotion conceived in too instrumental a fashion through the lens of Western self-interest, it threatens actually to increase instability and violence, especially in the Middle East.[12] Critics predict that the backlash against the West occasioned by efforts to "impose" democracy is likely to outweigh any internal benefits from political liberalization.

Unsurprisingly perhaps, but also beguilingly, such an incipient "backlash" has come from two, opposing directions. The US is pilloried for now seeking heavy-handedly to "impose" democratic values for its own interest, but also berated for still in practice being ambivalent over political opening in the Middle East. It is salutary for Western policy makers to note that many polls regularly confirm that Arab citizens do not believe the West, and the US in particular, to be genuinely interested in backing democratic change. This is particularly the case as the US seemed to have shifted back toward a more realist policy during the latter stages of the Bush administration. If Arab views are often frustrating—admonishing the West in one breath for backing authoritarian regimes, and in the next for "interfering" when modest criticism is forthcoming of democratic abuses—this to the skeptic merely reinforces the point that meddling in the region's internal politics can only be prejudicial for the West.

A further, and also long-standing, concern relates to the process of democratic change. It is commonly observed that transitions from authoritarianism to democracy have invariably involved instability, as new coalitions between domestic groups constantly shift and the frustration of newly raised expectations feeds into growing support for nationalist platforms. Afghanistan and Iraq might now be cited as dramatic examples of this transition predicament; instability coinciding with incipient change in Lebanon, Saudi Arabia, and Morocco could also be seen as offering it some corroboration.

Beyond these debates over how democracy would reconfigure internal Arab politics, other analysts have simply questioned the whole premise that security is a matter related to forms of political system. Traditional realists have continued to conceive of security as the product of the international system's structure far more than of the nature of domestic political systems. Strategic issues, they insist, must in this sense be interpreted as revolving around international alliances, not internal political changes. Structuralist, "core–periphery" interpretations of the Middle East see the struggle for effective autonomy as the primary factor explaining relations with the West. Incongruence between the artificial territorial boundaries imposed by colonial powers and Arab

Identity continue to militate against security-enhancing democratization in the Middle East. Antagonism toward the West and internal tensions emanate, it is argued, from overarching structural constraints, likely to endure beyond any changes to internal political structures.[13]

Such perspectives relate closely to the familiar argument that Middle Eastern antipathy toward the West derives principally from the nature of international policies toward the Arabs lack of democracy, for many it rather merely reinforced the urgency of Palestinian self-determination. It is, of course, habitually asserted that perceived Western connivance in the continuing absence of a Palestinian state does more than anything to drive young men, and increasingly women, to perpetrate violence. For many observers, Palestinian statehood continues massively to outweigh the issue of democratization in its relevance to insecurity's explanatory roots.

From the realist angle, it is in turn suggested that the West's own focus should be directly on Arab regimes' foreign policies and not on the nature of their internal power structures. It is suggested that efforts to promote democracy merely risk wasting negotiating capital more usefully expended directly on constraining states' external actions. From a more radical and economic perspective, it has long been held that conflict and instability are products of the unequal distribution of economic resources, and that as long as economic shortages and injustices remain embedded within the prevailing structure of the international system, national-level democracy appears an increasingly hollow vessel.

This argument does not so much suggest that Middle Eastern democratization would be harmful or that Western nations should not encourage change where possible, but rather contends that whether democracy is present or absent simply has little bearing on terrorism. Hence, it is routinely pointed out that terrorist acts have in recent decades wreaked havoc in democratic states such as the UK, Spain, Italy, and Germany. The fact that those who carried out the July 7, 2005 bombings in London were British citizens was one of the most sobering falsifications of the notion that all terrorists are citizens angered into violent action by their laboring under repressive Middle Eastern regimes. The India–China comparison is also routinely raised to democracy's disadvantage, violent acts in democratic India exceeding those in authoritarian China. Indeed, where the India–China contrast has for many years been suggested to cast doubt over the presumed link between democracy and economic development, it has more recently served to render questionable the link between democracy and security.

Skeptics also question the "pool of discontent" argument, pointing out that, even if terrorists benefit from a "support network" among politically repressed citizens, it still requires only a handful of individuals to execute a violent act. Even if a perfect, pristine form of democracy took root across the Middle East, to widespread popular support, it would be wholly unconvincing to think that even this scenario could placate every actual or potential radical. More than anything else, perhaps, modern conflict's asymmetry is democracy's impotence.

In a slightly weaker version of the skeptical perspective, the conclusion that many analysts have reached on the basis of conceptual doubts over democracy's virtue is that the key changes needed in the Middle East are not precisely democratic changes. Many analysts have suggested that international efforts should focus on strengthening local institutional forms that improve human rights norms without entailing wholesale democratization. An "Arab form" of political reform is often advocated, predicated on traditional organizations such as the mosque, the neighborhood or village, the tribe, professional associations, and syndicates, rather than Western-style civil society groups. This echoes a more general argument that illiberalism instead of democracy is best suited to attaining social calm and stability. A "thick web of liberal institutions" should, it has been argued, take precedence over any consideration of formal electoral democracy that can simply encourage competitive leaders to ratchet up hard-line, populist positions.[14] Notably, relatively technical good governance measures have often been advocated in order to secure cleaner, less arbitrary, and less corrupt government, with these values held to be of far greater concern to citizens than Western-style liberal democracy. Indeed, improved respect for basic rights has been advocated post-September 11 as a means of actually helping to head off the uncertainties of regime change and full democratization.[15]

Toward a more measured view

The challenge is to chart a course between these two poles of security debates in the Middle East. Western policy makers' focus on democracy promotion is a welcome and necessary corrective to traditional security doctrines that for so long failed to look inside the black box of the nation-state to investigate the domestic roots of instability. However, the danger must be avoided of expecting too much of democracy as an instrument for security enhancement. The design of Western policies must not presume democracy to be a panacea for post-September 11 challenges. Rather, the complex interrelationship between political reform and ongoing processes of economic and social change must be reflected upon critically if concrete policies aimed at promoting democracy are to have the positive security benefits desired of them. On the other hand, the apparent shift back to alliance-building realism risks pushing the pendulum too far in the opposite direction.

Both extremes of the argument over the relationship between democracy and security often tend toward the simplistic. Democracy's advocates risk holding the lack of political liberalization too overwhelmingly to be the primary cause of the Middle East's own ills, as well as of the region's "export" of international terrorism. The "democracy as panacea" exaggeration posits too direct a link between domestic political change and external security issues. But the "democracy will be harmful" line itself adopts too static a view. The familiar critique is to suggest that certain "preconditions"—economic development, a decline in nationalism, civic-building consensus—need to be fulfilled before democratization can be expected to proceed smoothly and beneficially. This underplays, however, the extent to which the nature of politics itself conditions progress on such "preconditions." It fails to factor in how democratic change itself impacts on cognitive identities and the worldviews of political actors as part of a process of adaptation.

Many skeptics also err in dismissing the importance of domestic politics, often coming close to suggesting that most problems associated with the region would dissipate if the US modified its foreign policies, in particular in relation to Palestine and Iraq. Curiously, this questioning of the independent impact of domestic politics has equally characterized conservative and progressive critiques of the democratization agenda.

It has become standard to warn that political change should rightfully be gradual. True, but scarcely illuminating, it might be felt. It should not be forgotten that debates over political reform have been on the agenda in the Middle East for over two decades, with initial changes having accompanied structural adjustment programs in the mid-1980s. It is of course undeniably the case that political liberalization can be destabilizing if undertaken "too quickly." But with activity around political reform having fluctuated back and forth for twenty years in the Middle East, one might enquire how much more "gradual" should "gradual change" be? Does the Middle East experience not suggest that "democracy deferred" can be as worrying a phenomenon as "democracy precipitated?" It is entirely convincing to caution that state infrastructure is warranted prior to democratic transition: but can étatiste Middle Eastern regimes really be said to suffer a deficit of state institutions? Moreover, this would hardly seem to represent a lacuna in international policies, given that for many years external actors have been funding state capacity-building even as they have eschewed democracy assistance proper.

Both sides forward their arguments with remarkable certainty. Yet the truth is that we can probably not predict with any convincing certainty how "democracy's drama" would unfold in the Middle East or what broad ramifications it would visit upon the region. If there is a convincing conclusion to be drawn from the rich literature on democracy and international relations, it is that democracy itself can have dramatically varying impact across different states, strategic contexts, and time periods. The potency of path-dependency in democratic change militates against overly confident prediction—especially when debate continues over the extent to which the Middle East's internal politics really offer the prospect of meaningful change.

Events in Iraq have complicated and even distorted the picture. Iraq's post-invasion turmoil has clearly provided strong argument to those emphasizing that violence is invariably associated with political transitions. At the very least, it must be recognized that the jury is still out on whether democratization in Iraq can eventually prove to be a stabilizing force. The situation in Iraq continues to fluctuate. Optimism has grown as violence has subsided since early 2008 but, as of this writing, it cannot be concluded that this progress will be sustained. What has been unconvincing is the tendency of both sides of the argument to generalize from their respective readings of events in Iraq to the issue of democratization more broadly across the Middle East. Iraq so far conclusively demonstrates neither that democracy is doomed to breed bloody insurrection or that the fall of dictatorship necessarily sets the foundations for rights-sensitive stabilization.

While many of the doubts raised against democracy are entirely convincing, the conceptual groundings from which they are argued commonly lead critics to be overly dismissive of democracy's potential merit. One shortcoming, witnessed especially in the US, is the tendency implicitly to assume that the situation is one of the US deciding whether democracy is a good thing or not in the face of a passive Middle East. In reality, of course, democracy's fate is unlikely to be the West's to decide. Western policy is more a reactive than an independent variable, and security calculations must be made with this in mind. Even if the skeptics' concerns are fully acknowledged, what can perhaps be argued with some certainty is that, as and when the Middle East's political plates begin to shift, it would breed resentment if the West sought actively to discourage change.

It is particularly irritating—for those both in the Middle East and in other Western states—that debates over democracy promotion are so often couched in a discourse of "US values." Both the enthusiasts and the skeptics regularly conflate—or seem constantly a hair's breadth away from conflating—their respective views on democracy with their position on the US seeking to spread its values. Democracy must be carefully judged on its own merits. Presenting the argument in terms of "our security" being served by spreading "our values"—in fact a favorite formulation not only of President Bush but also of former British Prime Minister Tony Blair—could hardly be better designed to engender counterproductive responses to democracy promotion efforts. Where democracy support is aimed at ensuring that Arabs' own values and aspirations are not hindered from outside, a more comprehensive approach to political change is invited.

Such a starting point offers greater possibility of teasing out democracy's potential, linking support for political reform organically to a broader range of requisite change in the region. A truly holistic approach would be attentive to the pitfalls of political rupture unsynchronized with underlying structural adaptation of economy and social life. A strategy that fully contextualized political reform within ongoing processes of social, religious, and economic change in the Arab world might not magic away strategic threats, but it would go some way to preparing the foundations for the kind of comprehensive transformation that would render containment-based security less necessary. The value of support for democracy should not be discounted, but must be made to mesh with issues of a structural nature—and certainly not merely take the form of backing easily accessible, pro-Western democracy activists.

Related to this, care must also be taken not to confuse the challenge of international terrorism with that of anti-Westernism. Again, from both sides of the debate, views on the latter come dangerously close to determining the advocated strategy toward democracy. This of course leads on to the broader point, well beyond the scope of this chapter, of what issues actually constitute (or are "intersubjectively constructed" to constitute, as constructivists would contend) "security threats" to the West. At a minimum, it would appear imperative less unthinkingly to conflate different forms or levels of "securitized" issue— international terrorism, for example, being subject to a set of causal dynamics in crucial ways quite distinct from the soft security challenges linked to internal state–society pathologies. It might indeed be asked whether the central issue is really that of governmental anti-Westernism. Governments highly critical of the West exist in many places of the world without these being seen to represent existential security threats. It might be proffered that a viable trade-off is at stake, with governments more critical of Western policies externally actually helping to provide a stabilizing "pressure valve" internally. Paradoxically, it might prove to be in the West's interest to promote democracy especially where it seems most strongly not to be in its interest to do so!

One conclusion to flow from the "either/or" extremes of prevailing debate is that the West should above all be selective in its focus on encouraging democracy in the Middle East. This argument contends that Western governments should back political change where secular pro-Western forces are currently strong and could be expected to gain significant power democratically—as, for example, in Morocco and Lebanon. Where this is not the case, it is suggested that the West should discourage democratization in the short term and seek rather to build up pro-Western secular forces as a precursor to any eventual democratic transition.[16] Whatever one's general degree of doubt over democracy, it would seem reasonable to caution that this is exactly what the West should not seek to do. If one thing would seem guaranteed to engender resentment among Arab populations, it would be an attempt directly to engineer politics to the West's perceived advantage, on the basis of applying different standards between Middle Eastern states.

It has, rightly, been argued that efforts to encourage democracy in the Arab world should be conceived as having potentially positive effects for security, both within and beyond the Middle East, but that democratization should also be recognized as only one among many pertinent variables.[17] The danger so far does not appear to lie in the West blindly imposing democracy, but rather in being ultra-cautious in according substance to rhetorical commitments to support political change—such caution probably being more pronounced in Europe than in the US. Indeed, it is the other elements of counterterrorism strategy that have in fact predominated, in particular through cooperation between Western and Arab security forces and intelligence services. Looking carefully at the substance and resource allocations of Western governments, it would seem entirely unconvincing to suggest that they have in practice imprudently abandoned the dictates of short-term realism. Rather, the challenge resides in ensuring that traditional and democracy-based security strategies, which Western governments will inevitably pursue in parallel, do not undermine each other. The tension between these dynamics is yet to be resolved, and if security and counterterrorist strategies are to assume an appropriately multifaceted form, this is a crucial issue on which much work remains to be done.

Notes

1 B. Russett and J. Oneal (2001) *Triangulating Peace: Democracy, Interdependence, and International Organizations.* New York: Norton; J.L. Ray (1995) *Democracy and International Conflict: An Evaluation of the Democratic Peace Proposition.* Columbia: University of South Carolina Press; International IDEA (1998) *Democracy and Deep-Rooted Conflict: Options for Negotiators.* Stockholm: International IDEA; T. Gurr (2001) "Ethnic Warfare on the Wane," *Foreign Affairs* 79 (3): 52–64; K. Schultz (1999) "Do Democratic Institutions Constrain or Inform? Contrasting Two Institutional Perspectives on Democracy and War," *International Organization* 53(2): 233–66.
2 United Nations (2002) *Arab Human Development Report.* Geneva: UN, ch. 10.
3 B. Kodmani (2005) "The Dangers of Political Exclusion: Egypt's Islamist Problem," Carnegie Working Paper 63, October 2005. Washington: Carnegie Endowment for Internal Peace.
4 F. Halliday (2002) *Two Hours that Shook the World.* London: Saqi, p. 124.
5 F. Gregory Gause III (2005) "Can Democracy Stop Terrorism?" *Foreign Affairs,* September/October, pp. 62–76.
6 J. Mearsheimer (1990) "Back to the Future: Instability in Europe after the Cold War," *International Security* 15: 5–56; E. Mansfield and J. Snyder (1995) "Democratization and the Danger of War," *International Security* 20: 5–38; C. Gelpi (1997) "Democratic Diversions: Governmental Structure and Externalization of Domestic Conflict," *Journal of Conflict Resolution* 41(2): 255–87; T. Barkawi and M. Laffey (1999) "The Imperial Peace: Democracy, Force and Globalization," *European Journal of International Relations* 5(4): 403–34; E. Cousens and C. Kumar, eds (2001) *Peacebuilding as Politics: Cultivating Peace in Fragile Societies.* Boulder, CO: Lynne Rienner; H. Kissinger (2001) *Does America Need a Foreign Policy?* New York: Simon and Schuster; E. Mansfield and J. Snyder (2002) "Democratic Transitions, Institutional Strength, and War," *International Organization* 56(2): 297–338; F. Zakaria (1997) "The Rise of Illiberal Democracy," *Foreign Affairs* 76: 22–43; J. Gowa (1999) *Ballots and Bullets: The Elusive Democratic Peace.* Princeton, NJ: Princeton University Press.
7 T. Carothers and M. Ottaway (2004) "Middle East Democracy," *Foreign Policy* Nov–Dec: 22–28.
8 "Engaging Egypt's Islamists? Easier Said Than Done", *Democracy Digest* 2/12, December 22, 2005: 2.
9 E. Mansfield and J. Snyder (2005/6) "Prone to Violence," *The National Interest,* Winter 2005/6.
10 D. Geller and J. Singer (1998) *Nations at War: A Scientific Study of International Conflict.* Cambridge: Cambridge University Press.
11 K. Gleditsch and M. Ward (2000) "War and Peace in Space and Time: The Role of Democratization," *International Studies Quarterly* 44(1): 1–29.
12 E. Hobsbawm (2004) "Spreading Democracy," *Foreign Policy* Sept–Oct: 40–41.
13 R. Hinnebusch (2003) *The International Politics of the Middle East.* Manchester: Manchester University Press.
14 J. Snyder (2001) *From Voting to Violence: Democratization and Nationalist Conflict.* New York: Norton.
15 M. Indyck (2002) "Back to the Bazaar," *Foreign Affairs* 81(1): 75–88; A.R. Norton (1997) "Political Reform in the Middle East" in L. Guazzone, ed., *The Middle East*

in Global Change. Basingstoke: Macmillan, pp. 3–22; M. Salla (1997) "Political Islam and the West: A New Cold War or Convergence?" *Third World Quarterly* 18 (4): 729–42; S. Sarsar (2000) "Can Democracy Prevail?" *Middle East Quarterly* 7 (1): 47; V. Langhor (2002) "An Exit for Arab Autocracy," *Journal of Democracy* 13 (3): 116–22.

16 F. Gregory Gause III, op. cit.

17 J. Windsor (2003) "Promoting Democratization Can Combat Terrorism," *Washington Quarterly* 26(3): 43–58.

4 The fantasy of Arab democracy without a constituency

Walid Kazziha

Introduction

The main objective of this chapter is to trace the emergence and development of the discourse on the democratization of the Arab world in recent years. The purpose is not to record every twist and turn in the course of that debate, but to depict those distinguishing features that characterized the various stages of its evolution and progress. Ultimately, it is the intention of this modest attempt to contribute to finding an explanation for the failure of the majority of Arab societies in achieving a reasonable level of public participation in the political sphere.

The absence of political constituencies, let alone democratic constituencies, is very often ignored in favor of explanations that tend to view Islamic heritage, Arab culture, lack of modern political institutions, and the social atomization of Arab societies as impediments to democratization.

In this chapter, a serious attempt is made to refocus the debate on the political constituency as a necessary condition for initializing any progress toward democracy. Egypt and Palestine are used as two examples illustrating the importance of the existence of political constituencies, or their absence, in the evolution or inhibition of the success of political representation.

In essence, it is neither the debate among ruling elites and intellectuals detached from the bulk of society, nor the imposition of formal measures even by force by outside powers that in the final analysis creates a democratic environment in the Arab world. The likelihood of such an occurrence could take place when genuine political constituencies appear on the scene and pave the way for the emergence of vibrant political life in Arab societies.

The political discourse among a great number of academics, politicians, and journalists in the Arab world as well as the West has recently become over-saturated with opinions, views, and determined obsessions with the necessity of democratizing the Arab countries. Guests from Europe and the US sponsored by their governments and embassies have become frequent travelers to the region, often stopping in Arab capitals to lecture or preach on the wisdom and benefits of adopting democracy. Arab intellectuals are increasingly finding themselves carried away by this new drive and sharing heatedly in the debate. Officials of Arab governments, despite their reservations, are being forced into a discussion in which they pay lip service to the new popular theme. The concept of democracy, the notions of participation, and the fashionable concept of women in politics are being celebrated on every occasion in a similar fashion to the way Muslim communities celebrate their traditional festivities in their annual Moulids. The Egyptians, with their sharp sense of humor, have coined a very expressive term to describe such a phenomenon. They call it a "Hoga." In a recent article in the *Ahram* newspaper, an Egyptian intellectual, Dr. Abdel Aziz Hammouda, defined Hoga as a sudden upsurge which surfaces for a while, and then as quickly disappears, leaving behind no trace at all. Its underlying causes persist without any change, but the Hoga itself passes away as if it has not been there.[1] In a sense, the Arab world is experiencing today the Hoga of democracy forced upon it by forces from outside.

However, the fact that the discourse has become oversaturated, and that some of those contributing to it have ulterior political motives should not detract from some of the serious attempts that have been made at the level of theory and practice.

It might be true that many intellectuals and government officials are joining the debate to be part of the new fashion, despite the fact that they may know it may not last too long. Nevertheless, it is important for them to keep a high profile, exhibit their input, and claim that they have a contribution to make to the subject. From their point of view, this is professionalism and survival. It does not matter if they discover later that they have to abandon the discourse and adopt a new more popular one. This is part of being up to date, open-minded, and changing with the times. Even when a discourse becomes repetitive, the ideas redundant, and the outcome at the level of political practice negligible, the momentum has to be maintained without much concern for where it is going or what it seeks to accomplish. Yet there are those who believe that, once a discourse reaches its intellectual and political limits, it loses its raison d'être, and it is time to reconsider its validity.

In a discussion on democracy in the Arab world, the time has come to evaluate what the intellectual and political communities have actually achieved, and assess the course that should be taken to promote the debate to a higher level, or abandon it altogether until such time that it might become more relevant to the Arab setting.

Since 1967, the democratic discourse in the Arab world seems to have passed through three distinct stages of development. The first was largely influenced by the aftermath of the Arab defeat. It came at the heels of a national tragedy which shook the roots of Arab societies. The second appeared in the late 1980s and gathered momentum throughout the 1990s, with a strong European involvement in the area of civil society. The third and last phase was initiated by pressures from the outside, particularly the US, soon after September 11.

Phase one

The response to the defeat in the Arab world included a wide range of reactions embodied in a variety of political and intellectual tendencies, which extended from the extreme right to the extreme left. In a very similar fashion to the 1948 defeat, the Arabs once more posed the eternal question they had always elaborated in times of crises: what is to be done? And sure enough the remedies were prescribed, from armed struggle and people's protracted war to handing over the Arab future to America. Somewhere in between, God's will was invoked to deliver the Arabs to the shores of safety and everlasting peace. Illusions and ambitions were mixed with calls for a return to reason and wisdom. And in the midst of all these conflicting currents, a new train of thought emerged. It was closer to a sentiment than a concrete, well-articulated, well-defined notion. In their quest for an answer to what went wrong, many Arab intellectuals expressed their anger with the fact that their people had been marched blindly into the catastrophe under the leadership of dictators and authoritarian regimes. In Egypt, it was rumored that, when Nasser met a representative group of Egyptian students who objected to the lenient court sentences meted out to the top army officers responsible for the military defeat, one of their members addressed the president by saying that, had the Egyptians fought as free men and not slaves, the outcome of the war would have been different.

Soon after the defeat, a strong sentiment emerged calling for the participation of the people in politics, urging that, in matters of great significance to the future of the Arab world, decisions should not be left to one individual or to one group of people. With the discrediting of the defeated Arab armies and their autocratic leadership, a new notion was idolized: it was now time for the people to step in and raise the banner of defiance against the external enemy as well as against the internal oppressor. The popularity of the Palestinian resistance movement partly stemmed from the fact that it was not sanctioned by the discredited Arab leadership, but by the people and their supporters across the Arab world.

The new sentiment unleashed after the 1967 defeat did not remain at the level of generalities, but it gradually began to acquire a more sophisticated form, with an increasing number of Arab thinkers exploring the various aspects of its possible implementation. Toward the mid-1980s, a body of literature in the Arab world had grown to become a major trend in the political discourse of the time.

Much of that literature revolved around the notion of democracy, which was advocated in the course of searching for remedies to the ills of Arab societies. The Arab defenses against their enemies had been shattered to pieces, their armies decimated, and their political and military leaderships rendered completely bankrupt. The need for the Arab peoples to take things into their own hands had become the only way to salvation. Democracy seemed to be the key to deliverance, and the Arabs were enjoined to walk in the company of the free nations of the world.

In the initial phase of the development of a democratic sentiment in the Arab world, several ideas were introduced in an effort to illustrate its potential applicability. Among the Palestinians, the concept of popular armed struggle was adopted to emphasize the shift in the task of liberating Palestine from the hands of the Arab regimes and political elites into the hands of the Palestinian people. In Egypt, Tawfiq Al-Hakim called for the return of consciousness among the Egyptians and the liberation of their minds from the spell of Nasser's charisma and the dominance of the state. He wrote: "The return of consciousness to Egypt means the return of its freedom to govern itself."[2] He claimed that, since 1952, the fate of Egypt had become the possession of the state, which exercised full control over society and determined its future.[3] These thoughts were repeated by Arab intellectuals in Syria and Lebanon who critically reviewed the disastrous performances of the Arab regimes in the areas of economic development and political liberalization. Yassin Al-Hafiz, a former leading member of the Ba'ath party in Syria, offered a devastating social critique of Nasserism and Ba'athism, focusing his main attack on what he claimed to be the betrayal of the Arab masses.[4] The left in the Arab world viewed the failure of Nasserism to be inherent in the social petty bourgeois nature of the movement, which had no confidence in the lower classes of society, and therefore failed in realizing the national ambitions of the Arab nation in socialism and the liberation of Palestine. According to Al-Hafiz, it was time for the Arab proletariat to take the responsibility of leading the nation to its victory.

Among the liberal intellectuals, some important questions were raised regarding the nature of the Arab regimes that were needed to save the Arabs from the consequences of defeat and underdevelopment. The commitment of the autocratic, dictatorial, authoritarian regimes fell miserably behind the political ambitions of the Arab masses. They had no legitimacy in the eyes of their own peoples. According to the late Egyptian intellectual, Ahmed Baha'a el-Din, the Arabs were facing numerous challenges. There were serious external threats facing the Arab nation, which inhibited its struggle for unity, social and economic development, and political independence. However, he seemed to be more concerned with what he identified as the internal challenges that the Arabs needed to meet, namely democracy, rationality, and legitimacy. He wrote that, without the existence of a strong moral bond between the rulers and the people, there can be no legitimacy for a regime. In that sense, he thought that most of the Arab regimes suffered from being illegitimate, or from a weak bond between the authority and the citizens. He stated "If events had taught us the importance of democracy and rationality, it was high time for us to be aware that the greatest importance is for legitimacy ... because in the final analysis it is legitimacy which brings about the harmony between the rulers and the ruled."[5]

Writing in 1984, Baha'a el-Din was highly impressed and perhaps influenced by the publication of Michael Hudson's book on *Arab Politics: A Study of Political Legitimacy* (1979). He referred admiringly to that book in his work on what constituted a legitimate authority in the Arab world.

Combined with the theme of legitimacy, there was also a call for upholding political rationality. Both Al-Hafiz and Baha'a el-Din objected to the continued exercise of political power and the making of policies on the basis of spontaneous, erratic, and emotional responses. They urged that politics had to have a rationale to it. In modern times, it could not be conducted on the basis of the personal whims of individual rulers. It had to be based on a scientific and objective analysis of the variables that go into the making of a political phenomenon and shaping of political events.

Thus, the responsibilities for making and implementing policies should be shared by all, and the governed ought to be involved in the historical processes that contribute to molding their future.

In 1987, Ghassan Salameh, a Lebanese scholar and politician, wrote a monograph entitled: "Toward a New Arab Social Contract," published by the Center for Arab Unity Studies in Beirut. In it, he stated that there was a growing consensus among Arab intellectuals, scholars, and experts that the Arab regimes were suffering from a crisis of legitimacy. In his view, the lack of legitimacy precipitated a state of fear and concern on the part of the Arab regimes for their own survival. Consequently, they were disinclined to invite their societies to participate in decisions relating to development, reform, and independence. The Arab world, according to him, needed to establish a new social contract based on constitutional legitimacy, which would preserve for the Arab individual his human rights and basic liberties. In this process, he urged civil society and the Arab regimes alike gradually to adopt a new culture based on the appropriation of democratic values, which he felt was lacking up to that time from both the rulers and the ruled.[6]

Toward the end of the 1980s, the democratic discourse tended to revolve around a few themes that were introduced in a prescriptive rather than an analytical fashion, except in very rare cases. Democracy, political participation, rational politics, legitimacy, human rights, civil society, and constitutionalism were some of the remedies prescribed for the Arab national illnesses. On a practical level, the discourse did not appear to have any significant consequences.

By late 1973, some of the Arab regimes, especially Syria and Egypt, regained part of their credibility in the aftermath of the October War. The position of the oil-rich countries and their ruling families was greatly advanced by the rise in oil prices. Eventually, as the Arab regimes resumed their old ways of exercising power, the demand for democratization among their intelligentsia was toned down into more modest ambitions such as civil society and human rights. At the same time, the discourse remained very much confined to a thin layer of Arab society and did not gain any grassroots following.

This did not mean that there were no serious attempts to give the debate a more articulate theoretical and institutional form. In 1978, Burhan Ghalyun, a Syrian scholar residing in Paris, published his well-known book, *A Communiqué for Democracy*. The book remains a very relevant intervention in today's political discourse. It examined the potentials for the democratization of the Arab world in relation to the social and economic transformation of societies. Ghalyun defined democracy as a political system that did not have the necessary ingredients for its erection in the Arab world. Despite the optimistic mood generated by the democratic discourse, the analytical approach of Ghalyun resulted in a negative conclusion. The time had not yet arrived for democracy to become a realistic option in the present circumstances of the Arab world. He wrote: "The continued absence of democracy is due today to the loss of the basic objective political and social balances, the escalation of the national and economic crisis, inequality of distribution, and the incompatibilities in the ideological and patriotic positions."[7]

On an institutional level, the Center for Arab Unity Studies, which was founded in 1975, made some serious effort to contribute to the discussions politically and ideologically. In 1983, it organized a conference and a seminar in Beirut to which a number of Arab intellectuals, academicians, and political thinkers were invited. The proceedings and papers of the conference were published in two volumes. The first was entitled "Seminar on the Crisis of Democracy in the Arab Nation" and the second "The Crisis of Democracy in the Arab Nation." The papers presented were of uneven quality, and the topics focused on the various political, social, and legal aspects of democratization, and on its relationship with Islam.

Salwa Ismail had adequately summarized much of the debate that took place under the auspices of the Center, and attempted to situate the discussions in a historical context. Once more, she clearly illustrated that the debates were disconnected, eclectic, and marked by the absence of consensus or a sustained theoretical effort. The issues raised somehow stood on their own separated from each other, and the contributions of the academic community in the region as well as in the West may have clarified some theoretical aspects of the debate, but did not yield any significant political results. Somehow, the discussions were confined to a limited number of intellectuals and interested parties, but did not penetrate into the roots of Arab societies. Politically, the Center for Arab Unity Studies extended its efforts to the institutional level. It became very instrumental in laying the foundations for the emergence of human rights organizations in the Arab world, by providing the moral and intellectual incentives, and sometimes even the financial means. In the next two decades, human rights organizations in the Arab world mushroomed and proliferated, eventually gaining some clout as a result of their associations with similar organizations and governments outside the region. However, their political impact remained very limited as some governments in the region began to circumvent their efforts by creating their own national human rights organizations, and as the process of empowering them by foreign states discredited their leading gurus and functionaries.[8]

The Center for Arab Unity Studies also attracted the attention of the Islamists who were included in the debate by suggesting common grounds for cooperation between them and the pan-Arabists. Several conferences were held to establish a new forum for a national–religious dialogue, which met annually to discuss jointly the threats facing the Arabs and Muslims. Similar to the nationalists, the Islamists did not have a consensus among them, nor did they seem to share with the pan-Arabists any particular vision of democracy.

To conclude, it is reasonable to claim that the 1967 defeat had ushered in, among other things, a sudden upsurge in the debate for political liberalization and democracy. Throughout the 1970s, critical evaluation of the Nasserite and Ba'ath era by Arab liberals and leftists yielded a strong condemnation of authoritarian rule. The student movements, which erupted in 1968 in Cairo University, Ain Shams, and Alexandria, had one thing in common, a demand for political freedom.[9] Even the newly emerging Palestinian resistance movement under the leadership of Fateh did not escape sharp criticisms when it was defeated in September 1970 in Jordan by King Hussein's army. Dr. Sadek Jalal Al-Azm wrote a critique of the movement at that time accusing it of ignoring the involvement of the Palestinian masses and failing to mobilize them.[10]

The demand for political freedom gained momentum, and the democratic discourse gradually expanded to include a wide range of topics. Two major views of democracy were put on the table for discussion. One derived its intellectual roots from liberal democracy, which focused on legitimacy and constitutionalism and the institutional requirements of liberalization. The other emphasized the social and economic content of democratization, which could only be achieved through economic equality and social justice. The two competing trends were not mutually exclusive; but together, they embodied the major elements of the democratic discourse that lasted until the end of the 1980s.

One of the most distinguishing features of the debate during that period was that democracy was not seen in isolation, as a domestic dilemma facing each Arab society on its own. Democracy was viewed in the context of the wider national concerns of the Arabs, as part and parcel of their yearning to end Israeli occupation and achieve independence from Western and, more specifically, American domination. US policy in the region appeared to play a dual role which linked together some of the major maladies of the Arabs. On the one hand, since 1967, the US adhered to a pro-Israeli policy which frustrated the hopes of the Arabs in a just and comprehensive resolution of the Palestinian–Israeli conflict. On the other, it often reinforced and perpetuated the position of some of the authoritarian regimes in the region. Democracy, independence, and liberation became not only the victims of the failed regimes of the Arab world but also the targets of Israeli intransigence and Western hegemony in the region. Consequently, when the democratic discourse was launched in the late 1960s, it was perceived to be an integral part of the wider national discourse. Democracy was not to be pursued for its own sake, but as an effective avenue toward development and independence, and as an instrument of liberation from Israeli occupation, Western domination, and domestic state oppression.

The discourse was indigenous, generated by Arabs for an Arab audience; it was genuine, stemming from a historical turn of events in the region following the Arab defeat; and it was pan-Arab in inception and intent. The West did not seem during that time to be too interested in the discourse. Michael

Hudson may have been a perceptive exception among Western specialists on the Middle East. Most of them overlooked the new phenomenon. However, some time in the early 1980s, the attention of the West was drawn to the issue of democracy in the region, and a new era was introduced, in which the involvement of Western specialists and Western governments gained an unprecedented momentum.

Phase two

The change in the attitude of the West may have occurred as a result of changes in Eastern Europe after the collapse of the Soviet Union, when hopes were heightened by a sweeping wave of democratization which was expected to engulf other regions of the world including the Arab countries. Another factor may have been the Gulf War in 1991. It represented a moment of intense contact between the Arab world and the Western powers led by the US, which gave the latter the opportunity to have a closer look at the domestic problems of the region. The two factors may have combined to render the growing interest of the West in the internal arrangements of Arab societies inevitable.

The early awareness of the West of the lack of democracy in the Arab world followed to some extent the general understanding, based on the linkage between national and domestic issues that the Arabs had of their own dilemmas. At that stage, the Western powers were not willing to alienate the Arab regimes by pressing hard for moves toward political liberalization. They opted for achieving a balance between nudging the regimes to liberalize and, at the same time, avoiding measures that would undermine the stability of their close allies in the region. The West understood that the Palestinian issue was a key issue in the process of opening the Arab world to become more receptive to their urgings. The US administration moved quickly to convene the Madrid conference, in October 1991, in an effort to remove once and for all an obstacle that had poisoned Arab–American relations for a very long time. Some limited success followed, with the signing of the Oslo Accord in 1993, and the conclusion of a Jordanian–Israeli agreement in 1994. In the meantime, the US and its European allies encouraged the Arab regimes to allow more space for non-governmental organizations (NGOs), civil society institutions, and human rights organizations. They gently urged their Arab friends to concede some liberties for the opposition parties, without jeopardizing the political stability of the regimes.

In 1995, the European Union (EU) announced the Barcelona Declaration, which focused on issues of mutual concern to Europe and the Middle East. At the head of the list of concerns was security, which emphasized the need for a resolution of the Arab-Israeli conflict. It also stressed the need for economic and trade cooperation as well as cultural interaction. During the 1990s, Western experts as well as advocates of liberalism seemed to turn their attention away from democratization, which in itself was a revolutionary idea, to a more modest objective, namely civil society. It is not very clear why this change in sentiment had taken place, but it is possible to make an intelligent guess based on some evidence.

It would seem that as long as the democratic discourse was confined to Arab intellectuals and institutions it remained predominantly focused on the demand for direct political participation. Such a demand was by definition threatening to the political and social status of the existing Arab regimes. However, when Western governments and institutions became interested in the process of political liberalization, the notion of civil society was thought to be more suitable because it did not threaten to disrupt the position of the regimes and alter the status quo in the region. Consequently, as the American administration and the European Union became increasingly involved in the discourse, the emphasis gradually shifted toward civil society. Somehow the Arab democratic discourse was either overlooked or won over. There was a sharp contrast in the discussions on the issue between the 1970s and 1980s, on the one hand, and the 1990s, on the other. As was mentioned earlier, the Center for Arab Unity Studies in the 1980s held numerous conferences and seminars, and encouraged Arab writers to contribute to its monthly publication, *Al Mostaqbal Al-Arabi*, editorials and articles analyzing the various aspects of democracy. In the 1990s the stress was on civil society. The Center took the initiative in 1992 and held a conference on civil society in the Arab world.[11]

In Cairo, Saad Eddin Ibrahim became the guru of civil society. He established the Ibn Khaldun Center for Development Studies which published in 1992 a newsletter, entitled *Civil Society*. This was followed by a series of books published by the Center on civil society in various Arab countries. The tendency was not to face the regimes head on by raising the slogan of democracy, but to lay the foundations for the creation of nongovernmental institutions and organizations that would mediate the relationship of society to the state and vice versa.

The impact of the West on the Arab discourse was not limited to highlighting the importance of civil society intellectually, but went beyond to support politically and financially the institutional development of research activities and encourage representative bodies on the national and local levels to acquire the means of empowering themselves, by gaining access to information and knowledge. Western specialists on the ME were also engaged in the effort to explain and promote the case of civil society. The Ford and Rockefeller Foundations funded in 1992 the Civil Society Middle East Project which was launched by Augustus Richard Norton. The project lasted until December 1994, and resulted in the publication of two volumes edited by Norton and a primer by one of his associates.[12] Suddenly, numerous grants, fellowships and scholarships, academic exchange programs and conferences became available to academicians, writers, human rights activists to enhance their understanding of the theory and practice of civil society. The new twist in the emphasis of the debate tended to ignore the pan-Arab and national issues which formed the basis for unleashing the democracy debate in the first place.

The objective of the discourse was no more the end of Israeli occupation, or the elimination of Western dominance, or even circulation of power. Its purpose had become more modest, the alleviation of the burdens of autocratic rule through the development of civil society.

A separation had set in between the national concerns of the Arab nation and the process of political liberalization. Civil society was considered within a very limited context that of domestic politics, isolated from any entanglement with Palestine or western domination. The nature of the Arab discourse was transformed through the adoption of civil society as a substitute for democracy. The Western argument that the search for liberalization did not have to await the favorable outcome of the peace process between the Arabs and Israelis became prevalent. Such argument was reinforced by the fact that the US administration under Clinton's presidency had launched its peace initiatives in the Middle East without any reference to the issue of democracy.

It is reasonable to conclude that, by the beginning of the twenty-first century, the Arab drive for democratization, which emerged after the 1967 Arab defeat, had been diverted from its national course, due to the intervention of the West. Western involvement had three detrimental effects on the debate:

1 It diluted the intensity of the democracy discourse and reduced it to a civil society debate.
2 It emptied the discourse of the initial driving force behind it by separating it from the national concerns of the peoples of the region.
3 It rendered many of the Arab champions of civil society, who were closely associated with the political and financial contributions of the West, political suspects and discredited them among their Arab compatriots.

On balance, the West did not possess the political determination to tip the scales significantly in favor of civil society. Its concern for maintaining stable relationships with the authoritarian regimes eventually took precedence over its encouragement of civil society. The final outcome of a decade of involvement by the West in the liberalization process in the Arab world was very modest. It was estimated that the Arab countries had experienced from the mid-1960s to the late 1980s an increase in the number of civil society organizations from 20,000 to 70,000. However, according to serious studies conducted by Dr. Amani Kandil, executive director of the Arab Network of Civil Society Organizations, the quantitative increase hardly had any practical results, due to the ineffective performance of these organizations. The Western countries and the UN may have contributed to increasing the numbers even further, but there are no indications to suggest that outside intervention had significantly altered the political or social effectiveness of those organizations. In most cases, the Arab governments were able to introduce new legislation, which brought most of the newly established so-called civil society organizations under their bureaucratic control and emasculated their operations.

Phase three

September 11 brought about a more forceful Western interventionist strategy to guide the Arabs toward democracy. President Bush and members of his administration often repeated that it was high time to give priority to the implementation of policies leading to the democratization of the Arab world rather than continuing to opt for stability. At some point, Condoleezza Rice talked about "creative anarchy" as a desirable prospect and a tolerable risk in the process of establishing democratic regimes in the area. President Bush declared that the US was abandoning its sixty years of tolerance for authoritarian regimes and institutions, and adopting a new policy characterized by a serious determination to democratize Arab societies.

The US argument after September 11 was largely based on a belief, almost a faith, in the magic powers of democracy once it engulfs the Arab world. Democracy was once more repositioned to take a central place in the order of things, as it did earlier after the Arab defeat in 1967, while civil society was pushed to a back seat position. The new initiative by the Bush administration sought to serve two purposes. First, it shifted the blame for the events of September 11 from the disastrous consequences of the US policies toward its Palestinian, Arab, and Muslim victims to the victims themselves. It argued that the attack was a direct outcome of the growing frustrations of these people, due to political and social oppression in their own countries, and a result of economic deprivation and lack of education. Second, the new initiative provided the administration with the legal and moral justification to pursue a more aggressive interventionist policy in the region, and intensify the pressures on its governments and peoples alike to respond to America's political and security demands.

Democracy gained a high priority on the US agenda in the Arab and Muslim countries, but together with it, there were other demands put forward which required from the Palestinians peaceful acquiescence to Israeli dictates, from the Arabs ready endorsement of the occupation of Iraq, and from the Muslims at large an end to Islamic intransigence and submission to US hegemony. The publication of the first volume of the *Arab Human Development Report* in 2002 reinforced the administration's conviction of the need for the Arabs to attend to their shortcomings. The report emphasized that the Arabs were suffering from political oppression, gender inequalities, and a low standard of education. Secretary Powell and members of the US administration quoted the report enthusiastically on several occasions, indicating that the ills of the Arabs were self-generated and had nothing to do with US policy in the Middle East. However, when the third volume of the report was published, and it critically addressed the US and Israeli roles in the region, the administration attempted in the first instance to block its publication, but later withdrew its objections as the authors of the report toned down those parts of it which were highly critical of US policies.

Many governments snapped to attention, and in the face of the political and military onslaught of the US on the region, some of them even took a few steps backward. In late 2002, the Arab summit in Beirut decided to go along with Bush's suggestion to accept a two-state solution to the Palestinian–Israeli conflict. Most Arab governments reluctantly introduced political and legislative steps, with plans for political reform to open the way for a greater measure of political participation, in accordance with pressures exerted upon them by Washington. With few exceptions, the Arab regimes joined the efforts of the US in its declared "war on terror." Those who showed any resistance were declared outcasts, or worse, were listed in the axis of evil. In the meantime, the national issues that seemed rightly or wrongly to occupy the minds and hearts of the Arabs were deliberately ignored. No effort of any significant magnitude was made to redress the grievances of the Palestinians, or to alleviate the catastrophic consequences of the war on Iraq.

In the absence of any linkage between the US drive for democracy in the Arab countries and the national concerns of the peoples of the region, the US obsession with democracy was regarded with great suspicion. Even regimes friendly to the US began to show signs of resentment, and contributed in no small measure to enhancing the sweeping wave of anti-Americanism. The more the Bush administration intensified its campaign in favor of democracy, but refrained at the same time from addressing the Arabs most cherished national concerns, the more democracy acquired a bad name. Finally, when the US refused to deal with the winners of the most democratic elections ever held in the Arab world in the Palestinian occupied territories, in January 2006, America's credibility as the champion of democracy received a major blow. This, however, was preceded by signs of American political exhaustion in Iraq, in which the US had already abandoned its democratic ideals for a more pragmatic approach of divide and rule, and thus alienated its Arab as well as its US audience.

The dilemma between theory and practice

Today, almost four decades have passed since the early calls for political liberalization made their way into the Arab national discourse. During that time, the debate has gone through several phases of development. In its initial phase, it focused on the need for the widest possible political participation of the masses to realize Arab ambitions in the development, freedom, and liberation of Palestine. Its champions were drawn mainly from among Arab intellectuals and political movements that were closely associated with the Palestinian resistance movement. In the second phase, from the late 1980s until September 11, Western governments, think tanks, intellectuals, and academicians joined the debate, and overwhelmed and transformed the discussions to emphasize the separation between democratization and the Arab national concerns. Simultaneously, the scope of the debate was narrowed down to focus on the creation of Arab civil society and institutions without disturbing the political status of the Arab authoritarian regimes. September 11 introduced a new phase in which the US became actively involved in the discourse with a particular neoconservative outlook. It envisaged the realization of democracy in the region within the context of a Greater Middle East project, in which the Arab national concerns continued to be ignored. In the new arrangement, the security of Israel took precedence over Palestinian human rights. On the other hand, the security of the Arab regimes was undermined as the US encouraged domestic political demands for reform, and Arab leaders were humiliated when American troops marched into Baghdad and served notice to other Arab capitals who dared to incur the displeasure of the Bush administration.

From 1967 to 2006, a long time had passed in which numerous theoretical and practical efforts to democratize the Arab world were made. Intellectuals, policy makers, regional as well as international organizations were involved in promoting the cause of democracy in the region, but to no avail. The meager outcome of those efforts had led some to believe that the Arab world was the exception. While the rest of the world was moving in the right direction, the Arabs seemed to lag behind unable to enter the new age of freedom. A search has been launched, since the early days of the debate, to examine why the Arabs have failed while others have succeeded. As a matter of fact, a good part of the democracy discourse has been deeply concerned with this particular issue. So much has been written, so many interpretations introduced, and so many theories articulated to explain the failure of Arab societies to democratize. True, there were some experiences which were promising, some that have been close to success, but on the whole the results have been less than impressive. Has the time come to declare the futility of the effort in an Arab context? Perhaps yes, if the debate continues to explore the same avenues and the practical experiences continue to consolidate the traditional and archaic forms of ethnic and confessional representation. It was rather depressing to watch the American, European, and UN spokesmen and high officials celebrating in a self-congratulatory mood the results of the elections in Iraq. It was a pure case of where the tools of democracy had been made to substitute for the soul of democracy. In doing so, the position of the warlords of the north and the status of the tribal–confessional leaderships of the central provinces and southern Iraq were enhanced on account of the Iraqi citizen.

In the present circumstances in the Arab world, a discourse on democracy may become relevant politically only if some basic conditions for its development are satisfied. The majority of Arab countries do not only suffer from the lack of grassroots democratic constituencies, but worse, they have hardly developed significant political constituencies per se. Without the latter, the first condition for the establishment of democratic regimes could prove to be extremely difficult. Most Arab countries that gained their independence after World War II have failed to produce political constituencies capable of providing the basis for the emergence of democratic systems of government. There is sometimes the odd exception here or there, an oasis or enclave where some measure of political participation is witnessed, but unfortunately, by and large, viable political constituencies have not materialized on a wide scale in the region.

Ultimately, whether the discourse on democracy, civil society, or political participation was generated domestically or imposed from outside did not make that much difference. The fact was that, in the absence of a political constituency, the discourse did not penetrate and capture the imagination of the people, nor was it integrated into the political consciousness of Arab society. The political and military intervention of the US in the region, whether through the use of coercive persuasion applied to some Arab leaders, or the simple military invasion of Iraq, did not produce anything except warlords and oligarchs sustained by the military might of America and the coalition of the willing.

The absence of political constituencies in most of the Arab countries can be attributed to a historical process that accompanied the emergence and development of most Arab political entities after their independence. Two types of entities prevailed: "A group of major Arab countries which included Egypt, Syria, Iraq, Algeria and others appeared to develop a type of state which was monopolistic in nature."[13] It took control of the political and security apparatus, centralized the economy, and appropriated the wealth of society. Political participation under these conditions was confined to an elite consisting of army officers, bureaucrats, and technocrats who established a state party and deprived the rest of society of its right to be engaged in any political activity. "Another group of countries, mainly the oil producing states developed"[14] an equally exclusive model, whereby the ruling families monopolized the reins of power and wealth, and kept the rest of society at bay. In this latter model, the state bribed its citizens from the oil revenue by subsidizing goods and services, but kept political power to itself in the hands of a few. Neither of the two models allowed or even encouraged political participation with the exception of the Islamists, who some time during the 1970s enjoyed the favors of some Arab governments and the blessings of the US.

Before the collapse of the Soviet Union in the early 1990s, the US and its Western allies had been keenly interested in basing their strategic posture in the Middle East on the premise that Islam represented an effective antidote to the expansion of Soviet influence in the region. The Baghdad Pact in essence was nothing but an attempt to gather together the governments and the leaders of the Middle East under the banner of Islamic solidarity. Eventually, when the Baghdad Pact failed, the US opted for closer ties with the leaders of the Islamic pact countries headed by King Faisal of Saudi Arabia and the Shah of Iran. The US continued to lend its support to the Islamists, even after Khomeini's revolution in Iran in 1979, which undermined the interests of the Western powers in the region. The Soviet invasion of Afghanistan toward the end of that year prompted the US to reinforce its support to the Islamists with the intention of defeating Moscow and rolling back communism.

Under these circumstances requiring a continued effort to stand against communism, the US and its allies relied heavily in the Middle East on the support of the local Islamic forces and the autocratic rulers in the region. Political constituencies of a democratic nature could hardly evolve under such political and strategic conditions. Very often, American and Western intervention tended to buttress the position of the ruling elite, and encourage further the oppressive nature of the authoritarian regimes and the rule of autocrats.

Egypt and Palestine: the test

Where there were no political constituencies, there was little hope for the emergence of democratic systems of government, but where political constituencies did exist, the move toward political participation was more likely. The real test for the emergence of a democratic system in the Arab world can best be illustrated by examining two recent attempts to realize such an ambition in two Arab countries, namely Egypt and Palestine.

In Egypt, despite the enormous pressure exercised on the regime by its superpower ally to open up the system for the participation of others, the result was rather modest, and to all intents and purposes negligible. The regime allowed the presidency to be contested by the free vote of the electorate. The constitution was modified to permit the leaders of the various political parties who did not have a significant representation in the People's Assembly to become eligible candidates. Six offered their names including of course Mubarak, who was running for a fifth term. Formally, Egypt has some seventeen political parties; however, with the exception of the Muslim Brothers, who are not officially recognized as a party, and the newly established Al-Ghad party, the rest are remnants of the past and hardly have any following. They have become stagnant and relatively dysfunctional. The ruling party, on the other hand, is the party of the state. It has been and continues to be. Its main assets are not its achievements nor its political program, but its ability to mobilize the apparatus and employees of the state and bring them to vote for the government candidates at the right time. Traditionally, the regime has perpetuated itself in power by basically eliminating its opponents and nationalizing all political activities in society. Accordingly, despite the fact that relatively freer elections were held in the recent presidential elections, when the time came for the electorate to cast its vote, the overwhelming majority voted for Mubarak. The leader of Al-Ghad polled some half a million votes, but was later arrested and sentenced to serve seven years in prison.

The real challenge to the regime was posed by one political party, which had sustained its independent existence from the state, despite the continuous campaigns against it to dissolve itself. The Muslim Brothers were able to gain some eighty-eight seats in the last parliamentary elections against all odds. That in itself is quite an achievement for a party that has survived more than five decades of political suppression in Egypt, with only a brief period of respite under President Sadat. During the cold war, the Saudi monarchy and the US also contributed to the political and financial sustenance of the Brothers.

What are the lessons to be learned from the Egyptian experience? First, in the absence of vibrant political constituencies, regime continuity is assured, and its ability to pass the reins of power to the younger generation within the same ruling elite is almost guaranteed in the future. Second, the only serious challenge to the existing order come from those areas where a political constituency was capable of fortifying itself against the continuous onslaughts of those in power, namely the Islamists.

The second example is Palestine where the experience has been radically different. Among the Palestinians, the opportunity for the leading party— Fateh—to nullify the existence of the other political groups within the resistance movement had not been a viable option. Palestinians in the diaspora and in the occupied territories had been relatively free, especially after 1967, to make their own choices, without a supreme state authority nationalizing all aspects of their lives. The Israeli occupation and the oppressive regimes in the Arab world often tried to suppress the Palestinians, but failed because these were mainly external challenges. On the contrary, the challenge seemed to enhance the Palestinian sense of resistance and intensify their commitment to their national aspirations. With the signing of the Oslo Accords in 1993, the newly emerging Palestinian Authority (PA) was inhibited from establishing its full control over its society. First, the Palestinians were already highly politicized and thoroughly mobilized in the ranks of the various organizations, which made it extremely difficult for Israel or the PA to subordinate them to their political or military will. Second, the PA was not provided with the necessary political leverage or the adequate military facilities of statehood effectively to exercise its authority over the land and the people. The state of conflict between the Palestinians and Israel that had erupted since September 2000 as a result of the ill-advised visit of Sharon to the Aqsa Mosque had undoubtedly kept the Palestinians actively involved in a continuous political and social struggle for survival.

In the elections to the legislative assembly held in January 2006, over 75 percent of the Palestinian electorate took part in the process. This was indeed a very high percentage compared with that in Egypt, where no more than 23 percent participated in the elections for the new People's Assembly.

A comparison with Iraq could be very misleading. There too the returns in the polls were quite high, but unlike the Palestinian case, the patterns of voting were not determined by a commitment to a political and ideological program of one organization or another, but to primary loyalties more related to a religious sect, ethnic affinity, or tribal solidarity. It was a case more like a shepherd bringing his flock to drink from his own well.

It might also be worth noting that, in Palestine, the democratic process was closely linked to a national struggle for liberation and an end to occupation, while in Iraq, the issue of occupation was submerged or marginalized and, thus, the national platform of any of the competing parties was parochial in nature and rather weak and insignificant.

Conclusion

For democracy in the Arab world to become a viable option, a strategy of relinking the national concerns of the Arab peoples with internal arrangements for the circulation of power and free elections based on citizenship rights ought to be generated. It would seem that, with a few exceptions, such a condition has not yet evolved. Pressures from outside are scratching the surface, without going deep into the grassroots of Arab societies. The call for political liberalization and democratization is appealing to only a very thin layer of Arab society, whose political and social interests might coincide with such a call. However, the majority of Arabs, including most Arab elites, remain largely ambivalent and suspicious of the sudden interest of the West in their conversion to democracy, without at the same time responding equally strongly to an end to Israeli occupation, rebuilding Iraq, and respecting the religious and cultural sensitivities of the Arab world. Perhaps no action has been more cynical and damaging to the cause of democracy in the region than the European and US threat to starve the Palestinians when they exercised their democratic right and elected a majority from Hamas to the legislative assembly. By continuously ignoring the Arab national concerns and denying the Palestinians their national rights, the West has been doing a great disservice to democracy. It deprives it of its grassroots constituency, and leaves it in the hands of a few individuals who rapidly lose their credibility when the West comes to their support against the oppressive measures of their governments. In many instances, the cause of democracy in the region, as far as the West is concerned, was reduced to an Ayman Nour or a Saad Eddin Ibrahim, while thousands of Arab young men remained in Arab prisons without a Western voice coming to the rescue.

The process of democratization in the Arab world will be a hard and long drawn out battle. There are no short cuts to it. Its only avenue passes through the regeneration of political constituencies in the form of genuine political parties, independent civil society organizations, and free currents of thought. The attempts of the US and the European powers to overflood the region with NGOs, private voluntary organizations (PVOs), and community development associations (CDAs) without providing a well-defined political framework derived from the concerns and ambitions of the Arab peoples might improve the technical capabilities or efficiency levels of a few individuals here or there, or even create jobs, but it does not generate a significant momentum for political participation. In any case, most of the organizations and associations newly founded by foreign money have been gradually brought under the sponsorship of the ruling elite and the control of the governments of the host countries.

In the future, the West may have a more effective role to play in promoting democratic rule by pushing the Arab regimes to expand the political space for the rise of political constituencies. However, if ever the US and its European allies hope to enhance participatory politics in the region, they have to regain the confidence of the Arab peoples. The credibility of the West has reached its lowest ebb in the region with its deadly silence on Israeli atrocities, the violation of human rights in Iraq and Afghanistan, the illegitimacy of Guantanamo, the humiliation of Arab leaders, and the deliberate disrespect for the symbols and values of Islam. Until the West can find a way to win the hearts and minds of the Arabs, and develop policies more consistent with the moral values it claims to uphold and pursue, there is little chance that it will attract the attention of its Arab audience.

More recently, it has become more evident that the drive toward democracy in the Arab world, which has been championed by the president of the US and supported by the major European powers, has lost much of its momentum. The growing failure of the US policy in Afghanistan, Palestine, and Iraq has prompted the Bush administration to seek once more, out of sheer expediency, the support of its old regional allies, none other than the Arab autocrats.

The Arab victims of the policies of the US and its European and regional allies have become too many. The long entertained hope of some Arabs for democracy has truly become the latest of these victims.

Notes

1 A. Hammouda (2006) *Ahram*, January 24, p. 12.
2 T. Al-Hakim (1974) *The Return of Consciousness*. Cairo: Awdat Al-Wai', p. 25.
3 Ibid, p. 70.
4 Y. Al-Hafiz (1978) *The Defeat and the Defeated Ideology*. Beirut: Alhazima, wa al-Ideologia al-Mahzuma, p. 144.
5 A. Baha'a el-Din (1984) *Legitimate Authority in the Arab World*. Cairo: Shariat Al-Sulta fi Al-Watan Al-Arabi, p. 14.
6 G. Salameh (1987) *Toward a New Arab Social Contract*. Beirut: Nahwa 'Aqd Ijtima'i Arabi Jadid, pp. 97–98.
7 B. Ghalyun (1986) *A Communiqué for Democracy*, 4th edn. Beirut: Bayan Min Ajl Al-Dimuqratiyya, p. 25.
8 For further information, see S. Ismael (1995) "Democracy in Arab Intellectual Discourse" in Rex Brynen et al., eds, *Political Liberalization and Democratization in the Arab World*, Vol. 1. Boulder, CO, and London: Lynne Rienner Publishers.
9 For further information, see W. Othman (1975) *The Secrets of the Student Movement, 1968–1975*. Cairo: Asrar Al-Haraka Al-Tullabiyya.
10 S. Jalal Al-Azm (1973) *A Critical Study of the Thought of the Palestinian Resistance*. Beirut: Dirasa Naqdiyya Lifikr Al-muqawama Al-Filistiniyya, Dar Al-Awda, pp. 213–14.
11 The contributions of the participants were published by the Center in a special volume during that year, but the debate continued for sometime afterward in the Center's monthly, Al-Mustaqbal Al-Arabi.
12 Kazziha, et al, Civil Society and the Middle East, Institute of Developing Economies, Tokyo, 1997, pp.13-14.
13 Kazziha (1998) "Political Consciousness and the Crisis of Political Liberalization in the Arab World," in Sven Behrendt and Christian Hanlet, eds, *Elections in the Middle East and North Africa*. Munich: Bertelsman Foundation, p. 6.
14 Ibid, p. 7.

5 Democracy and faith

The continuum of political Islam

Azza Karam[1]

The Taliban need to be engaged in the political process ... [otherwise] the US attacks are unifying Islamist radicals in Afghanistan today ... There is a split between al-Qaida and Afghan Taliban ... and if the Americans cannot see this, it is a lost opportunity for all of us.[2]

We are witnessing the collapse of the American Empire ... What's going on in America is a result of the violation of the rights of people in Palestine, Somalia, Iraq, Afghanistan and Muslims around the world.[3]

Introduction

In the recent period, there have been tectonic shifts in world power propelled by how faith features more prominently in politics, the collapsing economy of Western governments, and thriving markets in some Eastern states. This chapter argues that, because of these shifts, it is time to see Islamist political interlocutors, and deal with them, very differently.

The financial meltdown, a collapsing mortgage market in the United States, and record revenue from oil in petroleum-exporting states are combining to bring about radical transformations in economic power. These market shifts are made more complicated by the shifting political forces after the attacks on the World Trade Towers as Al Qaeda launched itself so graphically into world politics and everything that has followed from that important event.

Islamist political groups have been and continue to make major gains. In spite of major efforts to eliminate them, the Taliban have re-emerged with a vengeance in Afghanistan. Some political actors and security advisors in and out of the country even argue that it is necessary to engage them in the political process. Hizbullah are seen in many circles—in and out of Lebanon—as the moral, political, and military victors over Israel since their 2006 conflict. Hamas won legislative elections and, after international attempts to isolate them, staged a coup of sorts, which now leaves them reigning over the Gaza Strip. For the first time, the Egyptian Muslim Brotherhood has eighty seats in a parliament of over 400 seats, and is arguably slated to win free and fair elections in the country. Algeria's "North African Al Qaeda" is repeatedly vying for gruesome limelight through violent messages and terrorist attacks. Al Qaeda's Osama bin Laden is supposedly rooted in Waziristan, along the Afghan border, but "cells" operate throughout Europe. "Home-grown terrorism" is now as popular in academic and policy think-tank discussions as "democracy" was in the 1990s. Controversial Danish cartoonists and Dutch MPs (with cartoons and a film, respectively, on Islam) feature in nightly talk shows on televisions in different countries.

The Iranian Revolution of 1979 created shockwaves in political circles around the Western world, the ripples of which can still be felt in speeches made by the current President Ahmedinejad, and in the ongoing debates about the country's nuclear capacity. A legislative decision held that the government's revoking of the ban on the veil in Turkey was illegitimate. This decision almost decided the future of the country's government and governing party despite strong electoral success in August 2007. In a country struggling to hang on to its staunchly secular identity, these Islamic forces in government are causing considerable consternation in many circles.

All this has many politicians and students of politics around the world rather worried. After the events of September 11, 2001, one of the most oft-repeated questions in the US was "why do they hate us [sic]"? Many years later and after many political developments, those on the right of the Western political spectrum are speculating as to how far back this "hate" goes (all the way back to the Crusades?) and when will the US troops come home from Iraq and Afghanistan? At the same time, students of Western politics in countries as diverse as Argentina and Pakistan are concerned about the backlash generated by US foreign policy. The unpublicized question is: do all these developments mean more terrorism is here to stay?

Ten to twenty years ago, the confluence of religion and mainstream political activism was deemed by many scholars and politicians to be, at best, a "lack of awareness of secular realities." Today, religion and politics are the topics of many graduate courses in almost all universities, and they appear in the headlines of major books and publications. Religion and politics, the sacred and the political, and several other variations of the same theme, are definitely "in."[4] This trend is surely for good reasons. With the collapse of the Berlin Wall and the Soviet Union came a near eclipse of the grand political meta-narratives of communism and socialism. Virtually left alone as the victor, liberalism eventually became entangled with globalization. Globalization itself is littered with hypocritical and morally corrupt political regimes, serious global economic disparities, global warming and debilitating effects on the environment, armed civil conflicts, and with transnational acts of terrorism as icing on the cake. Ringing in the collective global ears are the mantras of charismatic religious personas and the ethos of religious–political parties working simultaneously, it would seem, on the mind (providing new mobilizing ideologies) and the body (serving many people's economic welfare in the form of education, health services, and even pension plans in some countries). Whether it is the Christian coalition of the US playing a strong role in the election and governance decisions of the Bush administration, the Hindu BJP Party in India ruling for many years and now in opposition, or the ongoing influence of Iranian religious clerics in the political decision making, the fact is that religion and politics are today's most well-known bedfellows.

When Islamism, or political Islam, as we know it today, emerged strongly in the 1980s in the Arab world, it grabbed Western headlines with events such as the assassination of the Egyptian President Anwar al-Sadat, various kidnappings, bombings, and armed conflict in Lebanon, Egypt, and Algeria, to name but a few. Almost since the 1980s then, political Islam was perceived in the Western public consciousness as synonymous with violence. This impression has almost solidified the Western collective consciousness by unfolding events in the Arab world together with ongoing bombings and attacks elsewhere (i.e., the Paris subway bombings, US embassy attacks in Nairobi and Dar es Salaam, World Trade Center in New York, and the Pentagon in Washington, followed by Bali, Madrid, London, Glasgow, and so on). Needless to say, the conflict between Hamas and Fateh, as it unfolded in the occupied Palestinian territories (oPt), has done nothing to enhance both the impression of terror and the fear of it.

Today, spokespersons of political Islam, or Islamism, find themselves, at best, on the defensive about their diversity and their aspirations and, at worst, cornered and fighting.[5] This is a dangerous state of affairs; it is problematic to have a popular political movement misunderstood and pushed into a corner at any time. It is also unwise to subsume a diverse political movement under one heading, such as "terrorism/terrorists," which dismisses, in one fell stroke, its varied protagonists from opportunities for representation and negotiation at any time. But it is dangerous to do all of this at a time when many within, and even outside, these movements feel they have legitimate grievances, and believe they are fighting for a just cause. It is also a downright waste when some members of these movements are potentially critical interlocutors, at a moment when all of us are seeking a socio-political meta-narrative that can inspire and move us forward in contemporary times.

This chapter will be divided into three parts. First, political Islam will be defined and described through what I term the Islamist continuum. I will argue that Islamist movements fall on a spectrum characterized by a nominal unity of purpose (i.e., a more just/Islamic governance), but a significant difference in methods. Second, I will discuss the fact that Islamist movements are given an unparalleled boost because of both the decline in secular movements and "blowback" from US foreign policy—the latter seen as being realized and endorsed by illegitimate Arab governments. And last, the chapter will discuss how it is that religion is not only an occurrence in the Muslim world, but part and parcel of an ideological echo in both Eastern and Western hemispheres. As such, I will conclude by arguing that certain Islamist tendencies should not be seen as enemies, but rather as potentially powerful ideological allies in a struggle against spiraling violent confrontations.

I Landscapes: the continuum of political Islam

> The Prophet is our Leader, Islam is our credo (ideology), and the Holy Qur'an is our Constitution.[6]

Islamism is only one stream of politics within and outside the Muslim world. It is but a fraction of the different forms of social and political mobilization that take place among Muslims in general—and certainly among Muslim communities in the Western hemisphere.[7]

Repeated statements by US President George W. Bush and other members of his administration immediately after the events of September 11, then echoed by other leaders such as Britain's Tony Blair, highlighted that the "war against terrorism" has nothing to do with Islam. And yet, "Islamic extremism," "Islamic terror," "Islamic militants," and "Islamic violence" have become part of the mainstream lexicon.

Various Western authors continue to analyze political Islam and, after the US invasion of Iraq, several have attempted to trace differences between Shia'a and Sunni trends. Often, terms such as Islamic fundamentalism, *salafi*, jihadi, and Islamic radicalism have been used to explain the roots and objectives of all these movements. Much debate took place, particularly in the late 1980s and 1990s, about appropriate nomenclature. For the context of this study, the term Islamism is considered more appropriate to describe a continuum of movements that have a quintessentially political agenda, revolving around Islamizing (rendering more Islamic, often with the implementation of Shari'a laws) the structures of governance and those of the overall society. It must also be stated at the outset that, as a political movement with an agenda of eventually ruling, or capturing, power, the distinction between Sunni or Shia'a origins, or such affiliations, may simply cause more confusion.

An Islamist is to be distinguished (see Figure 5.1) from her/his fundamentalist or conservative counterpart, in that s/he is not literal in their interpretations and understanding of text and, in fact, can be quite creative in the manner in which they implement their "religious" understanding. Islamists are invariably heavily engaged in public social work and invest in it.

Whereas a fundamentalist may or may not become engaged in political thought, debate, and activism, an Islamist, by definition, does. Political engagement is a sine qua non of being an Islamist. The latter distinction also clarifies the difference between an Islamist, a Muslim fundamentalist, and an average Muslim. In other words, it is the involvement in a movement or a group that is advocating or struggling for political change—specifically to render more "Islamic" the social and political governing principles (or government)—that is the principal hallmark of an Islamist.

For many Islamists, Islamization as a political agenda is a means to bring about justice—politically, economically, and socially. To be an Islamist, it is by no means enough to be a Muslim, nor is it even sufficient (or even necessary) to be a fundamentalist. Rather, an Islamist must be committed to active

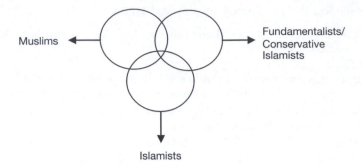

Figure 5.1 Muslim scapes: intersecting and distinct realities

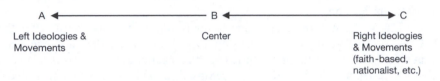

Figure 5.2 Political scapes: the political continuum

public engagement in the quest for a more Islamic (read: just) society. All Islamists will share this ultimate aim.[8]

But what constitutes an "Islamic" (or just) society and, therefore, Islamic governance? And what methods should be used to achieve this aim? These are among the most important questions around which Islamists will differ (often radically and, as we see in present-day Afghanistan and Iraq, often violently) from each other. There is no homogeneous Islamist entity. It is by now almost a cliché to say that not all Islamists are alike, and that there is a serious mis-representation when they are all lumped together as "fundamentalists," "fana-tics," or "terrorists." The latter obscures the significant differences within Islamist political thought and praxis.

When conceiving of Islamist movements, it is important to consider a continuum—which in itself is a constantly changing kaleidoscope. The Isla-mist continuum falls within a broader political one (see Figure 5.2). In other words, if we think of the political field as represented by a broad and ever-changing continuum of ideologies and/or movements, then we can distinguish between those of the extreme left, of the extreme right, and plenty that fall in between. On the right wing of this political spectrum are nationalist and religious-based parties (themselves very diverse).

If we were to take this right end of the political spectrum, where Islamists (and other faith-based and nationalist political parties) can be located, we would note that this ideology itself merits its own spectrum, or continuum (i.e., in Figure 5.2, if the broader political continuum goes from A to C, then the

Islamist one falls from B to C). On the left end of the continuum is the "moderate" tendency, while on the opposite side of it, the right, lie more radical/extremist/militant tendencies. Clearly, these are generalized and relative political categories (the moderate can only be described as such when juxtaposed with the extremist and vice versa). Where the different groups and organizations fall on the continuum and how they should be named (as moderate or radical) is a matter of great debate, not only among those outside the movements, but also within them.

Moderate Islamists[9] maintain that change will come about only through long-term education, social and economic engagement, constituency building, and advocacy, whereby increasing numbers of people become "followers" and eventually espouse the political ideology cum social action package. Moderates will generally advocate for and participate in elections, and in several majority Muslim countries and societies where this is permitted,[10] they will register as political parties and organize themselves as such. One notable and critical difference between Islamist parties and other political entities is that the moderate Islamists tend to have relatively well-defined social agenda(s) often exemplified by their provision of important social services (e.g., schools and clinics) in their respective communities. The latter lends them credibility and support among the various social classes (particularly the larger poorer ones) and thus constitutes an important factor in their political outreach and popularity.

The continuum is not etched in stone, but is fluid. Moderate Islamists, for instance, are themselves very diverse in terms of their aims and agendas, as well as the modality of their organization. It may happen that one moderate party, at certain times during its interaction and existence, or on specific issues, adopts a stance that sits more at the "radical" end of the continuum. The Egyptian Muslim Brotherhood, for example, remained relatively silent during a spate of attacks against foreign tourists in Egypt carried out by radical Islamists in the early 1990s. Some sectors of the Algerian Islamic Salvation Front (FIS) were radicalized into violence after the Algerian elections (which they were set to win) were cancelled by the intervention of the army in the early 1990s. Also, to this day, in spite of its evolution into mainstream political participation methods, Hamas's official documentation notes that the state of Israel must be eradicated.

Alternatively, some radical Islamists may veer toward the moderate end of the continuum on specific issues or at certain times. An example of this is the Lebanese Hizbullah (Party of Allah), which has a history of anti-Israeli struggle and became particularly notorious during the 1980s for the kidnapping of Westerners in Beirut. In the 1990s, Hizbullah formed itself into a legitimately recognized political party, ran for elections, and won seats in the Lebanese parliament. Their decision to participate in electoral politics was certainly based on realpolitik,[11] but it was also a choice for a relatively moderate strategy—selectively applied. Such a shift has implications for whether or not (and how) Shari'a[12] should be applied. For instance, it is worthwhile mentioning in this context a letter sent in 2007, shortly after the electoral success of Hamas, by its appointed foreign minister to the UN Secretary General. The letter noted a willingness to accept negotiations with the Israeli state (and its existence), a far cry from earlier positions maintained throughout by this party. Although the contents of this communication were denied once it was made public, the letter, with what was noted therein, stands.

Similarly, Egyptian Jihad announced a change in its policies with the renunciation of violence as a means to their envisioned end of an Islamic state. This renunciation began to take shape after the massacre of tourists in Luxor, Egypt, in 1997 and the ensuing anger on the part of many Egyptians (many of whom depend on the industry for their livelihoods and were thus adversely affected by the significant drop in revenues). Jihad's announcement in 2004 and the Hamas call for a ceasefire against Israel (which took place some time before the Palestinian legislative elections) were both treated scathingly by Al Qaeda's spokesman, Ayman al-Zawahri.[13] Nevertheless, by so doing, both Egyptian Jihad and Palestinian Hamas were effectively shifting on some issues at strategic moments toward the more moderate end of the Islamist political continuum (Figure 5.3).

Whereas moderate Islamists stress that change will come about gradually, peacefully, and with mass support, and indeed largely urge full participation in political processes, radical Islamists tend to be more Machiavellian in so far as they see violence as a (legitimate) means to an end. Although they may sometimes justify it as a form of self-defense, radical Islamists (e.g., the late al-Zarqawi's group and like-minded brethren in Iraq) will generally maintain that violence is retaliatory (and even pre-emptive) of more violence and aggression to come. This is evidenced by Bin Laden's insinuation in 2001 that, by targeting the unjust power (*dhalim*) of the US and other Western nations, what is taking place is a retaliation against Western actions, a "triumph by the injured," so to speak, and a pre-emption of future injustices. Once again, we are hearing an echo of Islamist discourse in that of the current US administration (as well as of that of the Israeli leadership). The above radical Islamist protagonists all iterate a similar rhetoric: in the pursuit of their vision of "justice" and for the sake of "self-defense," violence is legitimate.

Figure 5.3 Islamist scapes: the Islamist continuum

The fondest appeal of Islamism

What lies at the heart of the appeal of such groups, irrespective of where they are on the continuum at any given moment in time? There is nothing new in claims for and political manifestos about social, political, and economic justice. Marxist and socialist parties of various hues have had these claims for decades. Nevertheless, the claim to populist legitimacy that Islamism has should not be underestimated at a time when the shifting global topography has created enabling local–regional conditions: a fluctuating political economy, a political cum ideological vacuum, and a crisis of secularism.

Historically, economic globalization has entailed an experimentation with structural adjustment policies that has left governments of developing countries crippled as far as providing the basic economic needs of their populace, while multinational corporations have moved in to control ever-increasing shares of national resources. At the same time, privatization and free trade tariffs resulted in local markets becoming increasingly flooded with foreign produce, and locals found it difficult to compete. Collectively, these policies resulted in a shrinking formal job market, on the one hand, and the enlargement of an informal sector with little protection and fewer rights for workers, on the other. In the Arab context, in particular, the phenomenon of rentier economies (depending largely on oil in the Gulf countries and tourism in others) has further complicated the process of sustainable economic development. Recent developments in the world economy, however, are positioning some Gulf countries in a much stronger financial position, and bringing into focus the cultural and political debates within them.

At the same time, grand political meta-narratives (of Maoism, Leninism, Marxism, capitalism, and liberalism) all appeared to fail the expectations of achieving minimal utopias for the average Mohammed, Juan, or Joe. Where Islamists can claim a leading edge is precisely in the fact that they combined the allure of a grand political narrative (Islam) with a workable economic agenda. Who provided affordable clothes, books, medicine, and even transportation for the least privileged university students in Cairo in the 1970s? The Muslim Brotherhood. Who provides affordable (if not free) health care and pensions for families that have lost breadwinners in Lebanon? Hizbullah. Who organized pension schemes, arranged for alternative schooling in times of school closures, and ran an infrastructural network of services in the face of increasing corruption of a ruling party in the West Bank and Gaza? Hamas. Where is it possible to meet the religious needs, with political mobilization and economic efficacy (including both efficiently providing much needed charity and receiving it in a face-saving manner)? At the home of the Islamists. In many ways, Islamism seems to function as a one-stop shop for both politics and social services.

Furthermore, we are living in the age of crisis for secularism and secular values. For too long in the Arab and non-Arab Muslim worlds, secularism was the domain of the elite, many of whom were either part of the ruling clans or the few in opposition to them but who nevertheless emulated them in lifestyle and appearance. Whether rightly or wrongly, secularism is seen by the majority as synonymous with "liberalism" and sometimes, ironically, social-ism, "Western values," and "non-religious." In short, secularism is perceived as the domain of the rich, the few, the old, and the rulers, or the "other." As such, it holds increasingly less sway among a majority hungry for change, fed up with rhetoric that delivers to a few at the expense of the many, and with conditions that oppress in the name of democratization and liberalization, and believing that they have an untried solution sanctioned by the highest power on earth—God.

All this is taking place at a time when the Arab region, in particular, has become the youngest in the world—specifically with the largest population of youth aged between 15 and 25[14]—and with a continuity of largely illegitimate regimes seen to be supported, or propped up, by the US in particular. With all of the above features, it is not difficult to appreciate where and why Isla-mists host a strong appeal. This appeal has, if anything, increased and inten-sified through the continuously unfolding events in the Arab and Muslim world.

Common political platforms and distinctive positions

There are some common political platforms between Islamists and other secular liberal parties in the Muslim world at large. These two groups share general concerns around poverty and globalization, and a number of Islamists maintain key positions on democracy, human rights and, in some instances, also on women's roles.

On the Israeli–Palestinian dynamics

Almost all political parties in the Arab world are pro-Palestinian emotively and intellectually. Regardless of whether they are Muslim, Christian, or agnostic, all political parties (even those traditionally at odds and enemies of one another on other aspects) see Israel as an occupier of Palestinian land. Inter-estingly however, it is because the most vociferous supporters of Palestinians have been Islamists (dating back to the large contingent of Muslim Brother-hood members who fought alongside the Palestinians in 1948) that the issue of Palestine is seen and presented as an "Islamic" issue—as though there are no Christian Palestinians. This distortion of reality has contributed to the widespread misinterpretation and evocation of the Arab–Israeli conflict as though it were a Muslim and Jewish one. This in turn, feeds into current rhetoric employed by the various administrations in Israel, that they are "also" fighting the war against (Islamic) terrorists. In the words of one Syrian (Orthodox) scholar, Palestinian Christians are in "double jeopardy – not only do they suffer as all Palestinians under occupation, but they do not even exist in their struggle."

Arab ruling parties that have signed peace treaties with Israel (and non-Arab political parties in Muslim countries) continue to maintain (quoting international law and various UN resolutions) that Israeli government presence in Gaza and the West Bank constitutes an occupation, and that Israel should agree to East Jerusalem as the capital of a Palestinian state.

Islamists, moderate and radicals alike, tend to disagree with their political counterparts on whether peace and normalization of relations with Israel is wise and/or necessary at all. Radical Islamists argue that Israel's mere presence and existence is in itself a constant act of aggression against Palestinians and, as such, should be resisted. The precise form that resistance should take (and what constitutes "legitimate" armed struggle) is a matter of some discussion, debate, and as events in Iraq continue to unfold, of serious conflict between radical Islamists themselves. However, during the two Palestinian *Intifada*s (uprisings), Islamists across the Muslim world have been arguably among the most vocal and active in their solidarity with the Palestinian cause. On suicide bombings, moderate Islamists have joined with their radical counterparts to counter relatively more mainstream Islamic voices[15] by stating that, as long as the targets were Israeli (and/or American) soldiers, the suicides were a legitimate form of struggle. Most radical Islamists, however, maintain that the suicide bombings are a legitimate form of self-defense (or resistance) against continuous Israeli aggression, thus effectively not distinguishing between Israeli military and civilian populations.

On democracy and human rights

Significantly, matters related to advocacy for democracy and human rights are also shared by Islamist and non-Islamist parties in many parts of the Muslim world. The exception is countries where Islamists are the ruling regimes and either fraught with internal dissension on how to implement an "Islamic democracy" (e.g., Iran and Sudan) or not even willing to contemplate and/or engage publicly in such discussions on the topic (e.g., Saudi Arabia). Those opposed to Islamists heatedly maintain that Islamist espousal of democracy is opportunistic—as a means of achieving power themselves after which they will eliminate it. Such critics reference Khomeini and events prior to and after the Iranian Revolution of 1979, the Sudanese episode with the Turabi regime, the Taliban rule in Afghanistan, and the (brief) Islamist takeover in Somalia.

And yet, is it opportunism that has prompted several Islamist parties to "reform" their organizational structures? For example, the Islamist parties have advanced the political wing to lead the military/armed ones, they have developed an electoral platform, as both Hizbullah and Hamas have done, and contested elections. It is also opportunism that has prompted Islamist parties, as with Egypt's Muslim Brotherhood, to form strategic alliances with existing political parties, issue specific manifestoes outlining their positions vis-à-vis a woman's right to lead her community, and come up with public "open letters" to their country's political leadership condemning endless political office and decrying the abuse of democracy—as with the Syrian and Saudi Arabian Islamists? To what extent can all this be dismissed as a ploy? And if so, would these elaborate attempts at outlining their worldview and agendas not further underline the need to take these parties as serious political counterparts, rather than the current attempts which, at best, alienate and marginalize and, at worst, render their members as martyrs and their ethos as the "untried holy alternative"?

As for championing human rights, anti-Islamists and liberals claim that the motivation behind arguing for these principles is that Islamists themselves are among the victims of human rights abuses that certain regimes perpetrate. Once in power, these critics maintain, Islamists will have no qualms about perpetuating the same abuses against their opposition. These skeptical voices can now also be heard across the Muslim world and outside of it. And yet, a closer look at the dynamics of Arab politics, in particular, would point to a rather obvious feature: Islamist discourse only mirrors that of non-Islamist ruling parties—for where is there a transparent, accountable regime in power in the Arab region? In other words, the weaknesses and democratic deficit that characterizes ruling regimes are mirrored in their opposition too.

The Egyptian, Lebanese, Yemeni, Saudi, and Moroccan regimes, to name but a few, have gone through a retraction of promises on democracy that followed closely on the heels of the coalition forces' entry into Iraq. Already, several years down the road from events in Iraq, the Palestinian territories, Algeria, and Egypt, the ruling Arab regimes are letting their fear of extinction in the face of Islamists dictate their political behavior with the tacit blessing of their Western government supporters. These events do beg the question of whether Islamist parties would behave any differently when/if in power. This is particularly true as the Turkish example, with a strong secular infrastructure supported by both people and the military and which has several instances of military cooperation with Israel,[16] does not lend itself to repetition.

On women

Prior to the invasion of Afghanistan, much of the Western media was inundated with news and documentaries about the oppressive conditions that Afghan women were undergoing under the Taliban regime. However, this vast media machine failed to notice that the Taliban were in power for over fifteen years before September 11, 2001 happened, and none of these years was any different for Afghan women. Nevertheless, the impression was that the Western world was not only going into Afghanistan to eradicate terrorism, but was also to liberate the oppressed Afghani Muslim women. The same dynamic took place, and indeed continues to unfold, with Iraqi women. It has been conveniently forgotten that, under Saddam's notoriously oppressive rule, Iraq had the highest number of women in its legislative assembly and active within its political parties compared with any other Arab country. US and European policy makers are seemingly tripping over each other to debate and consider how "foreign intervention" can help Iraqi/Muslim/Arab (all in the same stead) women.

Interestingly, this is the same argument that former colonial powers have articulated as a way to legitimize their presence in any country. Leila Ahmad presents this fact in her seminal work on *Women and Gender in Islam*, and gives the example of Lord Cromer during British colonialism in Egypt. According to Ahmed, Cromer cited the "backward" condition of Muslim women as a means to partially justify why it was that the British had a civilizing mission to undertake in Egypt. "It seems the more things change, the more they stay the same." Why is this moralizing of a colonial agenda relevant to Islamism?

The clamor within the US establishment to "support" Muslim women all works to underline the argument that the great civilizing mission of the Western world includes, as a significant part of its mandate, the "liberation" of Muslim women.[17] And yet many Muslim women, in all their diversity and forms of activism, have been insistent that this is not necessarily the kind of assistance they require from their Western sisters and brothers.

There is a gender dimension to the interaction between Islamists and their non-Islamist counterparts, and this is simultaneously a flashback to the bad old days of colonialism. Activists for women's rights in the Muslim world, together with those intellectuals arguing for both moderate Islamic and secular political dynamics, are always attempting to ward off criticisms from two sides:[18] the religious right wing in their own countries for whom they are never "authentic" or "Islamic" enough and the Western right wing, which sees much of what takes place in the Muslim world as principally anti-Western.

In view of the contemporary political context, both right-wing discourses are aggravated, which tightens the noose around all topics of moderate discourse—including advocacy for women's rights. In this situation, a backlash against women's rights discourse and, by implication, a "third way" of thinking politically, socially, culturally, and economically in the Muslim world and among Muslim communities is muted. A vicious cycle is perpetrated: with the muted moderate discourse emerges a louder radical one, which in turn leads to further antagonisms and conflict.

Yet, assessing where various parties stand on the "question of women in the Muslim world" is incomplete without adding an important political twist. The outcome of the parliamentary elections in Egypt at the beginning of 2006, which, despite government harassment and intimidation, witnessed a rise in the Muslim Brotherhood presence to become approximately a fifth of the parliamentary representation, together with the success of Hamas in the Palestinian legislative elections, have been attributed—among many things— to the role of the women in these parties. Although the Egyptian Muslim Brotherhood does not have women in its *shura* (consultative) council (its main decision-making body), women are nevertheless a key part of its outreach as well as its constituency. The same applies to Hamas, which boasts a wide popularity among women as well as their representation in the newly formed Palestinian Assembly. Both as articulators and disseminators of the ideology and as voters, women have provided the edge to the ascent of the Islamist parties in these two countries. This is bound to have repercussions on the extent to which these parties formulate their policies on a range of critical social issues, and will undoubtedly play a role in the interaction these parties have with those in the Western world who are so concerned for Arab and Muslim women's well-being.

The decision-making and activist roles attributed to and played by women in these parties can also act as significant markers in distinguishing between moderate and radical Islamists. Moderate Islamists have women members active in the various echelons of the party structure, and different parties have differing numbers of women in various positions within the hierarchy. These women are not hidden from view, but on the contrary, play visible and public roles (e.g., the Turkish AK party's wives of the president and prime minister). Radical Islamists, however, as a rule, rarely have women in their decision-making structures and, if they did, it would not be public. Radical Islamists have not shied away from recruiting women to carry out acts associated with violence, whether to carry and deliver arms or even as suicide bombers. The distinction becomes far less clear cut, however, in the Palestinian context, where Hamas too has been alleged to recruit women suicide bombers and, indeed, where one Christian woman is rumored to have carried out a suicide mission.[19]

II Blowback and regional and international implications of the Islamist ascendancy to power

What of Islamism in a Western world? Although the radical Islamists will argue that they struggle for a world where Islam rules, the movements have different priorities when operating within the Western hemisphere. The first statements made by US President George W. Bush immediately after the World Trade Center attacks characterized the events as an "attack on freedom" and "on [American] values." However, Bin Laden referred to these events as a response to (if not retaliation against) "the triumph of the unjust over weak victims" (*nasrul-dhalim 'alal mustad'affin*), clearly referring to both US and Arab regimes as the unjust. This aspect of injustice features strongly in much of the discourse of Osama Bin Laden and the broader Islamist movement. Even the fear articulated by George W. Bush's administration falls short of believing that Islamists want to "Islamize" Western governments and/or society. Radical Islamists see certain Western governments (particularly the US, but also some of those in the European Union) as being the main props of corrupt and illegitimate regimes in various Islamic countries, and as the principal backers of the state of Israel.

From the oil fields of Saudi Arabia and Kuwait to China and South Africa, the US has a palpable presence—if not militarily, then politically and/or economically—in the world's smallest nooks and crannies. Barber (1996) refers to some of this economic hegemony as "McWorld," making a play on America's fast food chain, McDonald's, while Robertson (1992), Waters (1995), and others refer to aspects of this as the "globalization" of American influence. "Protecting [their] national interest" was a common and honest refrain of many US administrations, including the various plays the Bush administration makes on the theme of "making the world safe for our children." Since 2001, this refrain has been increasingly replaced by another one that is also used instead of the "war on terror," namely "the war of ideologies."[20] This war of ideologies, as maintained by its Western proponents, pits a supposedly "democratic," "freedom-loving," and "enlightened" discourse (that of the US) against the "ignorant," "evil," and "violent" one (ostensibly of Islamism). Reverse the owners of the terms, and we get a clear insight into why al-Zawahri and others are calling for a "jihad against the Americans." Each side sees itself as fighting for its interests: the US administration and their supporters for freedom, and Al Qaeda and offshoots for justice. These are, apparently, competing ideologies; each side sees itself as indelibly, and in the eyes of the Creator, in the right.

There are many "interests" that the US would seek to protect, yet few of them are spared a cynical perception by many of the world's inhabitants. The US is seen by many in the developing world, in general, and by Islamists, in particular, as the modern-day imperialist, with all the incumbent baggage of anger and resentment this engenders. When referring to Islamism, this attitude is often interpreted as hatred for "the West" and even for "modernity."

When it comes to acknowledging the extent of US involvement in the Muslim world, the list is long and laborious, especially taking into account the direct presence of US military personnel, along with the various economic, social, and cultural projects, programs, and institutions, and not forgetting the bitter aftertaste left in many Muslim mouths when they voice "Guantanamo." For many in the Muslim world, the US employs a double standard when dealing with certain Muslim countries—as evidenced in the latest debacle over Iraq, Iran, and what is perceived as US support for the Israeli destruction of Lebanon. Ordinary Muslims (Arabs and non-Arab) and non-Muslim Arabs are today asking: why is the US so insistent that the Iraqi regime and Hizbullah comply with all the UN resolutions, when Israel seems to be able to get away with non-compliance? And why is it that, despite the fact that North Korea has actually admitted to having nuclear weapons, the regime is known to be anything but democratic, and it has been identified as part of the "axis of evil" by George W. Bush, still the US is intent on bombing Iran while using diplomacy with North Korea? Islamists pose these questions to suggest that the US is intent on fighting Islam in the same way as it fought Soviet Union and communism. This image is reinforced by what is perceived as the US continuing to turn a blind eye toward the Israeli administration's treatment of Palestinian civilians.

Indeed, there are many theories that purport a historical antagonism (or struggle) between the "West" (sometimes represented by the US) and the "Islamic/Muslim" world (Huntington 1993; Kramer 1997; Emerson 2002).

But the resentment held by the Islamists vis-à-vis the US is not a matter that requires much delving into history. Instead, radical Islamism, such as that seen in the acts of September 11, 2001, events in Madrid, London, and elsewhere, is quite simply captured in the term elaborated upon by Chalmers Johnson: "blowback."

> The term "blowback", which officials of the Central Intelligence Agency first invented for their own use ... refers to the unintended consequences of policies that were kept secret from the American people. What the daily press reports as the malign acts of "terrorists" or "drug lords" or "rogue states" or "illegal arms merchants" often turn out to be blowback from earlier American operations.
>
> Johnson (2000: 8)

It is old news by now that present-day "terrorists," such as the Taliban and Saddam Hussein and the Iraqi regime, are all former "friends" of the US. In some instances, they were even financially and militarily supported by the US. Still lacking from the official rhetoric of the US regime is why (and at what point) did the former "good guys" become "bad guys"?

Whatever the explanation for the "change of heart," there is one good analogy for this form of blowback which "happened" to one of the regimes in the Middle East, which is both a regional leader and a close US ally: Egypt. In the early 1970s, the late Egyptian President Anwar al-Sadat came to power as president of Egypt after the death of the charismatic socialist and Arab nationalist leader Gamal Abdel Nasser. One of Sadat's key aims was to counter the overriding popularity of Nasser's socialist ideology. As a strategy to achieve this, he freed some of the Islamists imprisoned under the Nasser regime and turned a blind eye to their attempts to regroup. Eventually, Sadat's capitalism, which seemed to benefit a tiny elite, paled against Islamist ideology. The latter became more popular through the provision and management of an extensive network of social services to Egypt's most economically disenfranchised. And yet, when he turned against Islamists and all political opposition in his famous political "purge" of September 1981, Sadat only managed to enrage his population. Finally, on October 6, 1981, Sadat was murdered by precisely the same forces he had unleashed, and then attempted to "contain." His assassination was part of the blowback against his own actions and those of his regime.

Where the US boasts the Christian coalition,[21] mainland European countries in the 1990s and the first two years of the twenty-first century hosted a re-emergence of rightist political thought. It was championed by figures such as the French Le Pen and the late Dutch Pim Fortyn. Even where the star of the respective figureheads faded, much of their political rhetoric, which appealed to some of their economically disgruntled populations, was incorporated into mainstream political discourse.

It is risky to believe that control can be exerted once individuals have espoused an ideology about the implementation of "God's rules" or any absolutist values. And yet, it is remarkable how many regimes and individuals will attempt to do just that to either gain or consolidate power, locally and internationally. The formation of Jerry Falwell's moral majority in 1979, which initiated what is today referred to as the Christian coalition, or the "religious right," marked the entrance of religion into the political fray. It has now become common practice in contemporary and supposedly secular US politics. As Terence Samuel writes in an article entitled "The Peak of Political Power" on the US,

> [T]he evangelical movement is firmly entrenched in the nation's political life, lobbying and leveraging like any of the hundreds of other pressure groups in Washington out to advance their causes and promote their issues. The Christian Coalition's Web site is a beehive of political advocacy, and not just on traditional issues like abortion and school prayer … the Coalition worked doggedly on behalf of GOP candidates during the last election and might well take credit for swinging the Senate[22]
>
> Samuel (2002: 42)

The Christian coalition urges deeper and more active involvement of the US administration in Muslim countries. From supporting the civil war in the Sudan on behalf of the Christian and animist South, to assisting Israel by returning all the Jewish peoples to Jerusalem and the Promised Land in order to hasten the second coming of Christ, the legacy of the coalition and its like-minded allies can and does contribute to the violent blowback the US has and will witness. Even when a new US administration comes into power, which may attempt to distance itself from the Christian right, the rhetoric resulting from the mix of faith and politics will not diminish. In fact, one can argue that, once on the opposition side, this rhetoric may become even louder for a while.

The course George W. Bush's administration embarked on in Afghanistan and in Iraq, the "war on terror"/"war of ideologies," continues to boost the legitimacy and credibility of Islamism as a whole. Now, not only the US but increasingly most European nations are perceived to be clashing with the "ideology" of Islam. As current regimes cannot and do not appear to be able to resist, Islamists have profiled themselves as the "heroes"—defenders of Islam and Muslim nations.

Radical Islamist terror is increasingly seen as "understandable" by many desperate people from the slums of Baghdad to Chechnya. Nevertheless, radical Islamism, at best a thin sliver of the Islamist political tendency, is but part of the blowback against the US. Thus, it must be stressed that it is misleading to view Islamism as a whole as a blowback against US policy. Moderate Islamism has a different trajectory which requires distinction from acts of terror. Such acts have in the past seriously de-legitimized Islamism within and outside Islamic majority countries.[23] In such countries, Islamism is a multifaceted attempt to transform the ruling regime(s) and societies into a more Islamic and, purportedly, "just" reality. In Western contexts, where moderate Islamism has yet to be increasingly heard, pockets of radical Islamists (as with some fiery former imams of mosques in New York and London) are also intent on some form of "justice." Whereas there is nothing to justify the murders of hundreds of innocent civilians, why is it inconceivable that such Islamists also have their own version of "collateral damage"? If indeed this appears to be the case, then the strategy of the US administration is succeeding not in eradicating terrorism, but in furthering the raison d'être of radical Islamists who already believe that this is a war against Islam and Muslims, and thus requires a jihad. In other words, we are witnessing the age of repeated blowback.

III Can moderate Islamists be strategic allies?

Traditional opposition between nation-states and non-state actors has been replaced by morphings with non-state actors. Some, like Hizbullah, straddle both state and non-state perimeters. Many of these groups are lumped under the term "terrorists," a categorization that at once minimizes their differences and clarifies "an enemy" to intelligence institutions still comfortable thinking in terms of cold war binarisms. By rendering all Islamists as enemies, and thus failing to see the distinctions between the moderates and actively targeting them for negotiations and strategic alliances, Western countries risk furthering the image of themselves as crusaders against Islam, which in turn would consolidate the perception that some radical Islamists maintain of themselves as the (only) defenders of "justice." What is perpetuated is therefore a vicious cycle where misperceptions feed upon each other.

East and West are no longer worlds apart. They have, contrary to what Kipling noted nearly two centuries ago, already met. In fact, there are emerging variations among European and American and Asian forms of Islamic praxis. Distinctive forms of transnational political Islam, based not so much on Islamizing the state and implementing Shari'a laws, but instead bent on "justice" or vengeance for international acts perpetuated by a hegemonic nation and its allies, are also emerging. In a sense, the "wild west" tactics of "you're either with us or against us," and if you are against, then you and yours shall pay, rule the roost—on both sides of the so-called "war of ideologies."

It is ironic that religion, or self-proclaimed spokespersons of religion, feature strongly in these oppositional dynamics—whether on the side of the former George W. Bush regime or of radical Islamism. Engaged political voices on the right of the religious spectrum have been louder than at any other time in the twentieth and twenty-first centuries in the US and in the Muslim world. The question is whether it may be time to broaden the political space to include moderate religious voices. As "desecularization" becomes more acceptable, could this be a window of opportunity for religious peacemakers to intervene? In other words, if an alternative articulation of religion could be heard in this cacophony of right-wing "God talk," would it perhaps speak to the commonalities of culture and circumstance rather than the supposed clashes? Would it moderate the language of the US religious and political leadership, and mitigate against the sense of victimhood and injustice felt by Al Qaeda's and their other groups' supporters? Could an alternative religious discourse, which emerges through democratic praxis and espouses the rhetoric of democracy, as well as draws its legitimacy and inspiration from successes achieved by religious communities in their roles as peace-builders,[24] actually break the current impasse of violence?

I argued earlier that it is imperative to acknowledge the diversity between and among Islamists. I also maintain that not only is there a difference between moderate and radical Islamism, particularly with regard to the use of violence as a strategy to achieve their aims, their participation in democratic processes, and the role women play therein, but that some moderate Islamists find it counterproductive to be associated with terrorism. I further maintain that current political dynamics are leading to a boisterousness among the radical Islamists at the expense of moderate religious discourse.

My contention here is that moderate Islamists are, de facto, viable inter-locutors for any regime (in the West and in Islamic majority countries) intent on pre-empting violent attacks on their soil.[25] Engaging moderate Islamists is a necessary first step in the long-term direction of opening the political space, which is currently locked into an unrealistic Islamist/religious vs. non-Islamist/secular dialectic.

A wise approach would be to stop the vice of death by strangulation currently being imposed on the Hamas government by the US and Israeli administrations, and others, and instead to negotiate and form strategic alliances with some of the moderates in these sorts of Islamist parties. In the Islamic world, bringing the Taliban into political negotiations in Afghanistan, ceasing to attempt forceful isolation of the Muslim Brotherhood in Egypt, and opening the broader political space for different hues would be a critical start. The formation of strategic alliances with moderate Islamists would also, in the long run, contribute to deafening the noise raised by the radicals, while also validating the now largely ludicrous claim of some Western regimes that freedom and democracy are indeed what is desired.

Detractors, skeptics, and hawks would balk at this contention and question why it is that Western support would provide legitimacy for moderate religious discourse, when the same support seems to boost angry Islamists around the world? The answer to that is that Western support is currently provided by a Western administration that appears bent on pre-emptive war tactics to administrations with questionable legitimacy in the Muslim world. The moderate Islamists mentioned above are legitimately elected into power and are thus by and large representative of what peoples in these countries want. It is credible and expected that Western governments deal with these regimes elected by popular will, instead of continuing to endorse those who have no legitimacy. Besides, it is worthwhile reiterating that it is only a matter of time before regimes in Islamic majority countries themselves seek to make these alliances with the moderate Islamists.

Furthermore, if indeed the contention is to be believed that this is an ideological struggle, with the forces of democracy battling against those of darkness and dogmatism, then ignoring the democratic will as expressed by a majority stands as a clear contradiction. Even if we were to accept the rather tenuous assertion that Western governments are not obliged to deal with any ideological opponents simply because they are popularly elected (and here the list of countries from various continents in that category which Western governments nevertheless deal with is plentiful), then, equally, democratically elected governments should not be obliged to succumb to demands they are principally against. *That* would be the essence of a democratic engagement. There is little doubt in the minds of many Muslims today that ongoing events in the occupied Palestinian territories and in Lebanon will serve to enhance the stature of Islamism as a whole, while simultaneously emphasizing the legitimacy of the radical Islamists' urge to violent resistance. If this is a war of ideology, then the ideology of the oppressed has already triumphed. And across the Islamic world, Hamas is currently perceived as the oppressed, and Hizbullah as the liberator.

A further question would be why endorse or attempt to support any religious discourse, when, clearly, the over-involvement of religion is part of present-day dilemmas in the first place? The answer is simple: religion is here to stay, at least for a while, and after the litany of misjudgment undertaken by Western regimes in the Middle East, Islamism is not going anywhere in a hurry. Islamist thought and praxis shifts and adjusts with time, and as the Iraqi debacle, West Bank grief, and events in Lebanon continue to highlight, isolating and alienating religio-political moderates is counterproductive.

What is currently at play, whether in the Western hemisphere or in the Islamic majority countries, is radical religious discourse, which sees violence as legitimate whether it is labeled as self-defense, resistance, or pre-emption, harps on cultural clashes, and is diametrically opposed to international conventions honoring women and children[26] in the name of family values. This has to be distinguished from a religio-political discourse that spurns violence and indicates preparedness for those who will look and listen to work peacefully toward some semblance of international social justice.

Realpolitik imposes its own dynamics on the most intransigent of personalities and parties. This was witnessed to some extent in Turkey with the ascent of the Islamist Justice and Development Party (AKP) to power. This not only gives a chance to supporters to assess the party in light of actual achievements in power as opposed to being an untried—or victimized—alternative, it also gives the ideologues a chance to adjust both rhetoric and action to more workable parameters by creating strategic alliances both nationally and globally, engendering productivity, and delivering on people's economic and political expectations. When all is said and done about the deficiencies and specificities of the Turkish Islamist experiment, it remains one where moderate Islamism is clearly acclimatizing and adjusting, with ups and downs but overall relatively peacefully, to changing political exigencies.

IV Conclusion

It is politically unwise to alienate all Islamists and push them into overlooking their own differences. It is far more astute to monitor the natural schisms created among these groups by having some of them try their hand at governance—and indeed, to at least appear to assist them in doing the job they were democratically elected or popularly mandated to do. In this manner, strategic alliances would be created that would have an impact on the ideology, language, rhetoric, and trajectory of political Islam. This, in turn, would have a wider ripple effect on the evolution of political discourse within the Islamic majority countries and outside. Until Islamism is tried and tested in the everyday grit of the political street, it is conceived of in idealistic terms only. When it is tried in an environment that is not seen as inimical, it can become one of many political ideologies that can engender different offshoots in the long run as its predecessors, the Christian Democrats, eventually did.

This is not to argue that this evolution is necessarily only positive and will take place overnight. But it is a far safer bet than the current policy, which has effectively bankrupted Western political capital and that of its allies, and which boosts the language of victimization and armed struggle, as well as the "survival of the fittest" paradigm that currently dominates all sides of the debate in the Middle Eastern region. Thus far, the current paradigm has only resulted in cyclical episodes of violence and death. What we have today on all sides is the oldest form of a coalition of the righteous and fearful, hiding behind military might and binary rhetoric. What is called for is a new constellation of strategic alliances against all political violence, building on and embracing a discourse of justice for all. This new constellation must also be at once humble and brave enough to take a risk, acknowledge limits, and reach out to the unconventional.

Notes

1 The views expressed in this paper are entirely those of the author, and are not intended in any way to represent those of any organization and/or institution.
2 Pakistani Intelligence Officer, in a BBC Radio 4 documentary program, October 7, 2008.
3 Hamas's Ismail Haniya, quoted on October 11, 2008, in "Opponents of U.S. Gloat Over Fiscal Crisis: Mideast Hardliners Call Wall St. Meltdown Divine Retribution For U.S.'s Past Misdeeds Against Muslims." Online. Available www.cbsnews.com/stories/2008/10/11/world/main4515133.shtml?source=RSSattr=HOME_4515133 (accessed May 27, 2009).
4 See especially Rubenstein (1987); Benavides and Daly (1989); Berger (1999); Norris and Inglehart (2004).
5 Or "resisting" as some, such as Hamas's Ismail Haniya (the prime minister in the former Palestinian ruling coalition), would have it.
6 An old motto of the Egyptian Muslim Brotherhood which became prominent in the 1980s.
7 For more on the transnational connections between Islamist ideology in Muslim countries and Europe and the US, see Karam (2004).

8 Which partly explains why the (relatively new compared with others) Egyptian Islamist party *al-Wasat* boasted a couple of Christians as members.
9 An example of a moderate Islamist party in the Muslim world is the Muslim Brotherhood (*al-Ikhwan al-Muslimin*, which came into existence in Egypt 1928), and which has branched out into different countries since and is very diverse in its structure and organizational method(s). Today's Hamas in Palestine is a descendant and branch of the Brotherhood.
10 Lebanon, Jordan, the Palestinian territories, Algeria, Indonesia, Malaysia, and Pakistan, to name but a few.
11 It is maintained that the longevity of Hizbullah's claim to legitimacy is dependent on the dialectic with Israel. Needless to say, with the Lebanese–Israeli events of August 2006, the legitimacy of Hizbullah will not only cease to be an issue, but it has effectively become an icon to (reinstated) Arab pride after the humiliation of the 1967 war.
12 Commonly translated as Islamic law, it is worth noting that Shari'a is not one body of text or interpretation, but rather the sum of various juridical interpretations collated over a certain course of time. Thus, there is no one Shari'a law, but a whole set of man-made laws—some of which may differ according to the specific school of interpretation followed. This would also partly explain why certain applications of Shari'a differ from one Muslim country to another.
13 For more details on Al Qaeda's position on justice and violence, see also Karam (2004) and Rohan Gunaratne (2002/2003).
14 According to a 2006 report entitled *Arab Youth Strategising for the Millennium Development Goals*. Cairo: UNDP-UNDESA. Similar figures are referred to in the United Nations' World Youth Report of 2007, which also argued that "the region now holds the distinction of having both the highest rate of youth unemployment in the world and the lowest rate of labour force participation among young people" (p. 119).
15 Such as the Mufti of Bosnia and the Sheikh of al-Azhar in Egypt, both of whom maintained that suicide is against Islam—even if the resistance to Israeli occupation is legitimate. See also Capan (2004).
16 In spite of the Davos tiff between Turkish and Israeli political leaders.
17 For more reading on the emerging behavior of the US empire, see George Monbiot "The Logic of Empire" in *The Guardian Weekly*, August 15–20, 2002, p. 11; and Philip Golub (2002) "Westward the Course of Empire" in *Le Monde Diplomatique*, as quoted in *The Guardian Weekly*, September, p. 6.
18 I have elaborated on the relationship between political Islam and women's activism and the manner in which a gender discourse is intimately connected to the power dynamics that take place between Islamist political thought and governmental reactions, in *Women, Islamisms and the State: Contemporary Feminisms in Egypt*. New York: St Martin's Press, 1998.
19 See Victor (2003).
20 As articulated by Brigadier General Kimmet, deputy director of operations for the military coalition in Iraq, in a BBC World Service Radio interview, June 2006.
21 See also, for instance, Eck (2001) and Danforth (2006).
22 In *US News and World Report*, December 23, 2002, p. 42.
23 As referred to earlier in the aftermath of the Luxor massacre in Egypt, the massacres carried out by the Armed Islamic Group (GIA) during the civil war in Algeria, and the suicide bombings still carried out against civilians in Israel, for example.
24 For more on this, see Mohammed Abu-Nimer (2001); Marc Gopin (2000); Jonathan Fox (2001); Chadwick Alger (2002); Scott Appleby (1999); Douglas Johnston and Cynthia Sampson (1994); and Robert Johansen (1997).
25 A similar point is also articulated by Marc Lynch in *Foreign Policy* (September/October 2007), in an article entitled "Brothers in Arms," in which he maintains

that "the United States and the Muslim Brotherhood have more in common than they think" (pp. 70–74). Lynch, talking specifically to the Egyptian Muslim Brotherhood, argues that they need to win over American skeptics, especially as some Americans see them as "a relatively moderate force and a potential partner in a common struggle for democracy and against Islamic extremism" (p. 70).

26 It is interesting to note that, whether it is the Christian coalition of the US or radical Islamists such as the Taliban, both have serious problems with the United Nations as a viable entity, and with the Convention for the Elimination of All Forms of Discrimination Against Women (CEDAW) as well as the Convention on the Rights of the Child (CRC).

Part II
Country studies

6 Transformations in Eastern Europe and lessons for the Middle East

Shlomo Avineri

Fifteen years of post-communist transformations in Eastern Europe can be helpful, if analyzed critically, in assessing the challenges facing the prospects for democratization in the Middle East. The differential developments in various Eastern European countries suggest the need for a nuanced and measured approach that has to replace the ideological and rather uncritical euphoria which accompanied the collapse of communism and the disintegration of the Soviet Union.

This euphoria was twofold, relating both to the collapse of a totalitarian ideology as well as to the hope for a seamless future development toward political democracy and the introduction of a market economy. Conventional wisdom linked the two with an almost umbilical cord.

One should not overlook the fact that the rapid—and mainly peaceful—collapse of the communist regimes in Eastern Europe took practically everyone—politicians as well as academics, journalists as well as intelligence analysts—by surprise. When Mikhail Gorbachev began introducing the changes into the Soviet system which eventually became known as Glasnost and Perestroika, a lot of skepticism accompanied these developments among Western observes. Even those who saw in it the final vindication of the possibility of loosening up of the system by appearing to introduce something like "Socialism with a human face," à la Dubcek's 1968 brutally suppressed reforms, had great doubts whether these attempts would not ultimately fizzle out, as did so many of Khrushchev's steps, due to the entrenched power of Soviet bureaucracy and the recalcitrance or inability of totalitarian systems to reform.

Others expressed their skepticism in an even more radical fashion, arguing that Gorbachev's reforms were nothing else than a trick to lull the West's vigilance: communist tigers will never change their stripes.

When the final crash occurred in a reverse of the classical domino theory, epitomized by such high visibility dramatic events as the fall of the Berlin Wall, Prague's Velvet Revolution, the flight and execution of Ceausescu, and the final denouement of the failed Moscow coup followed by the disintegration of the Soviet Union itself into fifteen independent republics, one could well understand the almost messianic ("end of history") tones which accompanied these developments.

One should bear this atmosphere in mind in order to understand the somewhat uncritical euphoric triumphalism of the early 1990s. The fall of communism was understood not only as the failure of a deeply flawed system, which never managed to live up even to a minimal fulfillment of its own promises and ideological claims, but was also seen as a vindication of its ideological alternative: in the absence of the totalitarian repression inherent in the Soviet system, democracy and the market would now automatically flourish and triumph, as if guided by the hidden hand of the march of history. Ironically, this deterministic approach of seeing democracy and capitalism as the inevitable telos of all mankind was in a strange way a mirror image of the old Marxist–Leninist determinism, which claimed that all societies are doomed to follow the path of socio-economic development of the West, leading from feudalism to capitalism to socialism.

Paradoxically, those who believed that societies emancipated from the Soviet yoke would automatically move toward democracy and a market economy shared one of the major flaws of Marxist ideology: the almost total overlooking of cultural and historical societal ingredients, which cannot be reduced deterministically to what the Marxists used to call "economic infrastructure." Such a blindness to the relative autonomy of culture and historical heritage was even more ironical when one takes into account the fact that much of the Soviet failure had at its base the misguided attempt to transpose to pre-industrial and pre-capitalist 1917 Russia the analysis—and vision—embedded in Marxist theory, which was based, after all, on the experience of the industrialized capitalist West.

Looking at the Eastern and Central European scene a dozen years later, one has to account for the differentiated picture that has emerged in the post-Soviet orbit: far from moving forward as a more or less unified phalanx toward democracy and a market economy, post-communist societies present a most variegated picture. This should be even more surprising to those thinking in deterministic terms, as after all around 1990 all these societies were proceeding from more or less the same starting point: Soviet-style communism—with, one should admit, some variations (e.g., Poland and Hungary), but basically all were in the same one-party state, command economy mold. Why the enormous differences?

Today, one can discern four types of post-communist regimes:

1   Countries that basically succeeded in transforming their politics into working democracies and more or less achieved functioning market economies: Poland, Hungary, Czech Republic, Slovenia, Estonia—as well as Slovakia, Croatia, Lithuania, and Latvia.
2   Countries that encountered difficulties on the road to successful transformation and consolidation, but appear at least to be on track: Romania, Bulgaria; Serbia and Georgia should probably also be classified under this category.
3   Countries with some achievements yet with what appears to be a fundamental difficulty in achieving a meaningful transformation: both Russia

and Ukraine belong in this category, despite significant differences—Russia evolving under Putin into "authoritarianism with a human face," while Ukraine struggles to create a viable and functioning state structure based on an open society.

4 The failures: they range from such reconstituted autocracies as Belarus, Turkmenistan, and Uzbekistan to much more complex cases such as Armenia, Azerbaijan, and Moldova and the rest of the Central Asian Republics. This category includes a great variety of different regimes, but they have one characteristic in common: none of them can be classified as a functioning, consolidated democracy.

The question then arises as to how to account for these vast differences in development and achievement. While development toward democracy and the building of a viable market economy are obviously two distinct subjects and have to be discussed by different methodologies, it should be granted that they are, ultimately, somewhat related—even if one does not subscribe to a simplistic model of the link between the two. In what follows, we shall focus mainly on political development, although—mutatis mutandis—some of the same analysis could also be applied to the economic sphere.

There can be no purely economic explanation for the great differences and disparities in development enumerated above: degrees of industrialization and urbanization, regional differences in education or gross national product (GNP) per capita, population density, or other quantifiable data do not explain the differences among the countries—and any attempt to relate them to such criteria can be very easily faulted. Because of this, there has been great reluctance to ask these questions, and many observers preferred to focus on individual policies adopted—or not adopted—by various post-communist governments, or to focus on the merits or defects of individual leaders—be it Yeltsin or Putin, Yushchenko, Lukashenka, or Kerimov. The fallacies of such an approach are obvious, although they are driven by the personality-centered public reporting intrinsic to the TV age as well as the inability of many analysts to relate to issues and problems beyond daily developments.

If one looks carefully at those countries that have experienced successful transitions to democracy and also managed to consolidate the transition institutionally, and compare them with the less successful cases, one would find one criterion that would ultimately be the best predictor of a successful development toward democracy: the history and political culture of each of these societies before the communist takeover—be it the initial Soviet revolution of 1917 or the post-1945 imposition of Soviet-style communism on Central Eastern European countries liberated by the Red Army from German Nazi occupation or local variants of fascist or semi-fascist regimes. To use a variation of a metaphor sometimes mentioned in this context: once the Soviet Siberian permafrost was lifted after 1989, in those countries where the flowers had been blossoming before they came up again, and where there was dirt, it too came back to the surface.

Let us look first at Central Eastern Europe. There were not many countries with a full-blown democratic tradition in the region prior to 1939 or 1945, but the examples of the Czech Republic, Poland, and Hungary are illuminating, despite the differences among them. Between 1918 and 1939, Czechoslovakia was the one Central Eastern European country with the best democratic record—a multiparty democracy, free press, and religious tolerance. It was also the most industrialized country in the region, Bohemia and Moravia having been the major industrial heartland of the Austro-Hungarian monarchy. Obviously, Czechoslovakia's politics were not free from serious problems (e.g., Slovak–Czech relations, the position of the German-speaking minority), yet compared with its neighbors, it practiced a system that was certainly the most democratic and liberal one in the region. The Czech lands also had a long-standing tradition of political representation—going back to the medieval Bohemian estates and, later, active participation in the post-1867 Austrian Reichsrat in Vienna; this was coupled with a deeply entrenched culture of secularization and religious tolerance, going back to Jan Hus and the Reformation.

Poland and Hungary had a more complex experience between the two World Wars. The political discourse in both countries was marred by expressions of extreme nationalism, xenophobia, and anti-Semitism—drawing on the specific conditions in each country (in Poland, the fact that more than 30 percent of its population was made up of minorities—Germans, Jews, Ukrainians, Lithuanians; in Hungary, the double trauma of Trianon and the Béla Kun communist revolution and the White Terror). Yet both Poland and Hungary maintained a semblance of parliamentary representation between the wars, which while not fully functioning, did allow elections—albeit limited and circumscribed—even under the authoritarian regimes instituted, respectively, by Piłsudski and Horthy. Political parties did exist—despite severe limitations, especially on left-wing parties. Neither Poland nor Hungary, for all the non-democratic traits of their pre-1939 regimes, were straightforward fascist dictatorships.

To this should be added that both Poland and Hungary had traditions of political representations going back to medieval times: true, they were basically aristocratic in nature (but so, after all, were the origins of the English parliament); but over centuries, they functioned as effective breaks on royal authority and their memory was not totally obliterated. Similarly, while the religious histories of both countries were different, in both of them, the churches—in Poland the Catholic Church, in the Hungarian system mainly the Calvinist Church—have played a historical role which, for all the differences between both cases, did become a possible counterweight to power. Not totally separate from this was the fact that universities as well as cities had traditionally enjoyed relative corporatist autonomy from the central government.

To endow these historical outlines, rough as they are, with some more coherent theoretical dimension, what has been said here amounts to the claim that countries such as Czechoslovakia, Poland, and Hungary did have a centuries-old tradition of civil society—and it is not an accident that, in the last decades of communist rule, the slogan of "civil society" was a powerful weapon in the hands of dissidents in these countries—Solidarność in Poland, the Civic Forum and People Against Violence in Czechoslovakia, and the Democratic Forum (MDF) in Hungary. What turned this term from a mere abstract slogan to a political and social reality was the fact that traditions of civil society did exist in these countries and were not a mere desideratum.

Civil society—which has been considered the mainstay of modern democracy since Tocqueville—is the whole network of autonomous organizations and ways of behavior—voluntary associations, trade unions and professional associations, churches and religious groups, educational groups and academic institutions—which function independently of state power, have a high degree of legitimacy among the population, and draw on significant if not massive participation. Western democracies have been successful precisely in regions where these traditions of civil society have been well developed—the English-speaking world, the Netherlands, and the Scandinavian countries being the prime examples. In parenthesis, part of the weakness of the Weimar Republic was precisely the fact that civil society in Wilhelmine Germany was relatively weak, and many of its components—the professoriat and the students, many spheres of professional organizations on the right, and many working-class organizations on the left—did not view Weimar as a legitimate expression of their political will.

It was this salience of civil society in Czechoslovakia, Poland, and Hungary that may at least partially explain why the three attempts to reform communism from within occurred, albeit not successfully, precisely in these countries: in Poland in 1956 and again in 1968 and 1980, in Hungary in 1956, and in Czechoslovakia in 1968. While all these attempts were defeated by brutal force, they left a legacy that was picked up in the late 1980s.

The existence of a civil society, as well as the memory—whether "real" or "constructed"—of pre-communist structures that could be resurrected or reintroduced, gave dissidents, and later post-communist governments, both an internal legitimacy as well as a program that could appear as restorative in terms of historical experience. "Liberty" could be reintroduced, local traditions revived.

If one compares this with the Russian experience, one immediately sees the difference. Not only did communist rule last longer in the Soviet Union than in Central Eastern Europe: this is obvious. But pre-1917 Russia had very little tradition of civil society and citizens' participation in government to which the dissidents and reformers could hark back to.

Hundreds of years of Czarist rule created a political and social structure that was highly hierarchical and authoritarian, with very few elements of civil society in existence—by itself one of the causes of the failure of constitutional liberalism in Russia between 1905 and 1917. For centuries, the country has been run by a hierarchical bureaucracy, with the Czar at the top; there was no municipal or regional self-government; no representative institutions existed (until 1905, and after that their history was one of failure); legal political parties were basically not tolerated; the Orthodox Church was not an autonomous institution vis-à-vis state power, but combined the Cesaropapist Byzantine tradition of Orthodoxy in general with the total subjugation of the Church under Czarist rule at least since Petrine times; it became another arm of state control (paradoxically, the only ones relatively free from this yoke were the Jews and the Lutheran Baltic Germans); and—last and not least—the aristocracy, despite its wealth, was not an autonomous social power but was basically a caste in the service of the state, existing at its pleasure and mercy. With very little industrial development, no independent bourgeoisie appeared as an alternative counterweight to state power. The fact that Russian peasants were not freed from serfdom until the 1860s also meant that the peasantry—which in some Central Eastern European countries would be a focus of anti-state activity—was much more quiescent in Russia (in Ukraine, with its Cossack tradition, the situation was slightly different, as became tragically and brutally clear in the 1930s).

In short, institutional structures and societal behavior in pre-1917 Russia were anchored in totally different traditions from those of the three countries in Central Eastern Europe we discussed before. This weakness of civil society, coupled with a strong parallel tradition of authoritarian and hierarchical rule, meant that Russian dissidents had a much weaker anchoring in society: Russian dissidents were indeed basically limited to the two historical metropolises of Moscow and Leningrad, had a strong Jewish component (which again made them less attuned to the social norms of the countryside population), and had no memories, or institutional and normative structures, on which an alternative society could be built. This is also at the root of the fact that changes in Russia occurred not through a victory of dissenters outside the system, but through internal reforms from above within the system itself. Yet the lack of a civil society tradition meant that even the reformers themselves—Gorbachev or Yeltsin—did not have a "usable past" that could have helped them to either legitimate or construct their alternative society. For all his apparent liberal intentions, Gorbachev's vision of an alternative society was dismally poor if compared with that of Vaclav Havel or Adam Michnik. Reform in Russia remained an abstract slogan, not anchored in any Russian tradition: slogans about "socialism with a human face," just as a yearning after the (failed) tradition of the Constitutional Democrats ("Kadets") in the early twentieth century, were a poor substitute for the wealth of civil society traditions that were at the disposal of Polish or Czech dissidents. The weakness of present-day political parties in Russia—their virtual non-existence, except as short-term electoral vehicles for presidential elections, as they emerged under both Yeltsin and Putin—is another aspect of this deficit. That only the Communist Party exists in present-day Russia as a coherent political organization is another aspect of the same phenomenon: all other political formations are in constant flux.

It is a cruel irony of history—but probably not surprising under the circumstances—that the only historical model now somewhat operative in Russia is that of the Czar whose portrait adorns Putin's office: that of Peter the Great. True, a modernizer and a "Westernizer" in Russian terms: but the modernity he imported from the West was that of modern warfare, technological efficiency, streamlined bureaucratic control, and administrative hierarchy superseding the old anarchic semi-autonomy of the boyars. The way Putin was able to install Medvedev as his presidential successor, while maintaining at least some of his own power as prime minister, suggests how strong are the authoritarian streaks in Russian society.

Ukrainian observers occasionally maintain that the much more chaotic post-1991 development of Ukraine, compared with that of Russia, has also to be seen in a historical context—that of a lack of a strong state structure in Ukrainian history. Not only was Ukraine never an independent state in the past, but its political culture bears memories of the pluralistic, if not anarchic, Cossack tradition, whereas in western Ukraine, many pride themselves on Polish traditions that historically prevented the emergence of a strong, centralized Polish state (and eventually led to the demise of the Polish–Lithuanian Commonwealth). This may be compounded by the complexity of Ukrainian church history, very different from the statist traditions of the Russian Orthodox Church, with the Uniate Greek Catholic Church playing an important role in Ukrainian nationalism—but being basically a regional phenomenon in the west of the country, not common to all Ukrainians.

One could continue this analysis to include some of the cases enumerated above under category two. Again, Romania and Bulgaria did not have a vibrant civil society tradition prior to 1939; Romanian political life in the 1930s was characterized not only by violent nationalism and vociferous anti-Semitism but also by murderous changes of government among right-wing factions, with some of the political assassinations carried out under royal authority. Serbian political tradition in the nineteenth and twentieth centuries was particularly violent, and the violence continued under the different circumstances of the Serb-dominated post-1918 Yugoslavia. In this context, it should be mentioned that the Orthodox Churches in these countries, which developed into autocephalous national churches under the impact of nineteenth-century nationalism, only added another hierarchical element to the power of the state and became instruments of the state rather than possible countervailing powers.

In cases such as Slovakia and Croatia, the fact that a not very enlightened version of Catholicism became identified with a radical nationalist narrative, especially during World War II, certainly greatly hampered democratic developments in these countries—although they seem to have been able to overcome this legacy in the last few years. This shows that while historical cultural traditions are extremely important, they are not immutable and are—like all institutions and social traditions—malleable and subject to change.

Yet the fact of the matter remains that, once communism collapsed, Eastern European societies were not thrown back to a tabula rasa of a Lockean state of nature—but found themselves confronted with their own historical traditions. Where the building blocks that could be salvaged from these traditions included elements of civil society, tolerance, and pluralism, the potential for developing a democratic discourse was better than in cases where these elements were lacking.

Any such analysis that puts so much stress on historicist ingredients opens itself to the obvious criticism that it replaces one kind of determinism—economic—with another, based on cultural or political traditions. Hence a caveat is necessary, in order to make clear what is being argued here and what is not. What the argument here developed tries to suggest is that, in order to succeed in a transformation toward democratic political structures, societies need some preconditions: well-intentioned declaratory goals, or even reform-minded individual leaders, do not suffice. As the history of democratic developments in the West has shown, such a process is a multigenerational one: no society in the West has ever moved in a linear way from an oppressive regime to an open, democratic society. Moreover, the emergence of the multiplicity of societal norms, institutions, and patterns of behavior that we have subsumed under the rubric of "civil society" develops over time, and cannot be brought into life by legislative fiat or mere adoption of a desired model imported from outside. Even a superficial comparison between the US and Canada, on one hand, and Latin America, on the other, suggests that the societal differences between the patterns of British settlement in Northern America and those of the Spanish and Portuguese Conquista in South America have created such different preconditions, which to a large extent determined the different course of history in those two subcontinents.

Yet one has to underline the fact that these preconditions are not static and can change and be consciously changed over time, as mentioned earlier in the cases of Slovakia and Croatia. This also has policy consequences: any attempt to develop a democratic culture in societies in which such a culture has been historically weak or underdeveloped entails the necessity of identifying the ingredients of civil society already existing in that particular environment, even if they are weak, and a concerted effort to strengthen and develop them. Thus, elements of voluntary associations, trade unions, women's organizations, political parties, and the like should be the targets for further developments, as should traditions and memories of representation and pluralism. This may be much more helpful than attempts to craft a better sounding constitution or the promulgation of a set of laws (the adoption, numerous times, of copies of the US Constitution by practically all Latin American countries did much less to change the political environment in these countries than the arduous institution-building of elements of civil society). What is obvious is that this is a lengthy process, where ups and downs have to be expected. After all, French democracy did not spring out of Rousseau's head like a fully equipped Athena: it took France more than a century to develop the kind of consolidated and stable democracy it now enjoys—and the vicissitudes of countries such as Germany and Italy—eventually success stories, yet far from simple ones—should serve as a cautionary tale.

This should be borne in mind especially when confronting the future of Russia. As the main successor state of the Soviet Union, Russia has to undergo four transformations simultaneously: the building of democratic institutions, economic liberalization, the dismantling of an empire, and the creation (for the first time) of a Russian nation-state. To imagine that all four transformations could occur at the same time and that they are, indeed, complementary is the height of wishful thinking (or ignorance). No society can undertake such a multilayered transformation in a short period of time. The war in Chechnya suggests the far-reaching ramifications of what by itself could be seen as a minor conflict, but already had far-reaching consequences for the structure of power, the map of political parties and allegiances, the freedom of the press, etc. under both Yeltsin and Putin. Moreover, it is obvious that some aspects of economic liberalization may call for, at least initially, a consolidation of state power (e.g., vis-à-vis the so-called oligarchs), and this can be done, and is in fact done, by methods which greatly impair the rule of law and the processes of democratization. Western observers—be they academic analysts or policy makers—should approach the enormous burden bequeathed to the current political system of Russia by hundreds of years of Czarist autocracy and decades of Soviet totalitarianism with empathy and at least some humility. This should not be used as uncritical approval of or justification for Putin's neo-authoritarian system: but one should responsibly consider the available alternatives. Wishful thinking and condescension are poor substitutes for a studied analysis of options attuned to the realities of historical circumstances.

Some of the same issues came to a head in the wake of September 11. Because of the role of fundamentalist Islam in these terrorist attacks—as well as in similar acts in other regions involving suicide bombers—the question has been asked whether Islam as such is a hindrance for democratic development. Given the fact that few Islamic societies have developed in a democratic fashion—and that no Arab society is a democracy or can show a convincing attempt at democratization—this assertion appears not totally out of place.

Yet, like other types of cultural stereotyping, it is misleading and wrong. Islam is intrinsically not different from any other religion when it comes to issues of democracy or human rights. In nineteenth-century Europe, it was considered conventional wisdom that democracy and Catholicism are incompatible—and both democrats as well as Catholic theologians appeared to agree on this—from Mazzini to Pope Pius IX. Yet today, Christian Democrat parties are a mainstay of European democracy. There is no reason why the same could not happen, over time and given the right circumstances, with Islamic societies. Finding utterly distasteful quotes in the Quran regarding human rights as well as blood-curdling passages aimed at infidels is beside the point: similar quotes can be found in both the Hebrew Bible and the New Testament as well. Yet the fact that intolerant interpretations of Islam have recently appeared to gain ascendancy is obviously worrying.

That such an overall stereotyping of Islam is factually wrong can be seen if one looks at the recent histories of Islamic countries: over seven decades, Turkey has developed, through trial and error and many vicissitudes, a working democracy—obviously flawed, yet functioning; within this democratic institutional discourse, and through free elections, a party with Islamic roots came to power—and rather than turn the country into an intolerant theocracy, is doing its utmost to open up toward Europe and join the European Union. In the process of doing this, the Turkish Grand National Assembly has enacted, under the AK party identified with Islam, a set of liberalizing constitutional changes, which the previous Kemalist, supposedly "Westernizing" governments were never ready to entertain.

Muslim majority countries such as Bangladesh and Indonesia have witnessed developments toward democracy and liberalization which are truly remarkable, even if the last word has not yet been said. That a multiparty system, based on free elections, can function, albeit in a far from perfect manner, in a country like Bangladesh—one of the world's poorest—suggests both that Islam per se is not a hindrance, but also that poverty per se should not be viewed as an insurmountable stumbling block to democracy. Bangladesh is among the poorest and Saudi Arabia among the richest countries of the world—and both are Muslim countries, and the one has shown remarkable successes in the democratic direction, while the other is one of the most authoritarian societies currently in existence. Obviously, the enormous differences in their respective development cannot be attributed to Islam.

Perhaps the best example that Islam as such is not the cause of the lack of development toward democracy is the case of Iran. The last few years have shown that, within the political discourse of a country that views itself as an Islamic Republic, there are still options which may lead to encouraging results. The fact that there are elections in Iran—presidential as well as parliamentary—and that while they are conducted within a restricted Islamic discourse, they are still contested, with multiple candidates, with a variety of opinions presenting themselves to the electorate, suggests that an electoral process is not intrinsically alien to Islam as such. Iranian elections may not pass even the minimal criteria for democratic procedures—yet the fact that they are contested, that women have the vote, and that President Khatami was twice elected as representing a more moderate version of Islamic rule than the other candidate, and that, until the last, highly manipulated elections, there was a relatively moderate majority in the Iranian Majlis—all show how complex and differentiated the world of Islam is—and that a potential for further developments toward a more open system cannot be ruled out. Nor should one overlook the fact that, within the Iranian Islamic system, seats are reserved in parliament for the tolerated minorities (Christians, Jews, Zoroastrians). Given Islamic discourse, the Baha'is are excluded from this, being seen as renegades from Islam; and the Jewish representative is obviously expected to join—if not outdo—the official anti-Israeli stance of the Islamic Republic; yet the fact is that minorities are not ipso facto excluded from representation.

This should not be misunderstood or misrepresented as an uncritical attitude toward the Iranian system: certainly the elections that brought Ahmedinejad into power suggest how complex the picture is, but the fact remains that he came to power through contested elections, and in the second round. The June 2009 elections showed how public opinion may react, even under conditions of oppression. The Iranian system is oppressive and tyrannical, and is maintaining by force a particularly narrow interpretation of Shi'ite Islam, yet it is evolving with an inherent potential for further positive developments.

On the other hand, one cannot find such encouraging developments in any of the twenty-two member states of the Arab League: not only is none of them a democracy, but none can point to even such hopeful signs as those now visible in Iran. Whether traditional fundamentalist dynastic states such as Saudi Arabia, milder royal regimes such as Jordan, Morocco, Kuwait, and the Gulf states, or military one-party states of various degrees of oppression (from the milder Egyptian variety to the harsher Syrian one—not to speak of the abominable Iraqi variety deposed by force from the outside), no Arab society appears to be able to develop meaningful processes of democratization, either from above or from below: there are no Arab Gorbachevs, no Arab Wałęsas, no Arab Havels. Nor has there appeared an Arab Atatürk. Neither rich nor poor Arab societies seem to be able to develop the kind of civil society that is so central to democratic development, and all Arab societies experience different varieties of étatist economic structures—be it under the aegis of a Saudi dynasty or a Ba'athist National Socialist regime.

Recent development in Iraq and the Palestinian territories suggest a great difficulty in the development of consensual democratic structures. Granted that elections conducted under conditions of occupation are problematical by their very nature, it is the fact that, in both cases, neither the victorious majority parties nor the defeated minority parties were able, after the elections, to create a workable governing system: the newly empowered Shia'a majority conceived its victory as a license to marginalize the once dominant Sunni minority, and the Sunnis still have great difficulties in operating within a system that has deprived them of their historical hegemony, with many of them trying to reverse this by force and terrorism.

Something similar happened to the Palestinians after their legislative elections, in which Hamas became the largest party. The violent putsch of Hamas in June 2009 in Gaza makes the emergence of a coherent Palestinian polity look highly unlikely: that both Fateh and Hamas are not just political movements but also armed militias adds a built-in ingredient of violence into the complex relations between them.

Until September 11, this basic Arab democratic deficit had not been widely discussed, either by academics or by policy analysts for a variety of reasons. Yet the fact that fifteen out of the nineteen suicide murderers of September 11 were Saudis focused attention on the lack of political space in countries such as Saudi Arabia (and under different conditions in Egypt as well), and the argument has been made that this may be responsible for pushing young, well-educated people toward a terroristic option. Until recently, this has been a taboo subject in the Arab political discourse, and even outside the region, there has been little serious academic research on this Arab *Sonderweg*. The courageous UNDP *Arab Human Development Report*, which raised the issue publicly within an Arab discourse for the first time, is short on both analytical and prescriptive levels. Yet the issue has been raised openly for the first time.

That the situation is different in the non-Arab Muslim world may, perhaps, suggest at least a partial explanation. In such disparate cases as Turkey and Iran, Islam is obviously an important ingredient in the political and spiritual cultures of these societies: but there are other layers as well—Ottoman and Turkish ingredients in one case, the richness of Persian culture in the other. It may be that the combination of Islam and Arabism (and especially Sunni Islam and Arabism) is not helpful toward developing an autonomous civil society, given the hegemonistic tradition of Sunni Arabism in the Middle East. That Islam and Arabism seem to overlap in the consciousness of Arab societies underscores the difference. But this is a hypothesis that has to be further tested, yet it already has a number of possible policy implications.

Looking more closely at the predicament of Arab countries, one can see a number of obvious parallels with the situation in those post-communist Eastern European countries that were less than successful in the transformation process.

The first among them is the relative weakness of civil society as an autonomous actor: the strong statist, authoritarian tradition—common to countries such as Russia and Egypt, for example—has historically not left a public legitimate space for the emergence of that network of independent associations in which citizens act voluntarily for goals that are embedded in their personal views and orientations, but whose activities impact on the public sphere: the variety of social, economic, and educational organizations, religious and intellectual associations, and the like—that rich sphere that scholars since Tocqueville have seen as crucial to the emergence of a democratic, participatory culture. Only on the basis of such a rich culture and its institutions can political democracy—epitomized in elections, but not reducible to them—flourish successfully.

Second, the lack of historical memories of a "usable past," which can be reconstructed and then applied, with various degrees of embellishments and even some falsification, to current developments and grant internal legitimacy to democratic institutions and procedures. As mentioned, while Czechs and Poles could look back in pride to their historical representative and up to a point democratic traditions, Russia lacked this "usable past": the same can be said for most Arab societies.

It is true, as pointed out by some observers, that some Arab societies had experienced constitutional and representative institutions in the first half of the twentieth century: the cases of Egypt and Iraq are often cited. But there are three problems with these examples: first, these institutions were at least in part modeled on Western examples and were subsequently viewed as imperialist impositions on Arab societies, used to legitimate the power of the pro-Western elites; second, none of these institutions really grew out of popular demands or movements indigenous to Arab society, and hence lacked internal legitimacy; and third, unlike what happened in countries such as England and France, these limited, constitutional experiments were not followed by their widening to become more inclusive, truly democratic systems—on the contrary, when they collapsed in the 1950s, they were supplanted by non-democratic, populist revolutionary ideologies (Nasserism, Ba'athism, etc.).

Last and not least, given the mainly Sunni traditions of Arab societies, religion has historically been a vehicle in the hands of the secular powers-that-be (like the Orthodox Church in Russian), and hence did not create the kind of internal criticism of "speaking truth to power" (to use Edward Said's phrase in another context). When religious traditions and norms were eventually developed to confront power—from the *Ikhwan* to Al Qaeda—the consequences did not enhance a democratic discourse.

It should however be mentioned that, despite all this, there had been a constant internal critique in Arab societies of the lack of democracy: it is certainly not true that, until the US-led post 9/11 missionary zeal, Arab societies lacked voices of democratic dissent. Many intellectuals, mostly but not exclusively inspired by the Marxian tradition (e.g., Sadiq Jalal Al-Azm, Ghassan Salameh, and many others) had repeatedly raised their critical voices against the conformist and quietistic traditions prevalent in Arab societies and called for confronting the ruling authoritarian regimes. Their writings span a wide horizon of discourse, and their individual courage is exemplary: yet they never succeeded in creating the critical mass of public opinion in establishing strong protest organizations or political parties which would—like Solidarność in Poland—transform an intellectual discourse into a mass political movement, carrying out what Marx once called the transition from theory to praxis which can be achieved only when "theory grips the masses." This very impressive phenomenon still remains an elite phenomenon, and many of its spokesmen now grace European and American universities, rather than lead mass movements in their own countries: this is not a critique, but a sad commentary.

The current American call for the need for democratization in the Arab world is by itself a laudable policy orientation: for decades, the Arab world has enjoyed an immunity from the universal US-led campaign for human rights, which has certainly been influential in weakening the Soviet system (as well as helping processes of democratization in Latin America, the Philippines, Indonesia, etc.). Yet at a time when the US has—rightly—condemned in the harshest language Iran's infringements of human rights, it was virtually silent about the much more repressive Saudi regime and such secularist autocracies as Egypt.

This has now changed but, as is often the case with US policy orientations, current wisdom in Washington has moved to the other extreme: silence about the Arab democratic deficit has been replaced by an ideologically driven and almost naïve belief that democratization can be easily achieved in the Arab world when the major building blocks are so weak—and when the dangers of even worse developments cannot be ruled out (Algeria is an obvious warning alternative). This is coupled with a somewhat simplistic belief that the very holding of elections is tantamount to the establishment and consolidation of democracy. In its most extreme form, this almost messianic belief in quick democratization is evident in current US policies in Iraq.

Beyond the justifications for the US-led war in Iraq, the American attempt to introduce a democratic system into Iraq in a relatively short time is doomed to failure, and the debacle becomes clearer by the day. As mentioned before, there is no legitimate Arab model. Second, there are no indigenous Iraqi civil society ingredients—no effective democratic or constitutional historical memories or institutions to use as legitimizing factors. Third, introducing democracy under conditions of occupation is by itself problematic, and the post-1945 examples from Germany and Japan are problematic (where are the Iraqi Konrad Adenauers and Willy Brandts?).

Last and not least: the ethno-religious composition of Iraq makes the construction of a pluralistic, democratic regime in Iraq almost a mission impossible. To imagine that this can be solved or managed by promoting a constitution, which appears as imposed from outside as the current provisional government, is naïve if not pathetic. Perhaps eventually an independent Kurdistan may have better chances for democratic developments. But this would still not solve the problem how the rest of Iraq, deeply split between the historically dominant Sunni minority and the historically oppressed Shi'ite majority, can evolve toward a workable coherent form of government based on principles of democracy and pluralism when almost all the building blocks are lacking. It may be a bleak perspective, but to deny it is analytically wrong and politically dangerous.

The American debacle in Iraq raises another issue that should be mentioned in this context: the almost exclusive—and fallacious—identification of democratization with holding of elections. Free elections are, of course, the hallmark of democracy: yet they are, so to speak, merely the necessary but not sufficient superstructure of a democratic culture, or—to switch metaphors—the tip of the iceberg: to be meaningful, they have to be based upon and preceded by a vibrant civil society—again the comparison between Poland and Russia is illustrative of the ensuing difference between developments in a society that possesses a rich civil society and one that does not.

Three recent elections—each in a different context—show how problematic elections can be in the absence of these conditions: in Egypt, a relatively more relaxed election law did not strengthen the liberal, democratic forces (such as *Al-Ghad*, which lacked an organizational, mass infrastructure), but the *Ikwan* (who could build on their traditional grassroots support); in the Palestinian elections, it was Hamas that came out on top; and in Iraq, despite the high degree of participation in the parliamentary elections, so much touted initially by the US as a sign of successful democratization, the voting meant not democratization but a conformist rallying around ethnic/religious identities and affiliation. The last case is somewhat similar to what happened in

Yugoslavia in the 1990s, when the relative democratization of post-Titoist Yugoslavia gave democratic legitimacy to calls for the independence of the various nationalities (Croats, Slovenes, eventually Kosovo Albanians).

On the other hand, slow processes of relative opening—such as those in Kuwait, Bahrain, perhaps also in Morocco—suggest, paradoxically though it may seem, that piecemeal and partial reforms in some of the monarchical regimes may perhaps create the civil society infrastructure so necessary for successful democratic transformation. Holding local elections, or national elections to different varieties of shura councils, allowing women to partici-pate—even on a limited basis—in some elections may be important steps toward further, much more meaningful developments. It is too early to judge: much will depend on how far local rulers will allow these developments to proceed further and how successful the new leadership, thus emerging, will be in utilizing wisely its newly won powers; in the Gulf states, this may be com-plicated by the huge number of foreign workers, crucial to the local economy, but lacking political rights. Yet these developments may—if viewed through the prism of a *longue durée*— be extremely important: while the jury is still out, these steps should be watched carefully and with some hope, although nothing is predetermined and, once again, the same developments in different countries may give different results.

Developments in the two regions discussed above—post-communist Cen-tral Eastern Europe and the Arab Middle East—point to the fact that ignor-ing or overlooking issues of culture and history in any equation aiming at enhancing democratic development involves missing a major ingredient. This analysis is far from decreeing a cultural determinism, yet it strongly suggests that avoiding the issues of political culture and historical heritage makes one unable to account for the great differences in developments in societies which otherwise appear analogous—and, moreover, prevents one from charting a realistic course for democratic transformation in societies that are groping their way out of different forms of oppressive regimes.

7   Democratic transformation in Egypt

Controlled reforms ... frustrated hopes

Emad El-Din Shahin

The past few years have carried both great hopes and deep frustrations for the future of democratization in Egypt. The country witnessed a significant national referendum; two major elections, presidential and parliamentary, in September and November–December 2005 respectively; the formation of a pro-reform movement; and a remarkable political vitality. It is uncertain, however, whether these developments will place Egypt on the threshold of a sustainable democratic transformation. The regime is still well entrenched and in control of the agenda and the pace of reform. It continues to enjoy the support of external actors. The country's licensed political opposition is weak and divided, the newly emerging pro-reform movements have been unable to address the serious problem of public apathy, and their ability to sustain the reform momentum is questionable. Egypt presents a typical case of an authoritarian or a semi-authoritarian regime that suffers from an erosion of legitimacy and popularity, low capacity to address the economic and social problems of large segments of society, a crisis of political succession, and mounting domestic and external pressures for reform. This has prompted the regime to introduce a series of measures that allowed the country, for the first time in its post-1952 Revolution history, to have multicandidate presidential elections and relatively more contested legislative elections. These reforms still fall short of placing Egypt on the path of a serious democratic transition.

Introduction

Democratic transitions are neither simple nor certain. They are the product of a protracted process that may become subject to reversals. Compared with two or three decades ago, most Arab regimes have been transforming in response to increasing pressures for political liberalization. The main concern is that this political liberalization process is becoming an end in itself, giving rise to a new political system that is "neither/nor." It is neither a fully developed democracy nor a fully fledged autocracy.[1] Perhaps, this is precisely the meaning of transformation, which connotes the movement from one direction to another, from one political system to another. The real problem is that this neither/nor status may become a permanent nature of Arab regimes in the region for a long time to come. The tendency to bequeath power, establish "presidential monarchies," and resist changes to the structures of powers within the system falls into this vein. It clearly underscores the "exit dilemma" and the "succession crisis" which most, if not all, Arab leaders face. The transformation at the surface should not conceal the persisting extra-legal and authoritarian practices, absence of adequate channels of participation, the dismal human rights record, and lack of regime accountability in most Arab countries. The strategy of adopting political reforms from above does not necessarily limit the powers of the ruling elite or allow for real political competition. It simply masks the authoritarian nature of the regime and creates a superficial atmosphere of change that allows for a further manipulation of the political process through cunning appropriation of the opposition demands, wearing the opposition down, and deliberately coopting, de-legitimizing, or repressing them, whenever necessary.

This state of political opening seems advantageous to the regime, which can still prolong its rule, extract external handouts and support without losing power or making threatening concessions, changing the major structures of the system, or fundamentally changing the regime's ruling style. During this phase, the regime is willing to give some minor concessions to its opponents; allow for more freedoms; adopt less repressive measures; replace some of the old guards, particularly the unpopular ones, with more liberal elements; undertake anti-corruption cleaning up campaigns (particularly against middle-level elites); change some of the laws; and conduct regular elections in which its victory is always guaranteed. However, all these measures are taken in a way that assures the continuity of the regime and its control over the reform process. On the positive side, this process often generates rising demands for reform, leads to the emergence of protest and pro-reform movements, and creates frictions within the regime, giving hope that a democratic transition could be tenable. The downside is that this atmosphere of superficial liberalization is simultaneously marred by de-liberalizing and restrictive measures that divest the reforms of an effective impact, generate doubts about the entire process, and create a culture of apathy and indifference.

Regime's calculated reforms: democratization or prolonging authoritarianism?

Egypt is no exception to this situation. Since 2000, the Mubarak regime has embarked on a series of reforms to address the mounting popular discontent, eroding popularity of the National Democratic Party (NDP), and the succession crisis. Several of these reforms, at least on the surface, have indeed changed some aspects of the country's political landscape. Yet, democracy has not been the main value behind the regime's changes, but rather the need to deflate the domestic pressures and maintain the support of the external actors. Mubarak is characteristically known as a pro-status quo and anti-change president. He has adopted an extremely cautious attitude when it comes to the possibility of shaking the stability of his regime. His vision of reform reflects this attitude. According to Mubarak, "Reform has to be a well-calculated process and should be implemented through phases in an orderly manner."[2] He often equated democratization in Egypt to the state of a sick patient. An overdose of democracy can kill the patient, create chaos, and turn Egypt into another Algeria. Based on this patronizing attitude, the main objective behind reforms is thus to ensure continued control over the political process and prevent any deterioration that could pose a threat to the stability of the regime. Mubarak also needs to address the issue of regime transition and find a way to introduce his son Gamal to the political arena as a possible heir. This grooming would be best done through a package of reform measures that would generate a state of political opening and positive expectations that could allow for his election in a seemingly democratic way, and not through a "Syrian-style" handover of power. In sum, the regime's strategy behind the reforms is clear and could be summarized as aiming at the continuation of control, deflecting domestic and international pressures, and allowing for an acceptable succession of Gamal Mubarak.

The parliamentary elections of 2000 represented a moment of serious reckoning for the Egyptian regime, as well as an opportunity to implement its reform strategy. Prior to the elections, President Mubarak pledged that they would be clean and free and would be conducted under the supervision of the judiciary, not the ministry of the interior. The elections took place over three rounds. The first did not go well for the NDP, and consequently, the state had to resort to the old habit of "irregularities": ballot stuffing, intimidation of voters, bribery, rigging, and violence. Still, the state party performed poorly in the elections and failed to secure a majority. It fielded 442 candidates and won only 177 (38 percent) out of the parliament's 444 contested seats. The NDP was able to gain a majority, however, only after it had allowed former NDP members, who were not nominated by the party and ran as NDP independents, to rejoin the party, thus bringing its seats to a total of 388 (85.8 percent). The rest of the seats were distributed between the Muslim Brotherhood (17 seats), Independents (16), New Wafd (7), Tajamu' (6), Nasserites (5), Nasserite Party (2), and Liberal Party (1). The 2000 results come against a long, yet questionable, legacy of a landslide victory of the state party in almost all the parliamentary elections that have taken place since the adoption of a multiparty system in Egypt in 1976. In 1979, the NDP captured 90 percent of the seats; 1984, 80 percent; 1990, almost 80 percent; 1995, 95 percent.[3]

At the eighth NDP Congress in September 2002, Mubarak undertook a major restructuring of the party and leadership reshuffles that allowed for the emergence of new players, headed by his son. A new structure, the Policies Committee, was specially carved for Gamal who became its head. Gamal appointed over 120 members drawn from among university professors, intellectuals, and businessmen. Most of these new members have had very little political history; or more importantly, influence or popular following in society. The main objective of the committee was to devise the party's policies, draw the public policies of the government, and initiate draft laws for approval in parliament. At another level, the committee acted as a vehicle for Gamal to exercise influence within the party and over the government. The Congress also raised the slogan of "new thinking," in an attempt to project an image of change and a new vision for the future of the party and the country at large. Additional changes were made within the party. The NDP amended its bylaws to allow for the first time for competitive elections for the president of the party (Husni Mubarak); new members within Gamal's faction managed to secure twenty seats in the party's twenty-five-seat General Secretariat; and the powers of Kamal al-Shazli (the party's second man and one of its old barons) were reduced. These changes instigated debates about the emergence of a new guard within the party, more liberal and pro-reform, in opposition to an old guard that wanted to maintain the status quo and block change.[4] However, some signs gave reasons to question the new orientation of the party and its "new guards." The change among the old faces was rather limited. Mubarak appointed Safwat al-Sharif as the new secretary general. Al-Sharif could hardly be considered as fresh blood or a new guard. He has been in the corridors of power for almost three decades. Kamal al-Shazli, also close to the circles of power for four decades, kept his position as the party's secretary for organization/recruitment. The changes did not touch the lower structures of the party and remained confined to the top. Most notably, the changes focused on effecting internal reforms within the party rather than introducing reforms in society. The ascendancy of Gamal Mubarak and the possibility of using the party as a vehicle for taking over power provoked the opposition and other forces in society to press for genuine reforms. Their initial demands focused on rejecting a hereditary succession to power, amending the constitution, and ending the state of emergency (in effect since 1981).

To circumvent the growing demands for reform, the regime engaged some of the licensed opposition parties in a series of rounds of a closed dialogue, which excluded the Muslim Brothers and the socialist and Islamic-leaning Labor Party. The party's annual conference in September 2004 made it clear that the regime set and controlled the reform agenda. The party dismissed any discussion of the possibility of amending the constitution, changing the rules of the presidential elections, or lifting the state of emergency. It insisted on giving priority to economic reforms and proposed minor changes in some of the existing restrictive laws that regulate the formation of political parties and the electoral system (Party Formation law, the People's Assembly law, laws regulating the electoral processes, and the law of practicing political rights). All the proposed changes were made to ensure the party's grip over the pace of political reform. The opposition parties failed to extract any serious concessions from the regime and appeared utterly ineffective as they ended up accepting to put off discussions of amending the constitution. Ironically, some minor parties even went as far as endorsing Mubarak for a fifth term.

It became obvious that the regime was set on derailing the reforms. Most alarming was the fact that the country was being now prepared for a hereditary succession of power. President Husni Mubarak, who is the head of the party, did not participate in the congress proceedings, except for the concluding session. The president's son, Gamal Mubarak, received wide publicity and most of the attention during the congress, as he appeared to be spearheading the reforms and the "reformist wing" within the party. He assumed the role of explaining the party's plans, outlining the regime's future vision, and restructuring the party to increase the presence and influence of his own clients, the Party's "new guards." As the presidential elections were then only one year down the road, and despite official denials, it became clear that the way would be open for Gamal to become Egypt's next hereditary president— a scenario that all pro-reform forces in the country vehemently rejected and were willing to resist.

The NDP conference was followed by reform measures that included the release of detained prisoners of al-Jama'a al-Islamiyya; the cancellation of some martial laws that had been issued under the emergency law; abolishing hard labor sentences; forming a state-sponsored High Council for Human Rights; granting Egyptian women some additional rights; and calling for a continued national dialogue with some opposition parties. Most of these reforms have not addressed the reform demands of the opposition or affected directly the structure of power in the country. The regime seemed to engage in a strategy of outmaneuvering the reform process and divesting it of any serious impact. It continued to impose the state of emergency, rejected the removal of restrictions over the formation of new parties; failed to grant specific authorities to the High Council for Human Rights; and ignored the growing demands to grant more independence to the judiciary and to reform the existing press laws. More importantly, the regime was adamant on keeping the rules of electing the president unchanged and in getting Mubarak to assume power for a fifth term.

The amendment of Article 76: conditional contestation

The way the regime handled the amendment of Article 76 demonstrates its style of manipulating and circumventing reforms. This was clear in the timing and legal drafting of the amendment. On January 30, 2005, Mubarak described the call for amending the constitution as misguided.[5] He repeatedly reasserted his rejection of any constitutional change. He even accused those who were calling for a constitutional change of being spurred by external actors. Therefore, his decision in February 2005 to allow for an amendment of Article 76, which dealt with the rules for the selection of the president, came as a surprise. After all, after rounds of dialogues with the regime, the licensed opposition parties had already agreed to drop this demand for the time being, at least until Mubarak was re-elected.

Several factors explain Mubarak's decision to change his mind. The way the article was amended would clearly serve Mubarak to boost his legitimacy through low-risk competitive elections. It would also pave the way for his son to take over power in a seemingly more "democratic" way. It underscored the fact that only the regime was in a position to introduce reforms and that the licensed opposition had been too weak to extract meaningful concessions. The amendment would give a clear signal to the US and the EU that the regime was serious about reform and was proceeding to make a major structural change by changing the rules for the presidential elections. The amendment allowed for more than one candidate to run for the presidency. However, it introduced elaborate conditionalities that make it almost impossible for a non-NDP candidate, particularly independents, to stand a chance of being eligible to run for the presidency. The new amendment allows only candidates from political parties that won 5 percent of the seats in parliament to run. It requires independent candidates to secure 250 signatures of elected officials in the parliament, the shura council (upper house), and local councils in fourteen governorates. Despite the reservations of the opposition parties, the amendment was approved on May 25 by almost 83 percent in a popular referendum, in which only 25 percent (and according to the Judges Club, only less than 5 percent) turned out to vote. The referendum day was marred by state brutality against protesters who opposed the way the amendment was legally drafted. State-backed thugs sexually molested and beat several female journalists covering the protests. The violence triggered wide domestic anger as well as criticism from the outside world.

The presidential elections: new rules ... same president

The timing of the amendment and the referendum seems to be well calculated by the regime. The amendment was approved in May, just a little over three months before the presidential elections in September. This gave the political parties and potential presidential candidates little time to prepare for an event that they had never experienced before. Additionally, the presidential campaign ran through the month of August, which is almost a dead month for political activities. The result seemed to most people to be a foregone conclusion, particularly given the unlimited access the NPD candidate has to the resources of the state. Yet, ten candidates contested the presidential elections that took place on September 7. This was preceded by public election campaigns, in which the state-run TV, and not the state-owned press, maintained some degree of neutrality. For the first time, Egyptians were exposed to different views attempting to address their domestic problems. Mubarak, who was projected in a new look, made expansive campaign promises that included the creation of new jobs, providing housing, comprehensive medical coverage, doubling the salaries of civil servants, and introducing further political reforms.

It is clear from the results of the elections that what changed was the form, but not the outcome, of this particular aspect of Egyptian politics. Despite the fact that these were the first competitive elections in post-1952 Revolution Egypt, the voter turnout was strikingly low, reaching only 23 percent, according to official estimates. The majority of voters (77 percent) demonstrated a high level of apathy, perhaps sending a message of no confidence in the whole process. Mubarak still won more than 88.5 percent (6.3 million) of the valid votes (7.3 million); Ayman Nour, the leader of the newly formed Ghad (Tomorrow) Party, came second with 8 percent (540,000); Noman Gouma, the head of the historic Wafd Party, came third with less than 3 percent (200,000). A careful reading of the results shows that Mubarak won only 19.6 percent of the 32 million registered voters; and less than 12 percent of the eligible voters (48 million). Ayman Nour emerged as the major challenger to the president and a possible future threat. The results also reflected the profound structural weaknesses of the opposition parties in the country. Typically, the political parties were divided and failed to back a single opposition candidate to run against the incumbent president. Some opposition parties, such as the leftist Tajamu' and the Nasserites, boycotted the election, while the leadership of the Muslim Brotherhood allowed its members to vote, but refrained from backing a particular candidate. Seven party leaders who ran against the president received only a combined 2 percent of the votes, reflecting the lack of popularity of the political parties. Although his victory came as no surprise, the results of the presidential elections could hardly enable Mubarak to claim a new legitimacy.

The emerging protest movements and coalitions

Egyptian political life has for long been monopolized by an overdominant state party and characterized by deep political stagnation. The NDP strength was not driven by its popularity or clear vision, but simply from its close association with the state administration and control of an elaborate patronage system. Recently, several pro-reform movements have emerged to challenge the monopoly of the NDP over the political arena. Some managed to attract segments of the country's "dormant" and "ineffective" counterelites. Such reform movements have mushroomed in a relatively short time. In 2004 and 2005, more than fourteen pro-reform movements emerged in opposition to the possibility of renewing Mubarak's presidency for a fifth term and to a hereditary succession. "Change" seems to be the common denominator among all these movements. The list of recently formed movements include: *Kifaya* (The Egyptian Movement for Change), the National Rally for Democratic Transformation, Journalists for Change, Doctors for Change, Intellectuals for Change, Writers for Change, Youth for Change, the Association of Egyptian Mothers, and the Movement of White Ribbons. Obviously, these groups vary in influence and impact, but the rapid growth of such movements, which have repeatedly broken the fear barriers, taken to the streets, and organized demonstrations calling for change and reform, has several indications. It is a clear sign that the existing legal political parties are not effective in articulating the demands of the people; that professional or particular reform interests cannot be achieved unless overall reform is brought about; and that the movement for change requires the efforts of various groups. All these forces agree on a clear list of demands that includes ending the state of emergency; rejecting hereditary succession; free and clean elections; and changing the constitution.

Kifaya *[Enough]*

The Egyptian Movement for Change, *Kifaya*, is the most well known of these newly emerging protest movements. It appeared in August 2004, as a non-partisan, umbrella movement that reflects the major political trends in society. Its founders consist of a wide range of political activists, professionals, and intellectuals, representing the Nasserites, Islamists, liberals, and leftists, in addition to independents. *Kifaya* started with the formulation of basic reform demands on which all political forces could come to an agreement. The movement called for ending the state of emergency; ending the regime's monopoly over power; amending the constitution; and allowing for the transfer of power. It also expressed its opposition to any foreign intervention to push for reforms in the country. *Kifaya*'s objectives started to evolve as the movement gathered initial support from different political forces. It decided to take its demands directly to the streets. The movement organized its first demonstration on February 12, 2005, and since then it has organized several throughout the country. Despite its relatively short history and limited influence, it was able to organize fourteen demonstrations in different parts of the country on one day. As a sign of a further evolution, the movement is seeking to formulate a vision for the future of democracy in the country.[6]

Since its establishment, the *Kifaya* movement has become the focus of heated controversies. Even some of its founders are uncertain about its future or how it would evolve. Some question the objectives behind the formation and toleration of this movement. The licensed opposition parties are wary of the movement and have tried on different occasions to discredit it. They consider the movement as a sporadic phenomenon and accuse it of being elitist and of maintaining foreign links. The Muslim Brothers, who participated in the movement and in some of its demonstrations, expressed reservations regarding the language and the slogans the movement used in its demonstrations. They also seemed to harbor some concerns about the possibility that *Kifaya* might evolve or be used to undermine their popular influence and presence among the public. The regime, in a typical sign of a growing isolation from reality, accused the movement of being foreign inspired and of receiving finances from external sources.

In fact, *Kifaya* is an evolving political movement, with genuine concerns for reforms and for not leaving the political spectrum wide open to the main political forces in the country, the regime and the Muslim Brothers. Its main contribution lies in its ability to break the monotony in Egyptian political life and public discourse. It raises easy, direct, popular, and bold slogans: "No Extension for Mubarak; No to Hereditary Succession." Its approach is original in Egyptian political practices: high visibility, with small numbers. The movement adopted a short-term vision and succeeded in forming agreed-upon reform demands, which have already been popular. That might be a reason for its growing influence, despite the relatively limited number of its supporters (estimated at 20,000 in 2008). In addition, the movement has demonstrated great skills in using the Arab and foreign media. The phenomenon of *Kifaya* certainly reveals the ineffectiveness of the existing legal political parties and their inability to mobilize the people. It was able to transcend them in a short space of time. This may be the reason why the "tamed" political parties are suspicious of the movement. The movement also presents a clear source of pressure on the regime, which resorted to an unconvincing way to discredit the movement by accusing it of foreign links. However, *Kifaya* has its inherent limitations. It is unlikely that the movement will evolve into a political party because of the nature of its formation of representatives of various political parties and different ideological orientations. Unless the movement finds ways to renew its agenda, issues, and slogans, it would be difficult for it to maintain momentum. The leadership of *Kifaya* has acknowledged on several occasions that it has not articulated a comprehensive vision for reform. In fact, the movement was subject to several splits and the withdrawal of some of its leading members toward the end of 2006, in protest at the leadership style and the movement's inability to step up its opposition practices. Nonetheless, *Kifaya* as a movement could certainly assume a monitoring role for the process of democratization in Egypt and appeal to the street whenever violations occurred.

The National Rally for Democratic Transition

Another pro-change formation is the National Rally for Democratic Transition. It was formed by a group of politicians and intellectuals in June 2005. The Rally was led by the late Aziz Sidqi, a former prime minister, and included former officials, diplomats, university professors, and well-known experts in economics, education, diplomacy, media, and law. In a press conference that was attended by more than 100 prominent figures, the group appealed to all the political forces to join in forming a "national front" to crystallize and reach an agreement over a strategic vision of political change and democratic transition in Egypt. The founders confirmed their intentions not to organize demonstrations or compete for power, but to formulate ideas that would "rescue Egypt from the current state of stagnation and put checks on the alliance of corruption and authoritarianism that blocks reform."[7] The Rally eventually sought to hold a general conference of national and democratic forces and form a constituent committee representing all the political and intellectual trends. The main task of this committee was to write a new constitution for Egypt. The Rally tried to mediate between the competing opposition parties during the parliamentary elections, but failed to get them to reconcile their differences and form a coalition front against the regime. The most important aspect of the Rally, however, was the idea it stood for and the attempt to devise a futuristic vision to generate the agreement of the main political actors. This was not an easy challenge, given the fragmented state of the opposition in Egypt.

Despite their limited influence and low capacity to mobilize and engage the public in their reform agenda, these transient movements can still make some positive contributions. They can help generate reform demands and maintain them within focus. They can also raise the level of public discourse and debate over the proposed reforms. More important, they provide a forum where a new and younger generation of political leaders could possibly arise and acquire experience in political activism.

The licensed opposition parties

Party life in Egypt is highly fragmented. The country has over twenty lega-lized parties. The *Wafd*, the Arab Nasserite, and the leftist Tajamu' are con-sidered as the main opposition parties (some include the newly founded and now disintegrating *al-Ghad* to this group). Two parties, the Labor and Young Egypt, have been frozen by the regime. Thirteen parties are marginal and almost unknown to most people. A major opposition force, the Muslim Brothers, is not legally recognized; and two parties, the Islamic *al-Wasat* (Centrist) and Nasserite *al-Karama* (Dignity), are currently fighting protracted legal battles for legalization. Generally, the licensed opposition forces are characterized by a remarkable internal structural weakness, lack of popularity, and ineffec-tiveness in mobilizing the public or mounting pressures on the regime. Tradi-tionally, most of the regime's liberalizing measures came from above to address certain political or economic objectives and not in direct response to pressures from below. For example, the idea of dismantling the one-party system and establishing a pluralistic one was Sadat's initiative and was undertaken from within the ASU (the Arab Social Union), which is now the NDP. A more recent example, the formation of the High Council for Human Rights, came as a surprise to the opposition parties, and so did the decision to grant citi-zenship to the children of Egyptian mothers married to non-Egyptians, and the decision to amend Article 76 of the constitution. This has been an old and deliberate policy which the Egyptian regime has mastered to maintain control of the political agenda. However, reform from above weakens the political maturity of society and makes the legal opposition appear lacking in initiative and lagging behind the regime.

The liberal secular opposition has been ineffective and unpopular. The leaders of the legal opposition often attribute the ineptness of their parties to the regime's restrictive and repressive polices. Although this argument is often accepted by many analysts to explain the weakness of the liberal and secular opposition in Egypt, it cannot be entirely true. The Muslim Brothers, for example, who have been banned for decades, operate under much more restric-tive government policies. They have been exposed to sporadic harassment and arrests, and their leaders have faced frequent security crackdowns and military tribunals. Yet, the group has managed over the years, despite the regime's repression, to recruit a following from among the youth, maintain a highly disciplined constituency, maintain a coherent organizational structure, connect to large segments of the population, win seats in the national syndicates, and undertake well-organized demonstrations and election campaigns.

The weakness of the secular and liberal opposition lies primarily in their lack of vision and intellectual innovation, aging leadership, failure to institute democratic practices within their parties, inability to resolve their internal conflicts and prevent regular splits. All these obvious shortcomings render them unattractive and unable to recruit new elements, particularly among the youth. More damagingly, they have for long accepted many of the restrictions imposed on them by the regime and refrained from challenging them, which made them seem part and parcel of the authoritarian system and as pawns that help in its perpetuation. Over the past twenty-five years, the liberal and leftist parties have not organized a single demonstration in support of democracy or freedom, a clear sign of their lack of leadership, constituency, and will to defy the system. On some occasions, leaders of some secular parties publicly expressed their preference to be ruled by an authoritarian regime or even a dictatorship to a system run by Islamists, even if they came to power through democratic means.

The reformist judges

A significant and forceful group in the pro-reform movement are the judges, particularly the members of the Judges Club.[8] The case of the judges is worth elaboration, because it could have significant future political ramifications for a possible democratic transition in Egypt. Traditionally, Egyptian judges deliberately refrain from interfering in politics or taking a certain political stand in order to ensure the independence and neutrality of the judiciary branch. Since April 2004, many judges organized under the Judges Club finally joined the reform momentum and stressed the need for overall reforms. They pressed certain demands and conditions for the regime for their supervision of the presidential and parliamentary elections. Their demands included approving a new law for the judicial branch, which they had proposed but the regime had stalled since 1991, that would enhance the judicial branch and ensure its independence from government interference and administrative control. They insisted on complete supervision over the entire electoral process, starting with the preparation of the voters' lists to the announcement of the election results. The judges have been outspoken about past election irregularities and expressed their determination not to participate in future ones that could be rigged. Their stand received support from various organizations—the lawyers, journalists, engineers, and workers, the Muslim Brothers, and the *Kifaya* movement. They all considered the complete independence of the judiciary as a necessary safeguard for a democratic transition and the future of reform in the country.

The leadership of the Judges Club enjoys legitimacy and a reputation of integrity and credibility. They have played an extraordinary role in de-legitimizing the regime's tactics to outmaneuver reforms over the past years. They publicly opposed the proposed draft of the constitutional amendment of Article 76 and the measures taken by the regime to abort any possible questioning of the constitutionality of that amendment. They also questioned the regime's version of the results of the referendum and the voter turnout and gave damning statements and testimonies regarding the lack of integrity in the presidential and parliamentary elections. In other words, the reformist judges are gradually building a legacy of credibility, honesty, and defiance. The reformist judges could play an extremely significant role in any future democratic transition. They could easily act as guarantors of the legality of the democratization and consolidation processes. They could ensure the constitutionality of proposed laws, preside over an independent electoral high commission, exercise complete supervision over the electoral system and future elections, and enhance the integrity and independence of the judicial branch. Of course, the judges cannot mobilize society, but society needs to mobilize behind them. The regime was quick to realize this potential threat and harshly cracked down on the judges in May 2006. It put two popular reformist judges before a disciplinary court and applied violence against other judges who participated in peaceful protests, beating some of them in public. It crushed demonstrators who rallied in support of the judges and finally succeeded in bringing yet another reform momentum to a halt.

The Muslim Brothers: a change in strategy

The Muslim Brothers have emerged lately as the main contender to the NDP and as the most dynamic and well-organized opposition force in the country. They maintained a strong showing in the parliamentary elections of 2005 as they captured 20 percent of the parliament's seats. Unlike the secular opposition, the Brothers' remarkable performance was a result of long years of reasserting their presence at the public level, their direct engagement with the people, an appealing and pragmatic reform agenda, and willingness to confront the regime and pay the price for their defiance.

In a clear departure from their traditionally cautious attitude, the Muslim Brothers adopted an assertive strategy in their relationship with the regime and a more pragmatic orientation in the reform agenda they proposed. This change became quite noticeable in early 2005, when the Muslim Brothers insisted on reasserting their presence in an increasingly more dynamic political arena. They organized a public demonstration in March to demand a faster pace for the reforms and for public freedoms, despite the state security's rejection of permission to demonstrate. Defying the ban, the Muslim Brothers decided to go ahead and organized a "symbolic" demonstration in which 10,000 people participated. The regime responded by subsequent arrests of thousands of the Brothers' followers. The show of force between the regime and the Muslim Brothers seemed to be heading toward a major escalation, or what some have already called a "bone-crushing phase." In a clear break from past practices, the group refused to relent and continued with even larger intermittent demonstrations for a period of three weeks. The Muslim Brothers did not raise their usual traditional slogans in some of these demonstrations, but adopted an appealing reform agenda that called for ending the state of emergency, allowing public freedoms, precipitating the pace of reform, holding clean presidential elections under total judicial supervision, and releasing all political detainees (estimated at 20,000). In one day in May, they organized forty-one "surprise" rallies in which 70,000 people participated in eighteen governorates. The regime considered this continued defiance as a clear violation of all the red lines and stepped up its crackdown on the group by arresting some of its top leadership, particularly those in charge of preparing for the Brothers' participation in the parliamentary elections as well as many of the group's potential parliamentary candidates. Two days later, the group organized another demonstration. That day was dubbed "Black Friday" because of the violent confrontations that led to the death of one demonstrator, the injury of tens, and the arrest of hundreds. The violent regime response promoted the General Guide of the Brotherhood to threaten "civil disobedience if that was the only way to achieve freedom and justice for the Egyptian people" and to insist on achieving comprehensive reforms.[9]

The explanations behind the Brothers' change of strategy vary. The regime, its official media, and the critics of the group tried to attribute this change to external enticement. This explanation was widely publicized in order to discredit the group through claims of foreign affiliation and clandestine contacts and dialogue between the Muslim Brothers and the US and EU. They argued that the Muslim Brothers have become emboldened by statements from US officials, who expressed the administration's willingness to accept the results of a democratic process even if it brought Islamists to power, and from some EU officials considering engaging the moderate Islamic movements in the reform process.

In fact, the change in the Muslim Brothers' strategy relates directly to the rapid political developments that were taking place in the country over the preceding year and a half. The general political atmosphere was generating new (and reviving old) forces for change and reform in which various groups were competing for a place and a role. The emergence of new movements, particularly *Kifaya*, which succeeded in energizing the political arena through a series of street demonstrations and in rapidly acquiring de facto recognition, must have moved the Muslim Brothers to try to reassert their presence as a significant player and to reject being marginalized or perceived as non-recognized political actors. In addition, the regime and the licensed opposition deliberately excluded the Muslim Brothers, the most organized and main Islamic popular force, from the discussions over the reform process. In March 2004, the group issued a comprehensive reform initiative that reflected a noticeable change in its language and views. The main objective behind this initiative was to provide a common ground for discussion and agreement on basic reforms over which the opposition would rally against the regime. However, the legal opposition and the regime completely ignored the initiative, preferring to engage in a "national" exclusive dialogue with the regime.

Another significant explanation for the change in the Muslim Brothers' strategy is the mounting pressures on the regime and their feeling that the moment is ripe for extracting concessions and gaining new ground. The regime has been exposed to domestic and external pressures to introduce meaningful political reforms. All its attempts to pay lip service to reform and outmaneuver the pressures by introducing what could be described at this phase as more than cosmetic but less than profound changes have raised the expectations of its opponents and made the regime even more vulnerable. A calculated show of force and a popular presence on the part of the Muslim Brothers could add to these pressures and help them reach some form of arrangement that would perhaps grant them a larger representation in the parliamentary elections in return for preventing the street from plunging into total chaos. Ironically, even when the tension between the regime and the Brothers was escalating, both exchanged direct hints for easing the situation. At some point, the president declared that he did not hold any enmity toward the Brothers and would not mind their participation in the political process, not as a legalized political party but as members of already existing parties. The Muslim Brothers returned the courtesy. They continued to confirm that they were not seeking to topple the regime and that they were interested in a dialogue. The Brothers' General Guide, although a member of *Kifaya* himself, criticized the movement for not showing enough respect to the head of the state and for using insulting language against the president. In fact, it was in the interests of both sides to prevent an all-out escalation. The Brothers cannot afford the destruction of the organizational structures that they have worked for years to rebuild. There is no reason for the time being to offer themselves as the only scapegoat, particularly in the absence of a supportive stance from the liberal and secular opposition. Likewise, by crushing the Muslim Brothers, the regime would remove a moderate Islamist movement and indirectly contribute to the emergence of radical Islamic groups. This is not an imaginary scenario taking into consideration the re-emergence of such groups and the bombings that took place in 2004 and early 2005. The Brothers' strategy has paid off so far as they have managed to become the largest opposition block in the country's parliamentary history.

The parliamentary elections: the limits for the reforms

The parliamentary elections of 2005 clearly showed the limits to political reforms. Under no conditions was the regime willing to lose its grip over the parliament. The elections were marred by state violence, intimidation of voters, and plain rigging. They were held over three phases to ensure complete judicial supervision. Mubarak once again promised a clean and transparent electoral process. And once again, the elections were far from being clean or transparent. Similar to what happened in the 2000 elections, the second and third phases were characterized by severe irregularities, vote-stuffing, thuggery, and state violence that resulted in seven deaths and tens of casualities. The regime got what it wanted. The NDP won 314 out of 454 seats (70 percent) and secured its control over the parliament. However, the Muslim Brothers made a strong showing as they captured 88 seats (20 percent)—the highest number of seats an opposition group has captured over the past fifty years. The rest of the opposition parties combined won only sixteen seats (3.4 percent); and the independents captured 6 percent of the seats.

Although still in control of a two-thirds majority in parliament, the NDP's performance was astonishingly poor. In reality, the party candidates who ran on NDP's lists won only 33.5 percent of the seats (they lost 287 out of 432 contested seats). Had it not been for the direct interference of the security forces on the side of NDP candidates, the party would have lost even more seats. The NDP was rescued by allowing the winning party members, who were not originally nominated by the party and had to run as independents, to rejoin the party, thus bringing its seats in the parliament up to 314.[10]

The parliamentary elections have been revealing in many respects. They clearly show how far the regime would go with reforms. The Egyptian regime will allow reforms only as long as they do not alter the structures of power or threaten its complete control. It is not willing to share power or allow for meaningful reforms that would weaken its grip over the system, the reform agenda, and the reform process. The poor performance of the state party equally proves that the overhauling process of the NDP that Gamal Mubarak and the "new guards" have undertaken over the past years has been meaningless. The "new vision" has not enabled the party to improve its image, gain popularity, or connect with the ordinary people. In fact, it did worse than in the previous elections. Another alarming signal is the low turnout of voters. Less than 25 percent of registered voters went to the polls. This could be attributed to the atmosphere of intimidation and violence that accompanied the process; the low confidence in the integrity of the elections; and the inability of the opposition to engage the public in the democratization and reform process. The elections highlighted the place of the Muslim Brothers as the main opposition force in the country and allowed them to run on a broad pro-reform platform. They succeeded in getting 65 percent of the total number of their candidates (165) elected to the parliament, capturing 1.9 million votes (the NDP received 2.4 million votes, notwithstanding the vote-stuffing and rigging). With regard to the secular and liberal opposition parties, the elections once again underscored their weaknesses in society and their inability to mobilize a sizable popular support. All the heads of the legal opposition parties failed to win seats. The parliamentary elections of 2005 have definitely animated the political scene, but left Egypt's political reality almost unchanged.[11]

The aftermath of the elections

The Egyptian regime has endured the latest reform pressures and perhaps will continue to do so unless major structural changes take place. The state is still well entrenched and the opposition is too weak. In addition, two major issues frustrate the democratic transition in the country: the succession issue and the external support that the regime still garners. With regard to the former, the strong performance of the Muslim Brothers in the parliamentary elections helped the regime to show the "limited" range of alternatives—either a continuation of an NDP-led regime or the Islamists. As for the second issue, the US and the EU are still on the side of stability under reformed autocrats, until a liberal, and not an Islamic, constituency emerges. For the moment, they are for "change within stability." Ironically, this is exactly the same formula that the autocrats in the region have been implementing successfully. Moreover, the regime has cunningly been using regional issues (Gaza, Palestinian–Israeli conflict, negotiations between the Palestinian factions, Hamas's victory in 2006, the war on terrorism, Iraq, Iran, etc.) to demonstrate its relevance to the external players. It should not be surprising then if the regime focused in the coming years on putting checks on any meaningful or qualitative reforms, at least until the succession issue is resolved. After all, the external pressure seems to be easing gradually and domestic pressures are declining.

Following the elections, several secular and liberal opposition parties began to disintegrate because of internal power struggles, as well as direct regime intervention in some cases. Ayman Nour's newly established party, *al-Ghad*, split into two factions. Nour himself, a major contender against Mubarak during the September presidential elections, was sentenced on December 24, 2005 to five years in prison for allegedly forging membership signatures. The *Wafd* party underwent a major rift as members of its High Committee fired the party's leader, No'man Goma'a, because of his authoritarian leadership style, triggering a potential split and the possibility of a freeze in the party's activities. The leftist Tajamou' and the Nasserite parties experienced major internal dissents and increasing calls for an overhaul after their poor performance in the parliamentary elections.

The NDP too undertook a major reshuffle within its highest structures in January, as President Mubarak dismissed prominent elements of the party's old guard, expanded the membership of the General Secretariat, and appointed new members known to be close to his son Gamal. This move has been interpreted as marking the victory of the new guards, led by Gamal, within the party and as further consolidating Gamal's influence.

Following the elections, the regime stepped up its confrontation with the reformist judges in a clear attempt to weaken them and suppress their demands for reforms. It has made major changes to the proposal they had submitted for the reform of the judicial branch. The regime's draft has been submitted to the NDP-dominated parliament for approval. The regime-backed High

Judicial Council stripped some of the leading members of the Judges Club of their immunity and put them under investigation for offending some "judicial entities." These members had questioned the integrity of the elections on several occasions and accused the regime and some of the judges supervising the elections of rigging the results.

Since the conclusion of the elections, the regime has shown clear signs of retreat on reforms. In his December 19 speech before the newly elected parliament, Mubarak chose not to make any reference to the future of the state of emergency. The speaker of the house confirmed later that the emergency law will remain in effect and "on demand."[12] While being renewed until 2010, many have expressed concern that the emergency laws would be replaced in time by tougher and more restrictive anti-terrorism laws. The two main candidates who ran against the president, Ayman Nour and No'man Goma'a, were eliminated from the political process. Besides ignoring the demands of the reformist judges and the ongoing attempts to suppress the Judges Club, the regime has been reluctant to review the harsh penalties of the press law that impose prison sentences and fines for what journalists report. Several journalists have already been sent to prison and fined for publishing "false information" concerning the corruption of some state officials and/or raising questions regarding the state of the president's health. In January 2007, the state-dominated party formation committee refused to grant official recognition to eleven would-be political parties.

In a clear attempt to stop the Muslim Brothers from achieving further victories, the regime has decided to cripple the movement and downsize its presence in the political process. It postponed the local elections that were scheduled to take place in March 2006 for two years. The Muslim Brothers had planned to compete in these elections and hoped to make a strong showing. The regime used a parade that Muslim Brothers' students set up on Al-Azhar University campus in December 2006 as a pretext to launch a major crackdown and intensive media campaign against the group. Mubarak announced that the Muslim Brothers represented a threat to national security and would lead Egypt to isolation, ushering in a brutal suppression of the group. In this initial phase of confrontation, the state security arrested 150 students and twenty-nine leading members, freezing their corporate and personal assets. It closed down twenty-three of their companies and 123 franchises (with an estimated 1–1.5 billion Egyptian pounds in assets). Since then, the movement has been exposed to regular arrest campaigns. Despite their acquittal by the civil courts, Mubarak insisted on trying the movement's detained leaders before military tribunals. Given the extent of the arrests and the fierce media campaign that accompanied the process, this confrontation seems to mark a new confrontational stage in the relationship between the regime and the Muslim Brothers.

In addition to applying brutal force, the regime amended the constitution in order to regain full control over the political process following a period of relative toleration of dissent. It introduced several constitutional amendments that dashed hopes for true reforms.[13] The amendments that were approved in March 2007 by the state-dominated parliament and then in a referendum which the opposition forces boycotted have taken the country to a political impasse and a clear political setback. They ignored the most pressing reform demand to limit the tenure of the president to two terms; restricted the formation of political parties on a religious basis; banned any political activity on the basis of religion or religious reference (which clearly target the Muslim Brothers and their chances of forming a political party or even raising their religious slogans); gave the president the right to refer cases to military tribunals; institutionalized the extra-legal provisions of the emergency law (rights to privacy, searching homes without prior search warrants, bugging telephone conversations); restricted independent candidates from running for presidential elections; reduced the supervision of the judges over the electoral process; changed the electoral system from a single candidate-based into a party list-based system; and gave the president the authority to dissolve the "elected" parliament without reference to the people.

Concluding remarks

Egypt began the process of political liberalization over thirty years ago. It is still struggling through a three-decade-long transition whose end does not seem to be in sight and might even acquire a state of permanency. It is true that this situation has produced some positive effects (a higher degree of pluralism, pro-reform movements, political vitality, amendment of some laws, a more critical press, and more freedom of expression). However, these measures fall short of generating a true contestation for power or changing the basic structures of the system. They have failed to generate a qualitative transition toward democracy (the same constitution that was primarily designed for a socialist system, the same head of state for twenty-five years, the same state party for twenty-nine years, the same weak NDP-dominated parliament, and even the same speaker of the house for sixteen years). The licensed political parties are weak and incapable of imposing their reform demands or extracting concessions from the regime. That was clearly manifested following the national dialogue and the controversy over the amendment of Article 76 and the subsequent constitutional amendments of March 2007.

Holding regular elections which the regime always wins under the present rules cannot be an efficient means or an indication of a genuine democratic transition. They help the regime to prolong itself in power, enhance its legitimacy, and generate the approval of external actors. Better indications are the expansion of the scope and arena of effective political competition, effective constitution, rule of law, institutional and structural safeguards, right of political association, and free and fair elections. These changes could take place if the regime voluntarily gives up some of its powers and introduces real reforms, which is hard to imagine given the asymmetrical power relation between the regime and the opposition and short of an immense level of pressure or a sudden regime failure. The other more practical alternative to a democratic transition in Egypt is when the balance of power changes between the regime and the pro-reform forces as a result of the emergence of committed democratic actors who enjoy popularity, visionary skills, and efficient organizational and mobilizational capacity. They could then be in a position to pressure the ruling political elite to open up the scope of competition and break its monopoly over power and control of the political process.

Theoretically, two domestic actors can mount this pressure: pro-reform movements and political parties. However, both are remarkably weak at the moment. This means that the democratic transition has to wait until new social actors (protest movements or new political parties) become strong enough. So far, the current protest movements have not been able to connect effectively with a wide segment of society. They are still elitist, with an intermittent nature that prevents them from evolving into solid organizations with a clear vision for a future political system. Their role should not be underestimated, however, as they have generated a considerable level of vitality and have crystallized significant reform demands.

The issue of political parties in Egypt raises another serious problem for a democratic transition. The legalized political parties have been impoverished by state policies over the past thirty years, as well as by their aging leadership, undemocratic style of management, and lack of resourcefulness and innovation. They have in turn contributed to the impoverishment of Egypt's political life. Their meager performance in successive elections and the low voter turnout are good examples of their ineffectiveness and inability to mobilize people's support and confidence. The recent emergence of alternative protest movements, *Kifaya* and others, has been indicative of the need for some segments within society to transcend the political parties and their futile practices.

The change in the balance of power between the regime and the pro-reform forces will not be possible until the opposition forces augment their capacity to make it difficult for the regime to score easy political gains or make decisive victories. That might be untenable at this stage given the opposition's long record of ineptness and mutual distrust. Additionally, the process of regime-sponsored reforms and the way the regime has conducted itself in the constitutional amendment of Article 76, the referendum, the presidential and parliamentary elections, the constitutional amendments, the reformist judges, the critical journalists, and the Muslim Brothers have shown that a peaceful change cannot be achieved within the existing laws and current power dynamics.

The pro-reform forces need to adopt a new strategy for the next phase in the transition. They need to revisit some of their reform demands, particularly the ones that could give the regime the opportunity to score future gains. For example, the demand for ending the state of emergency could enable the regime to replace the emergency laws with tougher regular laws. Holding elections under the current arrangements will give the regime the opportunity to rig and win. Also, a new party formation law will generate more parties that will add to the weaknesses and factionalism of the already existing ones.

These are all legitimate demands and can put serious pressures on the regime, but might be counterproductive at present given the ongoing asymmetry of power. It might be more practical to focus on specific changes that could offset this imbalance and ensure an equal opportunity for all in any future political contestation. The next parliamentary elections are scheduled to take place in 2010. The pro-reform movement (Islamic and secular opposition and the protest movements) should aggressively contest these elections keeping two main objectives in mind: reducing the power of the NDP and addressing the problem of voter apathy. Until the elections take place, they should focus their demands on the separation between the NDP and the state apparatus and resources; the resignation of Mubarak from the leadership of the NDP; addressing the issue of the NDP independents; the establishment of an *independent* electoral commission; the full control of the judiciary over the electoral system (local and national); unfettered and complete domestic monitoring and foreign observation of future elections; and backing the reformist judges and proposals for ensuring the independence of the judiciary. Perhaps when people feel that there is some hope for change through elections, they may turn in larger numbers to the ballot boxes. These may seem short-term objectives, but they certainly represent major steps on the way to an effective democratic transition.

Notes

1 They have been often labeled as pseudo-democracy, liberalizing autocracy, semi-authoritarian, electoral authoritarianism, semi-democracy, virtual democracy, guided democracy, and so on. See Thomas Carothers (2002) "The End of the Transition Paradigm," *Journal of Democracy* 13(1): 5–21.
2 Muhammad Salah (2005) "Mubarak Criticizes Those Demanding Mis-Calculated Revolutionary Steps," *Al-Hayat* October 7: 5.
3 "Parliamentary Elections 2005," *Ahram Weekly* December 15–21, 2005. Online. Available http://weekly.ahram.org.eg/2005/parliamentary_elections.htm (accessed December 22, 2005). See also Omayma Abdel Latif (2001) "Egyptian Electoral Politics: New Rules, Old Game," *Review of African Political Economy* 28 (June).
4 I find it difficult to imagine the applicability of this situation to the Egyptian system for several reasons. In fact, both the new guards and the old guards are pro-status quo and anti-change. The difference is only in approach. The so-called new guards in the NDP have not yet produced a clear vision that clearly distinguishes them from the old guards. With the exception of a few big names, it is really hard to know who the old guards or the new guards really are. In a highly centralized and personalized system like Egypt's, both serve as custodians of that system and its head and have little room for autonomous decision making. This is evident when both were taken by surprise by Mubarak's decision to amend Article 76 of the constitution, as will be discussed in detail.
5 Ibrahim Nafi' (2005) "Mubarak in Abuja," *Ahram* January 30: 1.
6 Hamdy Al-Husseiny (2006) "Kifaya: A Beautiful Memory," Islamonline (December 12, 2006). Online. Available www.islamonline.net/Arabic/news/2006–12/12/03.shtml (accessed December 15, 2006).
7 "Egyptian Intellectuals Call for Rescuing the Country from Corruption and Despotism," *Al-Hayat* June 4, 2005.

8 See Nathan Brown and Hesham Nasr (2005) "Egypt's Judges Step Forward," Policy Outlook, Democracy and Rule of Law. Washington, DC: Carnegie Endowment.

9 Subhi Mujahid (2005) "Egypt's Muslim Brothers Threaten with Civil Disobedience," Islamonline (May 8, 2005). Online. Available www.islamonline.net/Arabic/news/2005–05/08/article12.shtml (accessed May 10, 2005).

10 For excellent analyses of the 2005 elections, see Mona El-Ghobashy (2006) "Egypt's Paradoxical Elections," *Middle East Report* 238, Spring; Mariz Tadros (2005) "Egypt's Election all about Image, Almost," *Middle East Report Online* September 6, 2005.

11 "Reforming Egypt: In Search of a Strategy," International Crisis Group, *Middle East/North Africa Report* 46, October 2005.

12 Mahmud Musallam and Nadya Ahmad (2006) "Surur: We will not End the Emergency Law," *Al-Masri al-Yaum* January 5, 2006. Online. Available www.almasry-alyoum.com/article2.aspx?ArticleID=4016 (accessed February 5, 2006).

13 See Amr Hamzawy (2007) "Amending Democracy out of Egypt's Constitution," *Washington Post* April 2, 2007; see also Nathan Brown, Michele Dunne and Amr Hamzawy (2007) "Egypt's Controversial Constitutional Amendments," Carnegie Endowment for International Peace, March 23, 2007.

8 Jordan

The myth of the democratizing monarchy

Shadi Hamid

It has been argued, in both policy circles and academic venues, that Arab monarchies are more conducive to liberalization and democratization than their republican counterparts.[1] Michael Herb, who conveys this view most cogently, posits that

> not only have many Middle Eastern monarchies survived, but some have even opened parliaments, suggesting that these regimes, once thought irredeemably anachronistic, might redeem themselves by making better progress toward democracy than the bulk of the region's ostensibly more politically advanced republics.[2]

The argument is an intuitive one. Monarchs who enjoyed popular legitimacy and political security would be more willing to take risks, gradually letting go of power and embarking on potentially destabilizing reforms. Daniel Brumberg notes that "Arab monarchs have more institutional and symbolic room to improvise reforms than do Arab presidents, who are invariably trapped by ruling parties and their constituencies."[3]

Kings are above the fray—umpires rather than partisans. As King Hassan II famously said, "I will never be put into an equation." As monarchies do not depend on elections to maintain power, they have less to fear from holding them. On the other hand, republican rulers, such as those in Egypt and Syria, do not "dispose of an inherent legitimacy, based on the hereditary transmission of the power to rule. As a consequence, [they remain] much more subject to contestation, at least from within ruling circles."[4] This fear of direct contestation has made them unwilling to take even minor steps toward substantive political reform. For these reasons, Herb concludes that "all other things equal, monarchism appears to provide a sound institutional base for the incremental emergence of democratic institutions."[5]

Such assertions, at first blush, seem to have some empirical grounding. Morocco, Jordan, and Kuwait, for example, have held relatively free and fair parliamentary elections and allowed for legal Islamist opposition. While these monarchies have proven to be effective initiators of reform, clear limits exist on how far such a process can go. Democratization need not lead to democracy. In the case of monarchies, it almost certainly does not.

For a short while, it did appear that the region's monarchs were bravely moving forward with bold democratic experiments where republican regimes had hit a political wall. For many, the notion of the modernizing monarch would find a home in its supposedly reform-minded embodiment, King Abdullah II of Jordan. When Abdullah first assumed power in 1999, observers were encouraged by the prospect of this charismatic Sandhurst- and Georgetown-educated monarch leading one of America's closest allies. Today, Western commentators and policy makers still regularly laud Jordan as a moderate, progressive nation, and, as Secretary of State Condoleezza Rice said in June 2005, a "model for what can be done in the region."[6]

There was, to be fair, a time when it seemed that Jordan, in contrast to its more recalcitrant neighbors, might fulfill its promise. On November 12, 1989, a carnival-like atmosphere pervaded the streets of Amman, as Jordanians proudly voted for their country's first freely elected parliament since 1957. This was not another cynical charade. The opposition—made up of Islamists and leftists—won a majority of parliamentary seats. Hisham Sharabi was understandably generous when he said that Jordan was playing a "heroic role" and had become "the conscience of the Arab world."[7] Throughout the 1990s, however, the democratization process would stall, suffering a series of debilitating setbacks.

With the passing of King Hussein in 1999, new hopes were placed upon the shoulders of his son. As Curtis Ryan notes, Jordanians were looking to "a young and reformist king to tip the scales back toward liberalization and away from the conservative retrenchment that has undone much of the process."[8] Yet Abdullah has not lived up to his reformist credentials. Instead, Jordan has fallen victim to a disturbing wave of de-liberalization, bringing back haunting memories of martial law.

Why has democratization in Jordan failed? I will argue that the most significant impediments to democracy lie not in ruling elites, electoral laws, or mismanaged policies, but rather in Jordan's very political structure, in particular its founding institution—the Hashemite monarchy. The authoritarian nature of the Jordanian state is enshrined as a legal matter, meaning that it is non-negotiable and outside the bounds of democratic contestation. In short, the problem is one of an institutional nature. As long as the institution of the monarchy retains both its hegemonic position and its many constitutionally guaranteed prerogatives, substantive reform will remain a remote possibility. Because the monarchy is well institutionalized and enjoys a substantial degree of historical and popular legitimacy, the likelihood that a peaceful transition to democracy will take place is extremely low.

The literature on democratic transitions provides us with a conceptual framework with which to capture the process of political change in Jordan. However, it leaves many questions unanswered. In the study of Middle East politics, there is a need to replenish institutions with explanatory power within the broader context of elite-led transition games.

The transitions paradigm and the role of institutions

The literature on transitions from authoritarian rule emphasizes the "high degree of indeterminacy embedded" in transitional situations.[9] There is good reason to believe, particularly if you ascribe causal power to institutions, that such an explicit emphasis on indeterminacy does not adequately account for the lasting impact of pre-transition political patterns and legacies, which manifest themselves in both macro-structural factors and institutional processes. In other words, transitions may very well be uncertain but less so than the transition paradigm would have us believe.

The transition paradigm, exemplified by Guillermo O'Donnell and Philippe C. Schmitter's seminal work, was groundbreaking in its willingness to handily do away with many structuralist–functionalist assumptions. Gone was the unrelenting obsession with preconditions and objective conditions. Simple monocausal processes were no longer evident. The emphasis had shifted, quite dramatically, to the contingent acts of the elite players who, in turn, were invested with the power to make critical decisions. When O'Donnell and Schmitter likened the process to a chessboard, the analogy was an apt one. During the transition, "assumptions about the relative stability and predictability" of "institutional parameters ... seem patently inadequate,"[10] they remarked. Moreover, macro-structural factors are "there" but "short-term political calculations ... cannot be 'deduced' from or 'imputed' to such structures except perhaps in an act of misguided faith."[11] Rather, in transition games, there are few constraints on bargaining elites, as institutional memory has presumably been erased by the violence of autocracy. For aspiring democrats, things are, at this point, truly open and the possibilities unbounded, leading to a feeling that became familiar in the near aftermath of fallen tyrants—the jubilation that freedom brings, and the abiding sense that, finally, real change can and will come.

But after the vaunted resurrection of civil society, many of the fragile polities in question, particularly in Latin America and post-communist Europe, have reverted to a conspicuous mix of pseudo-oligarchy, demagoguery, and clientelism run amok. Public attitudes toward democracy are unstable, evidence of an electorate that seems willing, under certain conditions, to experiment with plebiscitary populism.[12] Alarmingly, wide swaths of the electorate are losing democratic faith. As an urgent matter, then, it is not possible to ignore authoritarian legacies. In this context, the role of institutions must be re-evaluated and seen as playing a more central, determining role in the evolution of democratizing societies.

For rational choice scholars, however, institutions tend to be passive recipients, shaped and molded by the accumulated acts of individual elites. From this behavioral standpoint, "formally organized social institutions have come to be portrayed simply as arenas within which political behavior, driven by more fundamental factors, occurs."[13] Many institutionalists, thus, viewed the transition paradigm as ahistorical and narrow in scope. More importantly, for our purposes here, the paradigm had trouble accounting for an array of post-transition problems and dilemmas, many of which I will discuss in the following pages.

If institutions matter and hold within them explanatory power, then there are a few pessimistic realities to which we may have to resign ourselves. Nations, polities—and would-be democrats themselves—cannot simply start anew and create a fundamentally different politics than what existed before. The break can never be that sharp or conclusive. But, then, an elusive question is raised: if there is always a pre-existing configuration which affects that which comes after, then when, ultimately, are legacies born?

The institution of the monarchy in Jordan

The Hashemite monarchy is Jordan's oldest, most durable institution. It is the nation's backbone and serves as a unifying, integrative mechanism in a polity otherwise pulling apart due to divisions between Jordanians of Palestinian origin, who are in the majority, and "indigenous" Jordanians. If one wishes to account for the glaring failure of Jordanian democracy, after various intermittent efforts at reform since 1989, then one would be well served to look at how the monarchy has circumscribed available opportunity structures for the opposition and set severe constraints on potential paths of democratic development. The strategic context, thus, differs quite significantly from that of its republican neighbors.

I want to clarify again that by "monarchy," I do not mean the regime, the state, or even the monarch. I am referring to the institution itself. Peter Hall defines institutions as "the formal rules, compliance procedures, and standard operating practices that structure the relationship between individuals in various units of the polity and economy."[14] Per Samuel Huntington, institutionalization "is the process by which organizations and procedures acquire value and stability."[15] Using Huntington's specific measures, the Jordanian monarchy can rightly be considered "adaptable," "complex," "autonomous," and "coherent."[16] In sum, the monarchy enjoys a relatively high degree of institutionalization. The fact that Jordan is a monarchy—this decision was made long ago—determines the nature of formal (and informal) rules, the nature of opposition, and, more generally, what can and cannot be had in the world of politics.

This is an appropriate illustration of the blurry line between institutional determinism and path-dependence. Jordan was proclaimed a kingdom in 1921 and, nearly nine decades later, reform continues to take place only within such parameters. The anachronistic constitution guarantees the monarch's pre-eminent place at the head of the nation, above the law, and entirely unaccountable to the electorate. The constitution ensures that the king is "immune from any liability and responsibility" (Article 30). He "ratifies the laws and promulgates them" (Article 31) and "declares war, concludes peace and ratifies treaties and agreements" (Article 33). The king appoints the prime minister, cabinet ministers, and all forty members of the senate. He may dissolve parliament, if he so chooses.

Jordan is an autocracy, not just in practice, like almost all of its republican neighbors, but also in theory. Constitutionally, Jordan is an absolute monarchy. To alter this particular state of affairs would mean to destroy the modern Jordanian state, something that would require revolution, invasion, or magnanimous abdication, none of which are likely to happen any time soon.

A stalled transition: the National Charter of 1991

Because the monarchical institution enjoys religious and historical legitimacy, it deals with other political actors from a position of overwhelming strength. Where a republican regime may need to call on brute coercion to enforce its vision, a monarchy's task is made considerably easier. In Jordan, the monarch's "right" to guide and set the country's agenda is widely accepted as one of many kingly prerogatives. This strength, premised on soft rather than hard power, conditions future interaction in a way that perpetuates monarchical hegemony and, more problematically, further solidifies it. As Frances Hagopian observes,

> individuals rise who are adept at the political game as it is played, and they use their positions to perpetuate modes of political interaction that favor them. In this way, political arrangements, once in place, condition future political behavior and possibilities.[17]

Hagopian is referring to pact-making in Brazil, but her concerns could easily be applied to the Jordanian case. Jordan's then much heralded National Charter of 1991 appeared to fit relatively well into a linear model of democratic transitions. It was indeed, as Malik Mufti claimed, a "turning point,"[18] but one which, as it would turn out, did not portend well for the future of Jordan's fragile experiment with democracy.

Jordan's *apertura* (or opening) began with King Hussein's landmark decision to hold parliamentary elections in 1989, a response to the destabilizing Ma'an protests earlier that year. With gradual liberalization taking place and the opposition playing a greater role, there was an evident need to define the rules and boundaries of political contestation. The result was the National Charter. It was a "pact" of sorts, defined by O'Donnell and Schmitter as an "agreement among a select set of actors which seeks to define (or, better, to redefine) rules governing the exercise of power on the bases of mutual guarantees."[19] It proved, in reality, an unfortunate bargain for the king's erstwhile adversaries. The regime made opposition participation conditional upon acceptance of the legitimacy of the Hashemite regime and the institutional prerogatives of the monarch. By consolidating the monarchy's once contested position, the Charter de-legitimized any discussion of reducing the king's powers—a necessary step for Jordan to evolve from an absolute monarchy to a constitutional one. The most significant obstacle to democratization was, thus, removed from consideration and invested with yet more institutional legitimacy. The unaccountability of the executive was made a permanent feature of the nation's political system, this time with the official consent of all major opposition forces, including the Muslim Brotherhood and a once passionately anti-system left.

It is difficult to undo or reverse a decision such as this. Pacts—or any agreement over rules and institutions—are incredibly sticky. Understood through the prism of the transitions paradigm, it would have been fair to expect that Jordan was well on its way toward democracy, as many scholars thought at the time. A focus, however, on institutions, the rules of the game, and the general historical context would have likely given us pause regarding the country's progress.

The legitimacy of the monarchy, acquired and strengthened over decades, had produced an already lopsided playing field. In such a context, the regime was able to dictate and force its preferred outcomes on an opposition which was, after decades of debilitating martial law, more than eager simply to be allowed to re-enter the political system. As Russell Lucas notes, "first, the regime chose to whom among the opposition it wished to talk ... second, the regime also determined the ground rules for the talks."[20] The profound imbalance between regime and opposition doomed the process from the very beginning. This was a fait accompli.

One of the requisites of a successful democratic pact is that both sides have at least some degree of leverage and bargaining power. In pacts in the Arab world, this is rarely the case and, if it had been, no pact would be permitted in the first place. The objective of the Arab "pact" is not to provide the foundation for a reconstituted polity but to legitimize an otherwise illegitimate state of affairs. Where negotiated pacts are normally designed to lessen uncertainty, pacts initiated by Arab regimes are designed to preclude it altogether, to remove the possibility of not just drastic change but any change at all that redistributes power.

In short, Jordan's authoritarian legacy could not simply be ignored and cast aside as something that would be overcome by democracy's momentum. Just as democratization can achieve a kind of self-propelling logic, so too can institutions, particularly those that are highly adaptive and keenly responsive to internal and external challenges. It is in this manner that counterproductive pacts and "democratic bargains" are made. At the time, they are seen as qualified victories, when, in reality, they reveal themselves as unqualified defeats.

Authoritarian retrenchment under a new king: the professional associations' crisis of 2005

Just as institutions mattered in the failed pact of 1991, they would matter—with great consequence—nearly fifteen years later, during the professional associations' crisis of 2005, an important marker in Jordan's recent political development. The times had changed and the key players may have been different, but the results were strikingly similar.

On March 15, 2005, in an interview with the late broadcaster Peter Jennings, King Abdullah was asked whether Jordan would ever become a constitutional monarchy. More unexpected than the question itself was the king's answer. "Absolutely." Of course, few, if any, of Jordan's newspapers reported this particular exchange, as discussion of the king's prerogatives remains one of the country's "red lines." In any case, it was not meant for Jordanian consumption. The interview was part of a broader public relations effort directed at Western audiences.

In light of what was happening in the political arena in early 2005, Abdullah's comment must have induced a hint of confusion. At the time, the conflict between the increasingly active professional associations—one of Jordan's few remaining centers of robust opposition—and Prime Minister Faisal al-Fayez's government was intensifying. If anything, Jordan was moving toward a more vigorous absolutism, not away from it. The Jordanian government had been aggressively courting the United States, promoting itself as the West's indispensable ally in an otherwise unstable region. The king was consolidating his position as America's favorite Arab leader, and his access to US lawmakers, think tanks and President George W. Bush himself was unparalleled. As the Jordanian regime moved closer to the US and continued its normalization bid with Israel, it found the embened opposition of the professional associations an increasingly intolerable annoyance.

In January 2005, Interior Minister Samir Habashneh caught civil society off guard with a slew of unexpectedly harsh statements, demanding that associations "completely halt" all political activities and focus instead on promoting the skills of their members.[21] Ominously, Amman governor Abdul Karim Malahmeh announced that "any kind of event, gathering or meeting, save for weddings, should obtain prior approval."[22]

In early March, Prime Minister Faisal Fayez's government presented a draft professional associations' law to parliament. In one controversial section, the law would authorize the Audit Bureau to monitor each association's funds to ensure they are being spent only on internal activities. It would also change voting procedures so that professional councils would be elected indirectly through "intermediary commissions."[23] If there was ever any doubt over the government's intentions, Habashneh explained that the law aimed to eliminate the "prevalence of one current"—meaning Islamists—within the associations.[24]

The opposition launched a vigorous response, calling on parliament to fight the bill. Fifty-nine members of parliament signed a memorandum asking that the draft be withdrawn, although nearly twenty withdrew their signatures apparently due to government pressure. Several journalists went on record saying that the government pressed newspapers to refrain from publishing news on the crisis. Making an already volatile situation even more tense, the government proposed a new Political Parties Law, which would have prohibited the use of mosques, professional associations, and sports clubs for political party activities, banned recruiting and campaigning at educational institutions, and barred activities that could harm Jordan's relations with other countries.

With its knack for offending friends and foes alike, the Fayez government fell shortly thereafter and Samir Habashneh lost his job. At least temporarily, the brakes were put on Jordan's skid toward full-blown authoritarianism. The king reaffirmed his country's commitment to political reform and promised that the new cabinet's policies would be in line with Jordan's purportedly ambitious ten-year "national agenda."

Fayez's successor, Adnan Badran, used a less confrontational tone but proved largely ineffectual, hindered by what would develop into one of the most severe political crises in recent memory. MPs were angry that they were not consulted before the formation of Badran's cabinet. Even regime loyalists accused Badran of neglecting the country's southern regions in his appointments and catering to the Palestinian urban elite. With the very real threat of a no-confidence vote, Badran reshuffled his cabinet, sacrificing unpopular finance minister Bassem Awadallah and acceding to many of the opposition's demands. A political explosion was averted. The damage, however, had already been done. The king's patience had run out. On August 16, Abdullah gave a scathing nationally televised address, attacking the entirety of Jordan's political class. He reserved his harshest criticism for the political "salons" in "certain parts of the capital" and accused his opponents of allying with "foreign forces" to "intimidate our homeland."[25]

The months leading up to the king's speech had proven particularly contentious. The anger and frustration of Jordan's usually tame opposition could no longer be simply ignored or repressed. Yet, the conflict was illustrative of the problems that Jordan—as a monarchy—would continue to face. Jordan had experienced a profound political crisis. Yet, the monarchy's institutional prerogatives were, with very few exceptions, rarely brought up or discussed publicly. The "red lines" remained safely in place, immune to pressure of any kind. The limits of political contestation had, after all, been decided long ago. They had been institutionalized, normalized, and given a unique permanence over time. The decisions that were made in 1991 could be forgotten, but they could not be undone. The National Charter came back to haunt the opposition, as it bore the brunt of the regime's increasingly autocratic bent. The slide toward authoritarianism would culminate in the 2007 municipal and national elections, which many observers consider the least free and fair in Jordan's history.

It should be emphasized that, during the authoritarian retrenchment of 2005, King Abdullah was the one who appointed Prime Ministers Faisal al-Fayez and Adnan Badran. He had final say over all issues of "sovereignty" and enjoyed veto power over any decision made by the prime minister. He could dissolve parliament at any moment. (Indeed, he dissolved the senate in November 2005, using the pretext of the Amman hotel bombings of that month to promote a "security" agenda.) All of these things were well within Abdullah's constitutional jurisdiction. This was not an abuse of power on the part of a young, impetuous monarch. This was, rather, a confirmation of the power already invested in him by the kingdom's constitution. It was legitimate, acceptable, and—to make matters worse—*accepted*.

The constitution is nearly impossible to change as amendments require the approval of the senate. And, as noted earlier, all forty members of the senate are appointed by the king. It is a bleak portrait of a cycle of hegemony that is difficult to break. As Huntington presciently noted, "the more vigorously a monarch exercises authority, the more difficult it is to transfer that authority to another institution."[26] The power of institutions to not only reproduce and perpetuate themselves but preclude the possibility of alternate paths of reform cannot be overlooked. Thus, in the particular case of Jordan, there are no legal, constitutional mechanisms through which to affect structural political change. It is, in this way, a model autocracy.

Republican regimes

Where absolute monarchies do not necessarily aspire to be anything but absolute monarchies, republican regimes, by the very virtue of their republicanism, are deprived of similar luxuries. In an international context, where democracy has become a more or less uncontested moral good, republican autocracies find their means of legitimation constrained by discursive pressures. They cannot justify permanent autocracy, because they are—according to their own constitutions—parliamentary democracies with some degree of separation of powers. Nearly all Arab republican constitutions provide an institutional and at least nominally democratic mechanism for the election of both president and parliament. The head of state is either indirectly or directly accountable to the electorate. In short, while these regimes are undeniably authoritarian, they are not *supposed* to be. As O'Donnell and Schmitter note:

> They are regimes that practice dictatorship and repression in the present while promising democracy and freedom in the future. Thus, they can justify themselves in political terms only as transitional powers, while attempting to shift attention to their immediate substantive accomplishments … the often haphazard attempts of these regimes at institutionalizing themselves clash with the limits imposed by their own discourse.[27]

Egyptian President Husni Mubarak, when responding to criticisms of his country's slow pace of reform, counsels patience and explains that democratization is a long-term process (and that the Egyptian people are not yet ready for the travails of democratic life). He does not contest the assumption that democracy should be the ultimate goal. More importantly, there exists a widespread consensus among the nation's political elite that dictatorship is untenable in the long run.

Discussion of the executive's prerogatives was never taken off the table in Egypt as it was in Jordan. Moreover, it never could be because both the institutional and the constitutional grounds for doing so did not exist in the Egyptian context. It is true that most of the opposition in Egypt during the 1980s and 1990s refrained from directly criticizing Mubarak. However, this state of affairs was never institutionalized or given any legitimate permanence. There were no historical, religious, or political legacies which necessitated that the president be above the law and exempt from public accountability. Even during the worst phases of authoritarianism, the president's rule had to be legitimated by the electorate through, first, parliamentary nomination and, then, popular referendum. It may have been window-dressing but that did not change the fact that the head of state's legitimacy came not from some kind of divine right but rather from electoral acquiescence. Thus, the president could never be seen as a world apart. It was only a matter of time before his prerogatives were subject to a reassessment, and a harsh one at that.

Shifting the "red lines"

On December 12, 2004, the movement that would come to be known as *Kifaya* was born. An assorted group of leftists, nationalists, and Islamists staged a demonstration at the Supreme Judicial Court. They stood in silence, protesting against President Mubarak's plans to extend his quarter-century rule for six more years. Yellow stickers, scribbled with the Arabic word "*Kifaya*" ("enough"), covered their mouths. The protestors, perhaps not fully realizing the weighty nature of their act, had broken their country's long-standing taboos. It was the first explicitly anti-Mubarak protest Egypt had seen. "We've entered a new phase," said opposition activist Magdi Ahmed Hussein.[28]

The taboo of criticizing the president had been shattered. In responding to this unprecedented attack, President Mubarak could not argue for his office's inviolability. The very fact that Egypt was a republican regime constrained his menu of options. It would be both risky and difficult for the regime to simply arrest the offenders in question. Such an action would betray the illusion of Egyptian republicanism and its "transitional" status. In this case, the "red lines" could be shifted because they had failed to acquire any legitimacy in the eyes of the public or even, for that matter, the regime. To be sure, since the Muslim Brotherhood's success in the 2005 elections, the Mubarak regime has chosen a course of increased repression. But it has done so at a great cost, hemorrhaging the little legitimacy it had left. In contrast, the Jordanian regime's authoritarian slide has not diminished the monarch's legitimacy or overall claim to reign and rule. In this sense, monarchies have less to fear from holding elections. But they also have less to fear from repressing their opponents, who remain loyal to the regime and the monarchy despite such repression.

Conclusion

Institutionalist approaches are better equipped to situate the challenges of democratic consolidation, or lack thereof, in historical context. Furthermore, they can enrich our understanding of the hybrid regimes of the Middle East. In the case of Jordan, the anticipated and decisive break with autocracy never actually materialized. I have argued here that Jordan's failure to democratize is not surprising in light of its historically determined institutional makeup. In re-investing institutions with explanatory power, it is possible to arrive at a better understanding of the Hashemite kingdom's resistance to substantive political change.

On a variety of political indicators, Jordan appears to be in a better position than Egypt and other republican regimes. However, prospects for substantive reform, for the reasons I have laid out in this chapter, are more promising in Egypt because, there, the main barrier to democracy has been removed, if not in practice then in theory: authoritarianism is not and has not been legitimatized in Egypt, while in Jordan it has.

In Jordan, the legal opposition is opposed only to government policy and not the regime as such. The regime, and the hardened institutions that support it, are sacrosanct. The opposition therefore faces a debilitating set of constraints at the outset of every political battle it chooses to fight. Where the Egyptian political elite has in principle accepted the inevitability of democracy, the Jordanian political elite has accepted—somewhat unwittingly to be sure—the inviolability of absolute monarchy for the foreseeable future.

In discussing the prospects for Arab democracy, one must account for the lasting power of authoritarian legacies and the indelible, sometimes tragic mark they leave on the practice and process of politics. In the wake of autocracy, the delicate configuration of institutions, processes, and actors is irrevocably altered. Institutional memories—as the case of Jordan suggests—are overwhelming. Actors' preferences are not exogenous to the political system. They are, in a sense, determined. Indeed, the "dead weight of the past"[29]—to use Cardoso's evocative phrasing—has its consequences. Choices made in years and decades past structure future interactions. Put differently, "once a particular fork is chosen, it is very difficult to get back on the rejected path."[30] In those countries where the institution of the monarchy has acquired strength and legitimacy over time, transitions to democracy become much more difficult. With free and fair parliamentary elections and legal space for the opposition, democracy may appear close at hand. But without executive accountability and distribution of power, it remains just as illusive as before.

In Jordan, an institutional statis has set in and set roots. The country's institutional configuration has proven its stubborn durability. The hegemony of institutions can become so implacable, and so rooted, that one begins to wonder whether its enveloping reach and power can be resisted. Institutionalist approaches account quite well for the stickiness and pseudo-permanence of institutional arrangements. What is lacking, however, is a compelling theory of institutional change. Observers should be careful about succumbing to the perils of path-dependence and pessimism. However, it remains frustratingly difficult to envision how Jordan and the region's other apparently modernizing monarchies can possibly experience democratic change under the present circumstances. It may very well be that, for both better and worse, the impending transition can and will only come through an unexpected intrusion—an internal or external shock that will destroy the institutional resistance of recalcitrant regimes.

Notes

1 For variations of this argument, see Michael Herb (1999) *All in the Family: Absolutism, Revolution, and Democracy in the Middle Eastern Monarchies*. Albany, NY: State University of New York Press: 1, 4–5, 15–16, 267; Owen H. Kirby (2000) "Want Democracy? Get a King," *Middle East Quarterly* 7 (December 2000); Lisa Anderson (1991) "Absolutism and the Resilience of Monarchy in the Middle East," *Political Science Quarterly* 106 (Spring 1991): 3–4; Malik Mufti (1999) "Elite Bargains and the Onset of Political Liberalization in Jordan," *Comparative Political Studies* 32 (February 1999): 100–129.
2 Michael Herb, *All in the Family*, op. cit.: 4.
3 Daniel Brumberg (2002) "The Trap of Liberalized Autocracy," *Journal of Democracy* 13 (October 2002): 66.
4 Holger Albrecht and Eva Wegner (2006) "Autocrats and Islamists: Contenders and Containment in Egypt and Morocco," *The Journal of North African Studies* 11 (June 2006): 129.
5 Michael Herb, *All in the Family*, op. cit.: 15.
6 See also David Ignatius (2005) "Tragedy as Impetus in Jordan," *The Washington Post* November 16, 2005; Abdullah Schleifer (2005) "The Amman Initiative," *Islamica* Winter 2005 for similarly optimistic assessments.
7 *The Jordan Times*, January 21, 1990.
8 Curtis Ryan (2002) *Jordan in Transition: From Hussein to Abdullah*. Boulder, CO: Lynne Rienner: 123.
9 Guillermo O'Donnell and Philippe C. Schmitter (1986) *Transitions from Authoritarian Rule: Tentative Conclusions about Uncertain Democracies*. Baltimore, MD: Johns Hopkins University Press: 5.
10 Ibid.: 4.
11 Ibid.: 5.
12 For example, in one 1987 national survey, 58 percent of Chileans supported democratic rule as opposed to 9 percent who preferred authoritarianism; see Karen L. Remmer (1989) *Military Rule in Latin America*. Boston: Unwin Hyman: 2). However, five years later, in an April 1992 poll by the Peruvian Enterprise of Public Opinion, 73 percent of respondents expressed their support for President Alberto Fujimori's "auto-coup."
13 J.G. March and J.P. Olsen (1984) "The New Institutionalism: Organizational Factors in Political Life," *American Political Science Review* 78 (September 1984): 734.
14 Peter Hall (1986) *Governing the Economy: the Politics of State Intervention in Britain and France*. New York: Oxford University Press: 19.
15 Samuel P. Huntington (1968) *Political Order in Changing Societies*. New Haven: Yale University Press: 12.
16 Ibid., see 12–23 for an explanation of the different measures.
17 Frances Hagopian (1990) "Democracy by Undemocratic Means? Elites, Political Pacts, and Regime Transition in Brazil," *Comparative Political Studies* 23 (July 1990): 148.

18 Mufti, "Elite Bargains and the Onset of Political Liberalization in Jordan," op. cit.: 114.
19 O'Donnell and Schmitter, op. cit.: 37
20 Russell E. Lucas (2005) *Institutions and the Politics of Survival in Jordan: Domestic Responses to External Challenges: 1988–01.* Albany: State University of New York Press: 32.
21 *Jordan Times*, January 18, 2005.
22 *Jordan Times*, March 6, 2005.
23 *Jordan Times*, March 2, 2005.
24 *Jordan Times*, March 7, 2005.
25 Speech. Amman, Jordan, August 16, 2005.
26 Huntington, *Political Order in Changing Societies* op. cit.: 179.
27 O'Donnell and Schmitter, op. cit.: 15.
28 "Rare Anti-Mubarak Demo in Cairo," *BBC News*, December 13, 2004. Online. Available http://news.bbc.co.uk/2/hi/middle_east/4091983.stm.
29 Fernando Henrique Cardoso (1989) "Associated-Dependent Development and Democratic Theory" in Alfred Stepan, ed., *Democratizing Brazil: Problems of Transition and Consolidation*. New York: Oxford University Press: 307.
30 Stephen Krasner (1984) "Approaches to the State: Alternative Conceptions and Historical Dynamics," *Comparative Politics* 16 (January 1984): 225.

9 Democracy in Lebanon
The primacy of the sectarian system

Bassel F. Salloukh[1]

The withdrawal of Syrian troops from Lebanon on April 26, 2005 was cele-brated as a watershed event in Lebanon's path toward democratic recovery. Fifteen years of almost total Syrian control had reduced the Lebanese state to an institutional shell, dominated by a proxy security regime and allied former warlords, despite the trappings of civilian political participation. George W. Bush's promise of a Cedar Revolution in post-Syria Lebanon has turned sour, however, clashing against a rigid sectarian political system and the calcula-tions of domestic actors and their external allies. Democracy and national unity are the main casualties in the battle to redesign the political architecture of post-Syria Lebanon. Sectarian politicians advanced narrow political inter-ests at the expense of democratic standards and participation; and national sentiments have been replaced by a more aggressive and unabashed sectar-ianism. Moreover, Washington's democracy promotion discourse in Lebanon has been unmasked as a cover for a sinister plot to relocate Lebanon from one regional camp to another.

To be sure, the sectarian system in Lebanon is not without historical roots predating the establishment of the independent state in 1943; nor was it insulated from external interventions that were at times instrumental in negotiating sectarian peace, but at others served to aggravate sectarian ten-sions in the country. In fact, successive power-sharing arrangements nego-tiated first in Mount Lebanon and then in the independent Lebanese republic conditioned viable intercommunal coexistence on the principle of sectarian representation.[2] Once institutionalized, however, the priorities of the all pow-erful sectarian political edifice assumed precedence over proper democratic norms and practices. In fact, independent Lebanon's multiple consociational arrangements have stymied demands for better accountability, representation, and transparency, while sanctioning the neopatrimonial practices of sectarian politicians.

The omnipotent sectarian system

Plural societies make problematic democracies, especially in the so-called developing world where segmental cleavages are hard and often overlapping.[3]

In Lebanon, deep religious divisions predating independence produced a sectarian system celebrated by some as the hallmark of Lebanon's political pluralism.[4] This system was institutionalized in a rigid pre-war consociational power-sharing arrangement, the 1943 National Pact (*al-Mithaq al-Watani*). An unwritten gentlemen's agreement between the Maronite President Bishara al-Khouri and the Sunni Prime Minister Riyad al-Solh, the Pact reserved the presidency for the Maronites in what was supposed to be a consociational power-sharing arrangement for the nascent state. It declared Lebanon an independent state with a *visage Arabe* (*dhu wajh 'arabi*). This vague formulation was not without purpose. Christians took this to mean that Lebanon was geographically part of the Arab world, but was not itself an Arab state. The Muslims, on the other hand, assumed Lebanon's Arabness a matter of fact and history. The Pact committed Muslims to renounce any demands to reunite with Syria and accept the continued existence of Lebanon as an independent and sovereign state in the Arab world, provided it considered itself part of the Arab fold, and provided Christians renounced external, namely French, tutelage. Executive prerogatives in the newborn Lebanese state were not as vague, however.

The presidency possessed formal and informal constitutional powers that enabled the president to dominate the state's political, security, financial, and judicial institutions, thus contravening the National Pact's consensual spirit.[5] The constitution empowered the president to appoint prime ministers, appoint and dismiss cabinet ministers (Article 53), promulgate laws (Article 56), dissolve parliament (Article 55), and negotiate and ratify international treaties (Article 52). The president's prerogatives were buttressed by Maronite control over the most sensitive security, military, judicial, and monetary posts in the state. Maronites headed the Sûreté Générale, the army, military intelligence (Deuxième Bureau), the supreme justice council, and the central bank. In parliament, and to ameliorate Christian fears of being marginalized in a mainly Muslim Arab world, the ratio of Christian to Muslim deputies was fixed at six to five. These prerogatives gave the presidency substantial control over domestic and foreign politics.

The outbreak of the Lebanese civil war in 1975 was in part an expression of the outdated nature of the 1943 power-sharing formula. External variables may have determined the timing, duration, and intensity of the civil war, but by the early 1970s, the consociational power-sharing arrangement was under intense stress.[6] By then, as Table 9.1 maps out, Lebanon's political sociology had been transformed fundamentally since the days of the Mount Lebanon regime inaugurated in 1864, through French-created Greater Lebanon in 1920, and the early days of independent Lebanon after 1943. Hitherto docile sects—namely the Shia'a—were radicalized and resisted elite control by traditional neopatrimonial networks.[7] A number of power-sharing documents were promulgated during the war years, but all proved stillborn. Lebanon had to wait for the ripe moment, when domestic, regional, and international factors converged, to end the war, produce and allow the implementation of a new power-sharing agreement.

Table 9.1 Christian and Muslim Sects: 1913–2002[8]

Year	1913	1932	1975	2002
Christians				
Maronite	58.3	28.8	23	
Greek Orthodox	12.6	9.8	7	
Greek Catholic	7.7	5.9	5	
Other	0.8	6.8	5	
Total	**79.4**	**51.3**	**40**	**26.4–30**
Muslims				
Shi'a	5.6	19.6	27	
Sunni	3.5	22.4	26	
Druze	11.4	6.8	7	
Total	**20.5**	**48.8**	**60**	**70–73.6**
Total Population	**414,963**	**786,000**	**2.55M**	**3.3M**

The transition to post-war democracy in Lebanon was supposed to be governed by the terms of the constitutional amendments adopted in the Ta'if Accord of October 22, 1989.[9] The amendments amounted to a new power-sharing arrangement reflecting the post-war demographic and political realities in the country. Very little was done to shift politics away from sectarian to secular–national institutions, however. Article 95 of the post-Ta'if Constitution declares de-confessionalization an objective, but provides only general recommendations to achieve this objective without a fixed timetable.

Ta'if shifted the balance of executive power away from the Maronite president, placing it instead in cabinet in its collective capacity. Cabinet, a grand coalition, where sectarian communities are represented somewhat proportionally, became the real custodian of executive authority. This naturally empowered the Sunni prime minister's office, consecrating cabinet as an institution independent from the once all-powerful presidency. Decisions in cabinet are taken in a consociational manner, failing that then by majority vote. Important topics, however, require a two-thirds vote to pass in cabinet. Be that as it may, Ta'if proscribed any authority or policy that negates the "covenant of mutual coexistence" among all Lebanese sects.[10] This caveat was introduced to protect the consensual nature of the political system, and deny any group or sect the possibility to dominate it, a charge leveled against the pre-war power-sharing formula that gave the Maronite president control over the state's political, security, financial, and judicial institutions.

Ta'if tipped the institutional balance of power in favor of parliament. It strengthened parliamentary oversight over the executive, making it almost impossible for cabinet to dissolve parliament. The powers of the Shia'a speaker of parliament were increased vis-à-vis both cabinet and the parliamentary assembly. The speaker is elected for a four-year term, equal to parliament's tenure, and is subject to a very difficult two-thirds vote of confidence, but only at the end of the second year. The speaker may ignore bills sent to parliament by cabinet, and is under no obligation to convene parliament outside constitutionally prescribed regular sessions. These prerogatives allow the speaker to play a decisive role in the selection of the prime minister and the election of the president. Moreover, post-war parliamentary seats are divided equitably among Christians and Muslims, replacing the pre-Ta'if six to five ratio of seats in favor of Christian deputies.

The Ta'if Accord also addressed relations between Lebanon and Syria, a permanent bone of contention for the drafters of the constitutional reforms. It recognized that "distinct relations" link Lebanon and Syria. On the subject of the withdrawal of Syrian troops from Lebanon, Ta'if committed Syria to "redeploy" its troops to the Beqa' and its western approaches, but only two years after the promulgation of constitutional reforms. Most importantly, the future mission and duration of Syrian troops in Lebanon was considered a bilateral issue, to be determined by Syria and the future Lebanese government. Given the obvious power disparity between the two countries, and Syrian influence over a substantial number of Lebanese political groups, it was clear that in the absence of Arab and international pressure, this section of Ta'if was bound to follow Syrian priorities.

The long Syrian era

Lebanon's post-war democratic transition was obfuscated by Syrian fiat.[11] From 1990, and until the withdrawal of Syrian troops from Lebanon in April 2005, Damascus applied Ta'if whimsically and was the main spoiler of the post-war transition.[12] Rather than implementing the post-war consociational democracy promised in Ta'if, Syria ruled Lebanon with the heavy hand of its intelligence apparatus supported by loyal Lebanese counterparts and allies. The executive, legislative, and judicial institutions of the post-war state succumbed to the wishes of Syrian intelligence chiefs in Lebanon. Syrian operatives, and their Lebanese allies, penetrated almost all civil, political, and security institutions and organizations, establishing a coercive structure camouflaged by controlled political participation. Syria also imposed upon Lebanon bilateral treaties—the Treaty of Brotherhood, Cooperation, and Coordination of May 22, 1991, and the Defense and Security Agreement of September 1, 1991—which streamlined Lebanon's foreign and defense policies with its own, reducing post-war Lebanon to a "Syrian protectorate" serving Damascus' geopolitical agenda.[13]

Lebanon's post-war power-sharing arrangement was replaced by what opposition pundits later labeled a "combined security regime" (*al-nizam al-amni al-mushtarak*), intimidating Syria's opponents and rewarding its allies. The post-war Christian opposition to Syria's hegemony was smashed, its leaders jailed or exiled. A new phrase was coined in Lebanon's sectarian lexicon, *al-ihbat al-masihi*, reflecting Christian despair with post-war Syrian domination.

Muslim politicians unwilling to jump on the Syrian bandwagon were either marginalized or their powers constrained. Even Rafiq al-Hariri, who formed his first cabinet on October 31, 1992 with Syrian blessing, soon discovered that Damascus would not allow the emergence of a viable post-war consociational democracy regulated by the constitutional provisions enshrined in the Ta'if Accord. Hariri wanted to exercise the powers given by Ta'if to cabinet and the prime minister. Then president Elyas al-Hrawi, on the other hand, and always with Syrian support, preferred government by a para-institutional consensual "troika" consisting of the Maronite president, the Sunni prime minister, and the Shia'a speaker of parliament. This enabled the presidency to regain its pre-Ta'if position in the political system, forsaking cabinet as the chief executive consociational institution; it also negated the principle of separation of powers consecrated in Ta'if.

Parliamentary elections held in 1992, 1996, and 2000 served to manufacture a political class subservient to Syrian dictates. Syrian intelligence officers gerrymandered electoral districts, excluded candidates and parachuted others, and imposed electoral coalitions, often joining strange sectarian and ideological bedfellows, to ensure the victory of their electoral lists.[14] This gave Syria and its allies control over the state's legislative institution. Consequently, constitutional procedures were ignored, especially those pertaining to the redeployment of Syrian troops in Lebanon, limits on presidential tenures, and the comprehensive application of the Ta'if Accord. The façade of electoral elections was maintained, but within the context of structured electoral competition and—to a large extent—preordained electoral results.

Syrian politicians and intelligence officers, often in partnership with their Lebanese counterparts, ravaged the post-war economy. One study estimated the number of Syrian workers in Lebanon in the early 1990s, when the reconstruction boom was at its height, at around 850,000 workers, later declining after the economic recession of the late 1990s to 350,000–500,000 workers.[15] Syrian workers' remittances, some US$1 billion annually, resuscitated the economies of the Jazira and Hasaka regions, and postponed the introduction of deeper economic liberalization measures in Syria.[16] Almost all profitable sectors of the post-war economy, but especially high-interest Lebanese Treasury bills (T-bills), telecommunications, oil and gas, electricity, tourism, Casino du Liban, the lottery, concessions for quarries, and reconstruction projects, were penetrated by Syrian officials, siphoning billions of dollars in personal profits.[17] Total Syrian revenues extracted from Lebanon through licit and illicit activities in 1990–2005 amounted to some US$20 billion.[18] Lebanon thus served Syrian officials as a market for both wealth generation and the investment of wealth accumulated from state capitalist policies in Syria. This helped sustain neopatrimonial networks in Syria and served the logic of regime survival.

Israel's withdrawal from Lebanon—except from the Kfarshouba Hills and the contested Sheb'a farms—on May 24, 2000 triggered a fresh wave of mainly Maronite opposition against Syria's domination over Lebanon. On

September 20, 2000, a manifesto read following the annual conclave of Maronite archbishops demanded the rectification of Syrian–Lebanese relations and the full withdrawal of Syrian troops from Lebanon.[19] Months later, on April 30, 2001, the Qornat Shihwan Gathering (*Liqa' Qornat Shihwan*) was founded under the auspices of the Maronite Church. Joining a number of Christian politicians and intellectuals opposed to Syria's domination but supportive of the Ta'if Accord, it underscored the Church's unwillingness to further tolerate the tilt in the post-war confessional balance of power in favor of Muslim sects. Syria's control over post-war Lebanon had enabled the post-war Sunni and Shia'a political elite to inherit the Maronites' privileged position in the pre-war sectarian political system. The opposition crescendo climaxed during the Maronite patriarch's visit to Mount Lebanon on May 29 and August 3–5, 2001. The patriarch was welcomed by public demonstrations orchestrated by supporters of the exiled Michel 'Awn and the jailed Samir Ja'ja'. It was a public spectacle of defiance by opponents of Syria's policies and its control over Lebanon. Two days later, on August 7 and 9, 2001, the security regime retaliated. Hundreds of Free Patriotic Movement and Lebanese Forces activists were attacked and arrested by the intelligence services in an attempt to pulverize the opposition and restore control over society.

Syria's position in Lebanon soon became untenable, however. The fall of Baghdad on April 9, 2003 inaugurated a period of intense US–Syrian competition in Lebanon, with broader regional implications. US pressure on Syria was part of a more ambitious strategy to reshuffle the geopolitics of the Middle East and neutralize Israel's enemies.[20] Unable to elicit Syrian cooperation in Iraq and the occupied Palestinian territories, Washington now sought to undermine Syria's control over what Damascus had historically cherished as its own security backyard: Lebanon. The Syria Accountability and Lebanese Sovereignty Restoration Act introduced by Congress on April 12, 2003 was part of this strategy.[21] Similarly, on May 3, 2003, Secretary of State Colin Powell presented Bashar al-Asad with a long list of US demands aimed at, among other things, loosening Syria's grip on Lebanon.[22] This US pressure campaign against Syria intensified during summer 2004, as the pro-Syrian Emile Lahoud's presidency was drawing to an end. It climaxed with the promulgation of United Nations Security Council Resolution 1559 on September 2, 2004.

The resolution declared its support "for a free and fair electoral process in Lebanon's upcoming presidential election conducted according to Lebanese constitutional rules and devised without foreign interference or influence." It also called on "all remaining foreign forces to withdraw from Lebanon," and mandated the "disbanding and disarmament of all Lebanese and non-Lebanese militias" in the country.[23] Choosing confrontation rather than accommodation with the international community, Damascus renewed Lahoud's presidential tenure for an additional three years on September 3, 2004. But Hariri's assassination on February 14, 2005 created a domestic, regional, and international tidal wave that forced Syrian troops out of Lebanon on April

25, 2005. This, in turn, created great expectations for a post-Syria democratic transition in Lebanon.

Another stalled democratic transition?

Syria's withdrawal from Lebanon unleashed an intense contest in Lebanon: which sect or alliance of sects would control the post-Syria Lebanese state, and to what regional and international camp would this state subscribe? The overlap between these domestic and external contests complicated the post-Syria democratic transition, sacrificing the consociational power-sharing arrangement enshrined in the Ta'if Accord for narrower sectarian objectives, and unleashing a full-fledged contest for total state control.

During the post-war Syrian era, with the Christian political establishment ostracized politically, the sectarian balance of political power was tipped in favor of the Sunni and Shia'a political elites. Now that Syria was out of Lebanon, Christian politicians and the Maronite patriarch demanded the balance be restored. They demanded ultimate say in the selection of a new president, a redistribution of bureaucratic positions to rectify what they described as a Muslim invasion of the bureaucracy since 1990, and a reapportionment of posts throughout the state's multiple security institutions. With the return of the exiled 'Awn on May 7, 2005, and the release of the incarcerated Ja'ja' on July 26, 2005, prospects for a Maronite political restoration seemed positive. The May–June 2005 parliamentary elections proved otherwise, however.

Designed by the security regime in 2000, and later selected for narrow political considerations, the electoral law used in the 2005 elections produced some startling cross-sectarian and cross-ideological instrumental electoral alliances.[24] Some alliances gathered political factions opposed to Syria—such as Sa'd al-Hariri and Walid Jumblatt's—with parties more favorable to Damascus—such as Hizbullah and Nabih Berri's Amal Movement. Other alliances joined political extremes such as Hizbullah and the Lebanese Forces in cross-sectarian and cross-ideological electoral alliances. Most importantly, the elections created a split in Maronite political representation. A majority of Christian voters voted for electoral lists supported by 'Awn and his allies, with the balance of Christian voters voting for lists sponsored by the March 14 anti-Syrian coalition.[25]

Instead of inaugurating an inclusive, post-Syria, democratic transition, the elections resulted in de facto confessional cantonization, dividing the country into four tightly knit, closed, unipolar, sectarian communities: the Shia'a led by the Hizbullah–Amal alliance, the Sunnis by Sa'd al-Hariri, the Druze by Jumblatt, and the Maronites led by 'Awn and a bevy of less representative political leaders.[26] A more assertive and chauvinistic sectarianism replaced the outpouring of nationalist sentiments witnessed following Hariri's assassination.[27] The stage was now set for a showdown over the Lebanese state. Albeit shrouded by a discourse that underscored political rather than sectarian divisions, at heart the contest was a natural byproduct of the entrenched and omnipotent sectarian system: a sectarian contest for control of the post-Syrian state.

With cabinet dominated by the March 14 coalition, an unrelenting assassination wave targeting its figures, and the weight of the international community committed to relocate Lebanon away from the Iranian–Syrian camp into America's regional orbit, a systematic takeover by the Hariri–Jumblatt alliance of state and security positions commenced. A media campaign was launched to focus popular attention on the ongoing investigation into Hariri's assassination and deflect it from the reorganization of state institutions under way. New appointments in the judiciary, the state bureaucracy, the Sûreté Générale, internal security, the army, and military intelligence replaced elements of suspected loyalties with cadres politically affiliated with the March 14 coalition, especially Sa'd al-Hariri, Jumblatt, and Ja'ja' supporters.[28] The Maronite Archbishops' Council voiced concerns over a Sunni monopoly in public sector recruitment, and 'Awn accused the Hariri camp of turning the security forces into a state-controlled sectarian Sunni militia.[29] The post-Syria Lebanese state looked increasingly like a state dominated by Sa'd al-Hariri's Sunni cadres and political protégés.

The Hizbullah–Amal alliance felt especially targeted by the reorganization of the state's administrative and security structures. Changes in the security establishment threatened Hizbullah's security details in Beirut and South Lebanon. Shia'a clients in the bureaucracy were replaced by non-partisans without prior consultation with either party. Guarantees offered by Sa'd al-Hariri and Jumblatt against implementing 1559's domestic agenda, i.e., the demobilization and disarmament of Hizbullah, were slowly eroding. Most disturbing for Hizbullah was the unilateral manner in which decisions were being taken by Prime Minister Fuad al-Siniora and his March 14 allies, both inside and outside cabinet.[30] This threatened to erode post-war Shia'a political gains in the state's public and security institutions. The assassination of the prominent and vociferous anti-Syrian newspaper editor and member of parliament, Jubran Tueni, on December 12, 2005 led matters to the breaking point.

A decision by the majority ministers demanding the establishment of a court with an international character, and the expansion of the UN investigation commission's prerogatives to cover all assassinations since the attempt on Marwan Hemadé on October 1, 2004, led to a walkout by the Hizbullah–Amal ministers. Hizbullah, accused of bombing US targets in Lebanon during the civil war, feared that an international body with open-ended prerogatives might prosecute its own cadres retroactively. The Hizbullah–Amal ministers protested that the modalities and jurisdiction of the proposed court had not been finalized, and that further deliberations could lead to consensus obviating the need for a cabinet vote.[31] Hizbullah had actually accepted the principle of the international court. The cabinet crisis was over more than just the prerogatives of the prospective international court, however. It reflected a deeper structural chasm: what sort of Lebanon is being formed after the Syrian withdrawal? How are critical political decisions taken? Consensually, as prescribed by the Ta'if Accord, or by a two-thirds majority cabinet vote? What balance of political power will prevail among the different sects in the post-Syria era? What is the future political role for the Shia'a in this state? Could a cabinet vote neutralize the full demographic and political weight of the Shia'a community in the country? And what foreign policy orientation will this state assume?

Fearing political marginalization via the institutionalization of a voting precedent, the Hizbullah–Amal alliance boycotted cabinet meetings from December 12, 2005 until February 2, 2006. Hizbullah Secretary General Hassan Nasrallah attacked the unilateral and exclusivist manner in which the state was being run by the March 14 coalition. He charged that Hariri's assassination was being abused, especially by Jumblatt and Ja'ja', to legitimize the wholesale takeover of state institutions.[32] Nasrallah's position resonated with 'Awn's, who denounced the unilateral administration of state institutions by the Hariri–Jumblatt–Ja'ja' trio and their efforts to neutralize his overwhelming political representation of the Christian community. The Memorandum of Understanding, signed by Hizbullah and the Free Patriotic Movement on February 6, 2006, was meant to break Hizbullah's growing domestic isolation by providing its opposition to Siniora's unilateralism Christian political cover, strengthen 'Awn's presidential aspirations, balance against the growing power of the March 14 coalition, and halt their invasion of state institutions.[33]

Hizbullah reasoned that efforts to shift Lebanon's foreign policy orientation toward embracing Washington's regional agenda, coupled with demands to replace Lahoud, aimed at consecrating 1559 as a domestic reality, paving the way for besieging and disarming the resistance.[34] It thus demanded, and later received, assurances that decisions would be taken consensually rather than by cabinet vote, thereby institutionalizing consociation as the sole mechanism of decision making in post-Syria Lebanon, especially over decisive issues.[35] Siniora also acknowledged the national identity and mission of the resistance, thus indirectly refuting its paramilitary militia status. This met Hizbullah's condition for a return to cabinet, ending the cabinet crisis on February 2, 2006.

Hizbullah's intransigent position was rooted in the conviction that precedents set in the immediate post-Syria transitional phase will be as foundational for the future Lebanese political system as were the 1943 National Pact and the 1989 Ta'if Accord. Hence the insistence on Siniora's promises, despite charges, sometimes from within the Shia'a community, that Hizbullah was acting on Syrian orders to paralyze the new government. The National Dialogue inaugurated on March 2, 2006 between the principal political factions sought to negotiate the contours of the country's post-Syria political road map. It conceded that the political gridlock could not be resolved within state institutions, requiring an extra-constitutional forum. Agreement on most of the dialogue's items was unproblematic: support for the international investigation into Hariri's assassination; the formation of a court of an international nature; the assembly of Palestinian arms outside the camps and its reorganization inside them; that the Sheb'a farms are Lebanese territory under Israeli occupation and, concomitantly, Hizbullah's continued role as a legitimate armed resistance; and exchanging diplomatic relations with Damascus. However, arriving at an agreement over Lahoud's replacement, and Hizbullah's weapons arsenal, proved much more difficult. A new president affiliated with the March 14 coalition would remove the last obstacle impeding its complete takeover of state institutions. Hizbullah's disarmament prior to the adoption of a new national defense strategy exposes it to Israeli attacks and international sanction. The future of its arsenal is also tied to the wider regional confrontation between Washington and Tehran.

War by other means

Post-Syria Lebanon inherited the same contradictions of the post-war state inaugurated by the Ta'if Accord: a paralyzed state, penetrated by external actors, besieged by perpetual political crises, and divided by sectarian leaders into neopatrimonial fiefdoms. To be sure, the margin of political contestation and representation in Lebanon exceeds that found in most Arab states,[36] but it is constrained by a sectarian system that assumes primacy over democratic procedures, values, and standards. Sustained by the clientalistic neopatrimonial networks of parochial ethnic politicians, the sectarian system has always entailed a state with weak penetrative institutional capabilities, lacking transparency, and privileging exclusivist sectarian affiliations over inclusive national ones. In this regard, the constraining impact of the sectarian system on democratic practices remains unchanged despite the transformation of Lebanon's pre-war power-sharing arrangement.

The thirty-four days' war triggered by Hizbullah's abduction of two Israeli soldiers on July 12, 2006 revealed the contradictions besetting post-Syria Lebanon. Israel destroyed not only the bridges tying Lebanon's regions together, but also the bridges between the country's multiple sects. Despite talk of national unity in the face of external aggression, the deep divisions among Lebanese over a host of issues—whether in defining the common enemy, agreeing on the type of state Lebanon should have, or reaching a consensus on the actual results of the war in terms of winners and losers—re-emerged swiftly. The contest over the proper political weights of the respective sects inaugurated after Syria's withdrawal resumed unabated immediately after the "end of hostilities" on August 14, 2006. Hizbullah moved swiftly to use the political capital accumulated from its self-declared victory over Israel to recalibrate the domestic balance of power in its favor. It deployed core Shia'a symbols to rally around it a bludgeoned and fatigued constituency at a moment of domestic crisis. On its part, the March 14 coalition resumed its reorganization of state institutions and capture of sensitive security posts under the guise of implementing United Nations Security Council Resolution 1701 of August 11, 2006, signaling its unwillingness to relinquish control over domestic and foreign policy making.[37] Attempts by the March 14 wing of the government to sideline sensitive, but Shia'a-dominated, security organs, such as the Sûreté Générale and the Directorship of Airport Security, from new security details requested by Israel and the international community raised eyebrows and elicited a harsh rebuke from the Shia'a political leadership.[38]

The contest over post-Syria Lebanon took a new turn when all five Shia'a ministers resigned from Siniora's government on November 11, 2006, protesting the latter's unilateral decision to table the draft bylaws of the proposed international court investigating the Hariri assassination for a government vote. Siniora's intentional disregard of the consensual norm in government decision making breached a taboo in Lebanon's delicate sectarian system, and signaled to Hizbullah that the US–Israel July 2006 war to disarm and demobilize the organization was now being waged by other, political means and by proxy Lebanese actors.[39] The cabinet's decision to pass the draft bylaws on November 13, 2006 led to a massive opposition sit-in on December 1, 2006 in the central district of Beirut demanding the resignation of the Siniora government and the formation of a national unity one in which the opposition possessed veto power. The ensuing eighteen-month domestic crisis resulted in the paralysis and atrophy of state institutions, and the remilitarization of society along sectarian lines. A new sectarian balance of terror, especially between the Sunni and Shia'a communities, exploded in bloody clashes as sectarian militias rearmed themselves and the country's landscape was re-demarcated into sectarian zones. Militant, Saudi-financed Sunni Salafi groups in Tripoli and Sidon were permitted operational space by pro-government security agencies to balance Hizbullah's coercive capabilities; moreover, the Future Movement mobilized the Sunni religious establishment and masses against Hizbullah, intentionally underscoring the sectarian nature of the conflict, thus deploying the threat of a sectarian civil war to neutralize Hizbullah's campaign to dislodge Siniora's government.[40]

This protracted domestic crisis overlapped with a regional geopolitical contest pitting Iran and Syria against the US and its allies among the so-called "moderate" Arab states, namely Saudi Arabia and Egypt.[41] After the July 2006 war failed to dismantle Hizbullah's military structure,[42] both Riyadh and Washington spoiled any resolution of the political standoff in Lebanon lest this was interpreted as a victory for Hizbullah and its regional allies at the expense of the Siniora government and its regional and international sponsors.[43] After all, the Siniora government was "one of the few successes in the Bush administration's Middle East policy";[44] Washington spent close to US $1.3 billion to help it survive the confrontation with Hizbullah—a substantial part of which was used to upgrade pro-government security forces.[45] After all, Siniora's government signified a Lebanon controlled by pro-American moderate Sunni Islam, in the form of Hariri's Future Movement, secure from radical Islamist groups and serving as an antidote to anti-Americanism in the region.[46] Consequently, when Hizbullah launched its political campaign to topple this government, Saudi Arabia and the US led a concerted effort, in coordination with their Lebanese allies, to ensnare Hizbullah in a sectarian quagmire and deny its weapons arsenal regional and domestic legitimacy.[47]

Damascus and Tehran also used the political weight of their Lebanese allies, but especially Hizbullah, in their regional contests against Saudi Arabia, but also to balance against US and Israeli security threats. However Washington's spoiler role exposed the false promises of its democracy promotion agenda in the Middle East and the destructive "birth pangs of a new Middle East," to quote Condoleezza Rice's disturbing phrase.[48] Washington is thus no different than Tehran or Damascus in using Lebanon as a site for proxy confrontations. George W. Bush may console himself by declaring that the war between Hizbullah and Israel is part of a wider struggle "between freedom and terrorism," and that the "freedom agenda did not create the terrorists or their ideology" but will "defeat them both."[49] However, these mental reductions ring hollow with the peoples of the Arab world, for whom the "new Middle East" means more smart bombs to Israel, a freer hand for the coercive agencies of Washington's regional allies, and no democracy promotion whatsoever.

The domestic standoff reached a climax with the Siniora government's May 5, 2008 decisions to consider Hizbullah's clandestine telecommunications network illegal, demanding its dismantlement, and to replace pro-Hizbullah airport security chief General Wafiq Shuqayr.[50] Hizbullah viewed the decisions as a declaration of war by the Siniora government, instigated and supported by Washington, Saudi Arabia, and Terje Roed-Larsen at the UN, part of an escalatory scheme aimed at dismantling the party's military wing and prosecuting its leadership.[51] The Siniora government's decision to reshuffle Shuqayr from his sensitive security post was also a flagrant disregard of the mutual veto that the sects possess over appointments in the state's major posts in Lebanon's delicate sectarian system. Faced with government intransigence, Hizbullah and Berri's Amal Movement opted for a surgical military operation on May 8, 2008, occupying Beirut and decimating the Future Movement's skeletal military structure, while sidelining the Lebanese army and avoiding confrontation with it. Hizbullah's military operation forced the Siniora government to rescind its decisions, opening the door for an externally sponsored political settlement that ended the eighteen-month political stalemate. Albeit Hizbullah's violent takeover of Beirut betrayed earlier promises not to deploy its military might in domestic disputes, creating deep sectarian scares among Lebanon's Sunni population that threaten to unleash Salafi rage against Hizbullah, it was also not without context. It was the inevitable result of the Siniora government's disregard of the consensual principles of the sectarian system and its refusal to share power with the opposition, a position rooted not so much in Washington's and Riyadh's support for democratic principles and procedures in Lebanon, but rather in their geopolitical struggles with Iran and Syria, and their determined campaign to emasculate Hizbullah, an overlapping domestic–regional contest over post-Syria Lebanon that brought the country ominously close to all-out civil war.

Conclusion

The Qatari-negotiated May 21, 2008 Doha Accord amicably ended the opposition's military takeover of Beirut and organized a political settlement of the political crisis. The sit-in in Beirut's central district, labeled an "occupation" by the March 14 coalition, was ended the same day the accord was signed. The Doha Accord opened the way for the election of the consensus presidential candidate, army commander General Michel Suleiman, on May 25, 2008 and the formation on July 11, 2008 of a national unity government, one in which the opposition possessed veto power. The accord also stipulated that the upcoming 2009 elections be based on the middle-size electoral districts of the 1960 electoral law—a victory for the Christian faction of the opposition— with Beirut's electoral districts gerrymandered to satisfy mainly the electoral strategies of Hariri's Future Movement; it also delegated the new president the task of organizing a national dialogue to discuss the future role and status of Hizbullah's weapons arsenal—as demanded by the March 14 coalition. Hizbullah's unwavering position on this latter point was soon revealed in the protracted deliberations over the cabinet manifesto of the national unity government. The March 14 alliance sought to deny Hizbullah's military wing any role in the liberation of Israeli-occupied Lebanese land,[52] thus denying its weapons arsenal legitimacy and a future deterrence role. Hizbullah, on its part, insisted on the resistance's role not only in liberating occupied Lebanese land, but also as part of a defensive deterrence strategy.[53] In its final version, the cabinet manifesto recognized the right of Lebanon's "people and army and resistance" to "liberate or recover" occupied Lebanese territory and to "defend Lebanon against any attack,"[54] clearly a victory for Hizbullah's efforts to legitimize the role and future deterrence mission of its weapons arsenal. The Doha Accord is thus akin to a regionally brokered sectarian ceasefire, allowing the country and the new president some breathing space in preparation for the 2009 parliamentary elections, the next important contest in the ongoing struggle over post-Syria Lebanon. However, its electoral recommendations promise sectarian chauvinism at the expense of national, cross-sectarian alliances. Nor does it insulate Lebanon from externally instigated sectarian clashes that serve the geopolitical agendas of regional actors.[55]

Is there then no escape from the trap of the sectarian political system and the sectarianism embedded in Lebanese society and most civil society organizations? In the absence of a new sense of intersectarian citizenship, Lebanon will remain a collection of sects vying for political privileges in the context of a divisive and confessional system. The road to civic citizenship—or *muwatana*— is not without difficulties. At least, it entails the emergence, from within each sect, of a critical discourse, demystifying self and other, and opening the way for a new sense of civic engagement, tolerance, and intersectarian citizenship.[56] To be sure, at times of crisis, Lebanese tend to be proactive and mobilize at the civil society level and across sectarian lines. But gradually, this mobilization gives way to sectarian priorities, and loyalty to sectarian leaders takes precedence over national objectives.

Israel's devastating summer 2006 military campaign against Hizbullah triggered a critical debate within the Shia'a community, with many voices demanding a re-examination of Hizbullah's regional alliances and loyalties, especially its Iranian military and political connections.[57] However, the

March 14 coalition's unrelenting coordinated campaign to demonize the Shia'a as Lebanon's "other" community to undermine their political weight in post-Syria Lebanon backfired, rallying most Shia'a around Hizbullah and Berri's Amal Movement in defense of sectarian privileges.[58] Moreover, this deliberative exercise has remained confined to one sect, and must extend to other sects. It also requires practical institutional manifestations free from the hegemony of the sectarian system to open up possibilities for an intersectarian civic space. Otherwise, democracy in Lebanon will remain hostage to the whims of ethnic politicians versed in the clientalistic art of neopatrimonial politics, and the confessional state controlled by predatory politicians will persist.

Not unlike the experiences of other post-war states, constitutional engineering in Lebanon has hitherto proved an insufficient condition for a viable democratic transition.[59] Nor have external actors helped in the implementation of the peace agreement. The first post-war democratic transition was spoiled by Syria, who advanced its own geopolitical and economic interests over the principles enshrined in the post-war power-sharing arrangement. The second, post-Syria transition has collided against the hard realities of Lebanon's stubborn sectarian political system, and was abused by external actors bent on transforming Lebanon into a site for their grander geopolitical confrontations. The Ta'if Accord's consociational stipulations were again shelved to sanction a wholesale takeover of state institutions by the principal pillars of the March 14 coalition. Sectarian calculations have squandered a second opportunity for a viable post-war democratic transition.

Democracy building, Filippo Sabetti reminds us,

> requires a calculus of consent and commitment as well as love of country that cannot be imposed and must emerge from people willing to engage in a dialogue with one another and to practice the art of associating together.[60]

Since Hariri's assassination, and the sea changes that followed in Lebanon, most Lebanese have demonstrated infinite love of country. They have yet to demonstrate their ability to build a democratic Lebanon through dialogue and association beyond narrow sectarian loyalties and external agendas. Failing this challenge will only consecrate the primacy of the sectarian system at the expense of proper democratic standards in Lebanon.

Notes

1 Bassel F. Salloukh thanks Shoghig Mikaelian for her research assistance and comments on an earlier draft of this chapter.
2 For an overview, see Albert Hourani (1966) "Lebanon: The Development of a Political Society" in Leonard Binder, ed., *Politics in Lebanon*. New York: John Wiley & Sons: 22.
3 See Arend Lijphart (1977) *Democracy in Plural Societies: A Comparative Exploration*. New Haven: Yale University Press; Donald L. Horowitz (1985) *Ethnic*

Groups in Conflict. Berkeley: California University Press; Alain-G. Gagnon and James Tully, eds (2001) *Multinational Democracies.* Cambridge: Cambridge University Press.

4 See Farid el Khazen (2000) *The Breakdown of the State in Lebanon, 1967–1976.* Cambridge: Harvard University Press.

5 See Fawwaz Traboulsi (2007) *A History of Modern Lebanon.* London: Pluto Press: 110 and 244.

6 Compare el Khazen, *The Breakdown of the State in Lebanon, 1967–1976,* op. cit. with Michael C. Hudson (1988) "The Problem of Authoritative Power in Lebanese Politics: Why Consociationalism Failed" in Nadim Shehadi and Dana Haffar Mills, eds, *Lebanon: A History of Conflict and Consensus.* London: The Centre for Lebanese Studies and I.B. Tauris & Co Ltd: 224–39.

7 See, for example, Fouad Ajami (1986) *The Vanished Imam: Musa al Sadr and the Shia of Lebanon.* Ithaca: Cornell University Press; Augustus Richard Norton (1987) *Amal and the Shi'a of Lebanon: Struggle for the Soul of the South.* Austin, TX: University of Texas Press.

8 For 1913 figures, see Ghassan Salamé (1987) *Al-Mujtama' wa-l-Dawla fi-l-Mashriq al-'Arabi.* Beirut: Markaz Dirasat al-Wihda al-'Arabiya: 103. For 1932 and 1975, see Helena Cobban (1985) *The Making of Modern Lebanon.* London: Hutchinson: 16. Total population figures for 1932 include a small Jewish community. For 2002, see Walid Shuqayr (2002) "Lahoud wa-l-Hariri Ittafaqa 'ala Taghyeer al-Hukuma wa Dimashq Nasahat bi-Tajannub," *al-Hayat* October 23, 2002, quoting then Interior Minister Elyas al-Murr.

9 See 'Isam Sulayman (1998) *Al-Jumhuriya al-Thaniya Bayn al-Nusus wa-l-Mumarasa.* Beirut: n.p.

10 The preamble of the Ta'if Accord reads: "Illegitimate is the authority that negates the covenant of mutual coexistence." See the text reproduced in Albert Mansour (1993) *Al-Inqilab 'ala al-Ta'if.* Beirut: Dar al-Jadid: 250.

11 For a detailed discussion, see Bassel F. Salloukh (2007) "Opposition under Authoritarianism: The Case of Lebanon under Syria." Paper presented at the Eighth Mediterranean Social and Political Research Meeting, Florence and Montecatini Terme, March 21–25, 2007, organized by the Mediterranean Programme of the Robert Schuman Centre for Advanced Studies at the European University Institute.

12 See Stephen John Stedman (1997) "Spoiler Problems in Peace Processes," *International Security* 22(2), Fall 1997: 5–53.

13 See Samir Kassir (2003) "A Polity in an Uncertain Regional Environment" in Theodor Hanf and Nawaf Salam, eds, *Lebanon in Limbo: Postwar Society and State in an Uncertain Regional Environment.* Baden: Nomos Verlagsgesellschaft: 101.

14 See Bassel F. Salloukh (2006) "The Limits of Electoral Engineering in Divided Societies: Elections in Postwar Lebanon," *Canadian Journal of Political Science* 39 (3), September 2006: 635–55.

15 See the essay by Michel Murqus in *al-Nahar,* April 1, 2005.

16 Samir Kassir (2004) *Dimuqratiyat Suriya wa Istiqlal Lubnan: al-Bahth 'an Rabi' Dimashq.* Beirut: Dar al-Nahar lil-Nashr: 96. This estimate is quoted in Marwan Iskandar (2006) *Rafiq Hariri and the Fate of Lebanon.* Beirut: Saqi Books: 154.

17 See the Arabic version of Joe Faddoul's study "Etude sur la corruption au Liban." Online. Available http://forum.tayyar.org/f91/etude-sur-la-corruption-au-liban-22533/ (accessed May 8, 2009).

18 See Iskandar, *Rafiq Hariri and the Fate of Lebanon,* op. cit.: 156.

19 See "Declaration of the Maronite Archbishops' Council," *Middle East Intelligence Bulletin* 2(9), October 5, 2000. Online. Available www.meib.org/articles/0010_ldoc0920.htm (accessed May 8, 2009).

20 See John J. Mearsheimer and Stephen M. Walt (2007) *The Israel Lobby and U.S. Foreign Policy.* New York: Farrar, Straus and Giroux: 229–79.

21 See the text at: www.fas.org/asmp/resources/govern/108th/pl_108_175.pdf (accessed April 6, 2006). Bush signed the act into law on December 12, 2003.
22 See Nqoula Nasif (2004) "Ma Taquluh Washington wa Dimashq 'an Muhadathat Burns," *al-Nahar* September 14, 2004.
23 The text is at: www.un.org/News/Press/docs/2004/sc8181.doc.htm (accessed September 3, 2005).
24 See 'Abdo Sa'd (2005) *Al-Intikhabat al-Niyabiya li-'Am 2005: Qira'at wa Nata'ij.* Beirut: Markaz Beirut lil-Abhath wa-l-Ma'loumat.
25 Labeled thus in reference to the massive popular demonstration in downtown Beirut on March 14, 2005 commemorating the one-month anniversary of Hariri's assassination. After 'Awn split from it on the eve of the 2005 parliamentary elections, it included the Hariri and Jumblatt parliamentary blocs, the Lebanese Forces, the reunited Kata'eb, most of the members of Liqa' Qornat Shihwan, Haraket al-Yasar al-Dimuqrati, Harkat al-Tajadud al-Dimuqrati, and a number of independent MPs. Its opponents later renamed it the February 14, coalition.
26 See Jihad al-Zayn (2005) "Al-Nuduj al-Federali lil-Barlamaniya al-Lubnaniya," *al-Nahar* June 14, 2005.
27 See the accounts in International Crisis Group (2005) *Lebanon: Managing the Gathering Storm*, Middle East Report No. 48, December 5, 2005.
28 See Ibrahim al-Amin (2005) "'An al-Tawazun al-Sa'b wa-l-Ta'ayush al-Mustahil Bayna al-Aqtab wa-l-Tawa'if," *al-Safir* November 14 and 15, 2005.
29 See the Archbishops' monthly declaration in *al-Safir*, May 4, 2006; and 'Awn's speech commemorating the first anniversary of his return to Lebanon in *al-Nahar*, May 8, 2006.
30 These include the demand for border demarcations between Lebanon and Syria; deploying the Lebanese Army around Palestinian camps and training grounds; and inviting the Federal Bureau of Investigation (FBI) to help investigate the assassinations. See Nqoula Nasif (2005) "Hizbullah Yakhsha Inhiyar al-Tahaluf al-Ruba'i," *al-Nahar* November 25, 2005.
31 See Ibrahim al-Amin (2005) "Taraqub Shi'i Yasbuq al-Hasm al-Niha'i," *al-Safir* December 14, 2005.
32 See, for example, Nasrallah's speeches reproduced in *al-Safir*, February 11 and 17, 2006.
33 See the text of the document in *al-Nahar*, February 7, 2006.
34 See Joseph Smeha (2006) "Al-'Unwan: Iqalat Lahoud, al-Hadaf: Kasr al-Tawazun," *al-Safir* February 18, 2006.
35 Interestingly, before the cabinet crisis erupted, and given the Christians' demographic minority status, the consociational democratic nature of the political system was a primary theme underscored by the Maronite Patriarch and the Lebanese Forces. See Antoine Sa'd (2005) *al-Sadis wa-l-Sab'un: Mar Nasrallah Butrus Sfeir, al-Juz' al-Thani (1992–1998)*. Beirut: Sa'er al-Mashreq: 159 and 224–25; and Lebanese Forces MP George 'Adwan's comments in Toni Abi Najem (2005) "Al-Quwat al-Lubnaniya 'Ashiyat Mefsal Asasi fi Masiratiha al-Nidaliya," *al-Nahar* October 25 and 26, 2005.
36 Compare Lebanon's ratings with other Arab states on Freedom House's table on Comparative Measures of Freedom. Online. Available www.freedomhouse.org/uploads/pdf/Charts2006.pdf (accessed August 28, 2006).
37 The text is at: www.un.org/News/Press/docs/2006/sc8808.doc.htm (accessed August 30, 2006).
38 See Nabil Haytham (2006) "Limaza Tashakalat 'Lajnat al-Sahar 'ala al-Ma'aber' … wa hal Ghoyeba al-Amn al-'Am?" *al-Safir* August 31, 2006.
39 See Nasrallah's speech reproduced in *al-Safir*, August 4, 2007.
40 See Joseph Smaha (2006) "Al-Ihtiqan al-Mazhabi Bayna al-Hizb wa-l-Tayyar," *al-Akhbar* December 12, 2006; Fida' Itani (2008) *Al-Jihadiyun fi Lubnan: Min "Quwat al-Fajr" ila "Fath al-Islam."* Beirut: Dar Al-Saqi; Ghaseb al-Mukhtar (2008) "Al-Khuruj men Fakh al-Tahrid al-Mazhabi," *al-Safir* May 16, 2008.

41 See Bassel F. Salloukh (2008) "The Art of the Impossible: The Foreign Policy of Lebanon" in Bahgat Korany and Ali E. Hillal Dessouki, eds, *The Foreign Policies of Arab States: The Challenge of Globalization*, new rev. edn. Cairo: American University in Cairo Press, pp. 283–317.
42 See Amos Harel and Avi Issacharoff (2008) *34 Days: Israel, Hezbollah, and the War in Lebanon*. New York: Palgrave.
43 See Khudur Taleb (2007) "Kibash al-Mintaqa Yutih Bitaswiyat al-Hukuma," *al-Safir* June 16, 2007.
44 Mearsheimer and Walt, *The Israel Lobby and U.S. Foreign Policy*, op. cit.: 307.
45 See Robin Wright (2008) "Fighting in Beirut Threatens a Top Bush Administration Priority," *Washington Post* May 10, 2008.
46 Comments made by Jean Aziz on NTV's program *Al-Usbou' fi Sa'a*, June 10, 2007.
47 See Seymour M. Hersh (2007) "The Redirection," *New Yorker* March 5, 2007.
48 Rice's comments were made in a news conference on July 21, 2006. Online. Available www.washingtonpost.com/wp-dyn/content/article/2006/07/21/AR2006072100889.html (accessed May 8, 2009).
49 Quoted in Michael A. Fletcher (2006) "Hezbollah the Loser in Battle, Bush Says," *Washington Post* August 15, 2006.
50 For a sober analysis of the immediate backdrop and consequences of these decisions, see Jim Quilty (2008) "Lebanon's Brush with Civil War," *Middle East Report Online* May 20, 2008. Online. Available www.merip.org/mero/mero052008.html (accessed July 28, 2008).
51 See Nasrallah's press conference reproduced in *al-Safir*, May 9, 2008; Nabil Haytham (2008) "Al-Mu'arada wa-l-Muwalat Bayna al-Ribh wa-l-Khisara," *al-Safir* May 12, 2008; Fida' Itani (2008) "Hakaza Khattatat al-Mu'arada li-Isqat al-Muwalat," *al-Akhbar* May 10, 2008; Nabil Haytham (2008) "Al-Hamla 'ala Hizbullah wa-l-Jaysh Tha'riya," *al-Safir* August 11, 2008.
52 Namely, the contested Sheb'a farms, the Kfarshouba Hills, and the Lebanese section of Ghajar village—the last occupied during the July 2006 war.
53 See Nasrallah's speech reproduced in *al-Safir*, May 27, 2008.
54 See the text of the cabinet manifesto in *al-Nahar*, August 6, 2008.
55 Reports suggest a Saudi hand in the May–August 2008 Sunni–Alawi clashes in Tripoli. On this view, the sectarian clashes are part of Riyadh's war of attrition against Hizbullah, Syria, and Iran in the post-Doha Accord period. Riyadh's and Washington's insistence that Siniora head the national unity government is another manifestation of this war. See Ibrahim al-Amin (2008) "Ma-l-Lazi Yuqliq al-Riyadh men Tafahum Hizbullah wa-l-Salafiyyin," *al-Akhbar* August 21, 2008.
56 For a philosophical and practical argument on Canada's intercultural practices, see James Tully (2005) *Strange Multiplicity: Constitutionalism in an Age of Diversity*. Cambridge: Cambridge University Press.
57 See Jihad al-Zayn (2006) "Musaraha ma' al-Sayyed Khamenei," *al-Nahar* June 26, 2006; Muna Fayad (2006) "An Takuna Shi'iyan al-An … ," *al-Nahar* August 7, 2006; Hani Fahs (2006) "Nahwa Ta'if Ijtima'i min Aj al-Ta'if al-Dusturi," *al-Safir* August 16, 2006.
58 See, for example, Sa'd al-Hariri's speech reproduced in *al-Nahar*, February 8, 2008; Jumblatt's interview on ANB television reproduced in *al-Nahar*, January 3, 2008; and Jumblatt's speech reproduced in *al-Nahar*, February 11, 2008.
59 For a comparative perspective, see Pippa Norris (2005) "Stable Democracy and Good Governance in Divided Societies: Do Powersharing Institutions Work?" John F. Kennedy School of Government, Faculty Research Working Paper Series, No. RWP05–014, February 2005.
60 Filippo Sabetti (2000) *The Search for Good Government: Understanding the Paradox of Italian Democracy*. Montreal: McGill–Queen's University Press: 264.

10 Democracy, Islam, and secularism in Turkey

*Ersin Kalaycioglu**

Introduction

Turkey belongs to a club of nation-states that inherited the legacy of a former empire. Turkey inherited the Ottoman cultural and political baggage, as well as the bulk of its foreign debt with the Treaty of Lausanne (July 24, 1923), which also erected the new Turkish state, and later a republic (October 29, 1923). It was established by means of a war of national liberation, which the Turkish nationalist forces won against great odds. Turkey emerged from the same cultural milieu and political system of the Ottoman Empire, as did almost all of the states of the Middle East and the Balkans. Turkey is home to more than seventy million Muslims most of who belong to the Sunni sect, although a small but still sizable minority are Alevi.[1] Although no reliable data exist, many citizens of Turkey can and do trace their roots to the Balkan, Caucasian, Central Asian, and Middle Eastern provinces of the Ottoman Empire. Thus, Turkey also qualifies as an immigrant nation or a nation of immigrants, most of whom identify with Turks and being Turkish. Many in those regions neighboring Turkey continue, with some enmity or envy and mostly with a complex ambiguity, to perceive of Turkey and the Turks as their former masters. Turkey shares many cultural traits and political characteristics with her Middle Eastern, Balkan, and Caucasian neighbors, and continues to enjoy complicated cultural, political, and economic relations with those regions.

Turkey started negotiations for full membership of the European Union (EU) in 2005, as the only candidate for full membership with a large Muslim population; she has been serving as a member of the North Atlantic Treaty Organization (NATO) since 1952, and also functions as a bona fide member of the Organization of Islamic Countries (OIC). Turkey has also been striving to establish a democratic form of government since the end of World War II, and is now considered to have satisfied the Copenhagen Criteria of the EU and thus become eligible for candidacy in that organization. In the meantime, Turkish troops take part in NATO operations in such disparate geographies as the Kosovo, the Baltic Sea, and Afghanistan. The list can be extended to include many more examples of United Nations (UN) peace operations in Palestine, Lebanon, and the like. Such a record distinguishes Turkey from the rest of the Balkan and Middle Eastern countries, with which she shares a long, rich history and culture. Two major characteristics of Turkish society and polity seem to stick out very clearly in differentiating Turkey from the other post-Ottoman societies and states: they are secularism and democracy. This chapter is devoted to the examination and explanation of the secular and democratic records of Turkey, which seem to differentiate her from other polities with large Muslim populations.

The republican cultural revolution

The Turkish republican regime inherited the Ottoman political culture and style of governance. In that cultural baggage of the Ottoman legacy, a deeply entrenched cultural cleavage had also been present. From the eighteenth century onwards, Ottoman and later republican Turkish political systems had been under the spell of two irreconcilable images of "good society," which were shared by two warring parties or *kulturkampfs*. One of these consisted of those who believed in the image of "good society" built around the core values of science and reason, and the other those who adhered to the image of "good society" constructed on the core values of tradition and religion, which in practice consisted of the teachings of the Sunni–Hanefi school of law; they had been involved in an existential struggle for ages. Although the former seemed to have enjoyed greater power and influence since the *Tanzimat* reforms of 1839–76, the latter managed to assert itself upon the realm of politics from time to time. However, at the time of the establishment of the republican regime in the early 1920s, it seemed as if a moment of reckoning had finally arrived in the perennial struggle of the positivist–secular and Islamic revivalist *kulturkampfs*.

The charisma of Mustafa Kemal Atatürk, who led the War of Liberation, became the founder of the republic and its first president, and his nationalist followers enabled them to liquidate what they considered to be the institutions of decadence and resistance to development of the Islamic revivalists from 1924 to 1928. In 1928, the constitution was amended, and the article that defined the official religion of the Turkish state as Islam was omitted from the text. In 1937, another sweeping constitutional amendment introduced "laicism"[2] as a major characteristic of the political regime of the Turkish state. Once again, the positivist–secular camp had drawn upon its source of inspiration from France to define the relationship between religion and the state in the young republic. It was the French concept of "*laïcité*" that came to their aid in describing the nature of secularism in the new Turkish practice.[3] A strict separation of religion from politics and simultaneously from public life was thus introduced as the gist of the Turkish practice of secularism by 1937. There was hardly any major national reaction or challenge to such a development. The urban middle classes seem to have wholeheartedly supported these changes. However, a Sunni (*Nakshibendi*) Kurdish uprising in the eastern town of Genç in 1925 and another Sunni uprising in the small western town of Menemen in 1931 were the only two incidents that may be considered as parochial reactions to the laicist policies of the republican state.[4] A huge majority of the population seemed to go along with and tolerated such changes as prayer calls in Turkish, Turkish as the language of prayer, the public sale and consumption of alcoholic beverages, women and men donning Western attire, the banning of such religious attire as the turban (*sarik*) for laymen, and the donning of religious garb by religious officials only during religious ceremonies and prayers and the like. It seemed as if Turkey had made a dramatic socio-cultural shift by the end of the 1930s. However, nothing could be more deceptive.

World War II and democracy

Turkey did not take part in World War II. In spite of not taking part in the war, Turkey kept a big army on full alert for six years. Such a defense posture had a big economic cost. The recently built pre-war industrial infrastructure was mainly left idle throughout the war, and the industrialization drive of the country suffered dearly. In the meantime, commercial activities were corrupted as a burgeoning black market emerged. A new class of war rich emerged from the black market operations. When the Republican People's Party (CHP)[5] government moved to confiscate the corrupt wealth of the *nouveau riches* in 1943, the emerging middle class of the country feared that their well-being was put in jeopardy. The same measures taken to tax the black market gains of the few also devastated the businesses of many merchants, who belonged to the Christian and Jewish communities of Istanbul and other major cities. The businesses owned and operated by the Christian and Jewish businessmen were either sold or given away to Muslim entrepreneurs. The emerging Turkish Muslim middle class did not feel secure from the encroachments of the CHP government either. They began to seek protection from the CHP government in the ranks of a pro-business opposition party.[6]

At the end of World War II, Turkey started to test the waters in Moscow for a renewal of the non-aggression treaty between the two countries.[7] The Turkish diplomats who visited Moscow came back with demands from the Soviet government. The Soviets proposed to change the Turkish–Soviet border at Kars and Ardahan of Turkey and western Georgia, and deploy Red Army troops at the Turkish straits to protect Turkey from further threats.[8] The CHP government rejected the proposals, but immediately started a search for a new alliance to deter the new Stalinist designs for Turkey. The obvious option was an alliance with the new superpower of the world, the United States. An iron curtain was falling on Eastern Europe, and the Turkish government decided to move swiftly to stay on the western side of that curtain. However, the single-party regime of the country with its nationalist credentials looked far too authoritarian for such an alliance to be forged. The Grand National Assembly (TBMM) moved new legislation to start multiparty politics in the country, and multiparty elections were announced for 1946. The burgeoning middle classes of the country could now obtain the protection they deemed essential from a pro-business party. Indeed, more than a few pro-business parties were established in 1945 and 1946, but the Democrat Party (DP) emerged from the ranks of the CHP and became the favorite of the anti-CHP middle classes, communities, and interests of the periphery. In 1947, President Truman declared that the US would come to the aid of Greece and Turkey to protect freedom in those countries. Turkey soon applied for full membership of NATO, participated in the establishment of the Council of Europe in 1949, and became a NATO member in 1952. Turkish domestic politics made a parallel move for a regime change to accommodate multiparty democracy.

Democracy and Islamic revivalism

The president of the country and the leader of the CHP, General Ismet Inönü, met the leader of the DP, Mr. Celal Bayar, to establish an accord for a smooth transition to democracy.[9] They agreed upon not involving religious jargon and symbolism and Kurdish nationalist themes in their partisan interactions. It seems as if it was Inönü himself who made these suggestions, with which Bayar concurred. However, it did not take long for the CHP leadership to renege upon its promises. The CHP government of the late 1940s lifted the ban upon public visits to tombs of religious figures and also established religious institutions of higher education in the late 1940s. Such a shift in the former secularist policies of the CHP enabled the DP to take bolder actions in carrying out other changes in the public role of religion when it came to power in 1950. The Democrats also won the 1954 and 1957 general elections. During the reign of the Democrats, the Turkish economy changed from economic growth through state-built industry to market liberalism and a mixed economy. The Democrats abandoned the emphasis on railroads, and instead began to build roads, which they had hoped to use to bring services to the periphery. However, the roads provided the rural masses with the opportunity to pack up and leave for the urban centers for a better life. Urban populations and industry began to be inundated with peasants fleeing their villages, which precipitated a rapid social mobilization process in Turkey.

The DP also provided a great opportunity for all those who opposed the CHP to join its ranks. It presented itself as the party of the people (the periphery, *taşra*), which the CHP had formerly tried so much to modernize and secularize, and failed. The DP provided them with new economic opportunities and jobs in the burgeoning private sector of the country, and did not show any eagerness to promote laicism. Such a stance enabled the formerly banned and outlawed religious orders (*tarikat*) to participate in the DP organization and establish various factions within that party. The front bench of the DP had come from the same background as the CHP elite, and they had served in close proximity to Mustafa Kemal Atatürk as well. Therefore, there is little reason to assume that the DP front bench was composed of revivalists. However, they tried to follow a policy of tolerance toward Islamic revivalism.

Under the circumstances, various brotherhoods began to surface and prose-lytize. For example, the leader of the *Nurcu's*, Said-i Nursi, found various opportunities to appear in public and rub shoulders with the DP elites. The DP governments quickly moved to re-install Arabic as the language of prayer and prayer call, and opened new religious schools and institutions of higher learning, such as Islamic institutes (*Islam Enstitüleri*), and new tombs were refurbished for public visits. The 1950s was a period of testing of the political waters for the revivalists. They began to establish their seminaries and could now work with less chance of being harassed by the political authorities. However, it took them another decade to become organized into a political party and vie for political power.

The military coup of 1960 ousted the DP from power. It did not take long for the parties of the periphery to organize and compete with the CHP. In the 1961 elections, the CHP managed to get the plurality of the vote, yet in 1965, the inheritor of the DP's legacy, the Justice Party (AP), received the support of the majority under an electoral system of immaculate proportional repre-sentation. The AP leadership did not shy away from using religious symbolism, and took even bolder steps in providing greater opportunity for the revivalists to organize and proselytize when it came to power in the 1965 elections. Reli-gious (vocational) secondary schools, legally named as the *Imam Hatip* High Schools (IHLs), were promoted, with the official aim of educating "enligh-tened imams," while they seem to have propagated an alternative education to secular schools, whereby their students were trained to stick to their "moral values" while they became engineers, lawyers, doctors, etc., just as their par-ents aspired.[10] It was a popular call. By the late 1960s, increasing numbers of students were graduating from the religious schools with anti-secular instruc-tion and training, and a deep suspicion, if not hatred, for the secularizing cultural revolution instilled in their minds. It was around that time that Prof. Dr. Necmettin Erbakan and associates established the National Order Party (MNP) as the first overtly political Islamist party in the country.[11]

Erbakan had been a professor of mechanical engineering at the Istanbul Technical University (ITU), and an unsuccessful businessman. He had estab-lished an engine manufacturing plant, which failed to succeed in the Turkish market, and he had to sell his enterprise. He blamed the secular political economy of Turkey for the failure of his business venture. He tried to run for the office of the presidency of the Turkish Chambers of Business and Stock Exchanges (TOBB). He was not successful in gaining the presidency of the TOBB, yet he managed to get into a row with Prime Minister Demirel. When the police evicted him from the directorship of the TOBB, he decided to move into politics. He established the MNP, which was almost immediately banned by a decision of the country's constitutional court, for the 1961 Constitution and the Political Parties Act of 1965 (Act no. 648) outlawed religious parties. He went into exile in Europe, as Turkish democracy experienced another breakdown in 1971.

He returned from exile in 1973 and established the National Salvation Party (MSP), which was careful not to make any overt claims about Islam or

Şeriat (Shar'ia). The MSP turned out to be much more successful. It participated in the 1973 elections and received 11 percent of the national vote. The
CHP obtained the plurality of the votes and the legislative seats in the
TBMM, but failed to gain enough to form a government by itself. The CHP
of 1973 was under the leadership of a young politician, Mr. Bülent Ecevit,
and his similarly young associates. They had tried to re-create the party in
their own image of a left of center party. They had campaigned for a change
in the political and economic order of the country. The CHP leadership discovered that the MSP was also using a similar quasi-socialist jargon, and similarly opposed the political and economic order of the country. They joined
forces and established a coalition government of the CHP and MSP. It was a
superb irony for the secular, revolutionary, nationalist CHP to ally itself with
an anti-revolutionary, internationalist party of political Islam to create a "fair
order" (*hakça düzen*)! What the CHP and the MSP understood by "fair order"
was worlds apart and quite irreconcilable. It took the CHP about a year and
the Cyprus war (1974) to discover that the MSP was after a totally different
change in the establishment than what they had hoped and envisioned to
accomplish. However, the CHP had managed to extend legitimacy to the MSP,
the party of political Islam in Turkey. If the bastion of secularism CHP could
establish a coalition with the MSP, who could legitimately condemn the conservative Justice Party (AP) for doing the same? Indeed, when the CHP–MSP
coalition fell apart in late 1974, the AP was waiting in the wings to strike an
accord with the MSP and the ultra-nationalist, anti-communist MHP to
establish a new coalition government. They managed to rule Turkey until
1978. For five years, political Islamists gained some representation in the state
ministries of the republic, who seemed to establish and run their own autonomous government within the context of the coalition in power. It was the
first and biggest dent in the secular state.

In 1978, the CHP made a comeback, established a coalition government
with eleven ex-members of the AP, yet were not effective in ruling the country.
The economy continued to fail under the weight of the 1973 oil crisis and the
US arms embargo, which was imposed upon Turkey in the aftermath of the
Cyprus war of 1974. Various Marxist–Leninist, Maoist, Fascist, and other
radical groups had established their militia and were involved in a bloody
struggle to topple the democratic regime of the country. As the country was
rapidly veering toward a civil war, the military stepped in again in 1980.

The military government and the "Turkish–Islamic synthesis"

The military coup of 1980 acted on the presumption that the main political
problem in Turkey was to cope with the Marxist–Leninist challenge for power.
The turmoil of the 1970s was diagnosed as being caused by the communists
seeking to divide the country into two and create a safe haven in the east,
which then would rise up against the republic and declare independence with
Soviet support.[12] In order to prevent such a scenario, the military junta set

out to crush Marxism–Leninism by force, and forge the national solidarity of the country through enhanced nationalist propaganda combined with Sunni Islam. The men and women in the streets were instructed in the common religious (Sunni Muslim) bonds uniting the country, while the academic and political elites were indoctrinated in nationalism and Kemalism, as if the two messages were reconcilable. A think tank, called the *Aydınlar Ocağı* (The Hearth of Intellectuals), which was a congregation of conservative, religious, and nationalist academics and intellectuals, began to serve the junta. The ideological output of these efforts was branded the "Turkish–Islamic synthesis" (*Türk–İslâm Sentezi*), and almost functioned as the official ideology of the country until the end of the rule of President Kenan Evren in 1987.[13]

The period from 1980 to 1983 was one of utter ideological confusion. The military junta was supposedly the bastion of Kemalism, although it was cooperating with the most conservative and even anti-Kemalist think tanks and intellectuals, on the one hand, its head was reciting the Holy Qur'an in public, preaching "true Islam," closing down the party of Mustafa Kemal, the CHP, at the same time, and proselytizing the ideas of Kemal Atatürk in secular schools and universities, commemorating his birth and his accomplishments with fanfare. In the meantime, 1980–83 was a period in which student enrolment in the IHLs increased by leaps and bounds, although no new IHLs were established. The graduates of the IHLs began to enroll in such undergraduate programs as law and political science with the intent of serving in the Ministries of Interior Affairs and Justice. Concerns began to mount among the secular *kulturkampf* over whether these students had any ulterior political motives or not.

The international system was also going through a major transformation in the 1980s. The Red Army had invaded Afghanistan in the late 1970s, and the US started to toy with the idea of fighting communism with Islam. A green crescent was to be built under the soft belly of the Soviet Union, which would target the Muslim populations of Central Asia and other parts of Russia. Stiff resistance to the Soviet armies in Afghanistan began to impress political Islamists. Pakistan was also under the rule of another military junta led by General Zia ul-Haq, who was a staunch ally of the US. Eventually, Pakistan began increasingly and simultaneously to get involved in Afghanistan and Islam. The Turkish military junta veered into close alliance with Pakistan, where Zia and Evren began to refer to each other as "brother" in public. Both seemed to have taken their respective places in the "green crescent" surrounding the former Soviet Union, under the US umbrella.

When Turkey reverted back to multiparty politics under the hegemony of the junta in 1983, the Islamic revivalists had already solidly consolidated their place in Turkish politics. In the 1983 elections, three parties were permitted to take part. Only the party established by Mr. Turgut Özal,[14] the conservative Motherland Party (ANAP), was semi-independent. ANAP received 45 percent of the national vote and established a party government in the aftermath of the 1983 general elections.

Table 10.1 Election results and the distribution of seats in the TBMM (1983–2007) (%)

Political Parties	CHP	MHP	ANAP	HP	MDP	SHP	DYP	RP/FP+	DSP	AKP
Elections	%	%	%	%	%	%	%	%	%	%
1983 Vote			45,1	30,5	23,3					
Seat			52,8	29,2	17,7					
1987 Vote			36,3	—	—	24,4	19,9	—	—	
Seat			64,9	—	—	22,0	13,1	—	—	
1991 Vote			24,0	—	—	20,6	27,2	16.7(*)	—	
Seat			25,7	—	—	19,7	39,7	13.1(*)	—	
1995 Vote	10,7	—	19,6	—	—	—	19,2	21,4	14,6	
Seat	8,9	—	24,0	—	—	—	24,5	28,7	13,8	
1999 Vote	—	18,0	13,2	—	—	—	12,0	15,4	22,2	
Seat	—	23,5	15,6	—	—	—	15,5	20,2	24,7	
2002 Vote	19,4	—	—	—	—	—	—	—	—	34,3
Seat	32,4	—	—	—	—	—	—	—	—	66,0
2007 Vote	20,9	14,3	—	—	—	—	—	—	—	46,5
Seat	20,4	12,9	—	—	—	—	—	—	—	62,0

Notes:
Only those parties that could win enough votes to go over the 10 percent national threshold and gain representation in the National Assembly are included in the table. Seats refer to the percentage of seats obtained by the corresponding party in the National Assembly in the immediate aftermath of general elections.

*FP, Virtue Party in the 1999 elections, which was more or less a continuation of the RP under a different name, after the former was banned by the constitutional court. The FP was also banned, and the AKP and Felicity Party (SP, Sunni Islamist) were established in 2001 to replace the FP.

†These cells refer to the Welfare Party Alliance, which includes the RP, the Nationalist Work Party (MÇP), which was later converted into the MHP, and the Reformist Democracy Party (IDP), which is now the Nation Party (MP).

CHP, Republican People's Party (left of center, secular); MHP, Nationalist Action Party (ultra-nationalist, anti-communist); ANAP, Motherland Party (right of center, liberal/conservative); HP, Populist Party (praetorian, left of center); MDP, Nationalist Democracy Party (praetorian, right of center); RP, Welfare Party (Islamist, "National Outlook"); SHP, Social Democratic Populist Party (left of center, secular); DYP, True Path Party (right of center, nationalist, conservative); DSP, Democratic Left Party (left of center, nationalist); AKP, Justice and Development Party (socially and culturally conservative, with leadership from Islamic revivalist background, economic liberal, political reformist).

Blank cells indicate that the party represented in the column was not in existence at the time of the corresponding national election.

Sources: Ersin Kalaycioglu (1999) "The Shaping of Party Preferences in Turkey: Coping with the Post Cold War Era," New Perspectives on Turkey 20, Spring: 48. Official Gazette (Resmi Gazete) November 10, 2002, no. 24932; and Official Gazette (Resmi Gazete) July 30, 2007, no. 26598 (first repetitive issue). Kalaycioglu (2005) Turkish Dynamics: 139. The data for 2006 is from the Ali Carkoglu-Ersin Kalaycioglu field survey on socio-political attitudes and political choices in Turkey.[17]

Table 10.2 Volatility and fragmentation in the party system (1961–2007)

Elections	Volatility	Fragmentation of Votes	Fragmentation of Seats	Effective Number of Parties
1961	–	0.71	0.70	3.3
1965	24.5	0.63	0.63	2.6
1969	11.4	0.70	0.59	2.3
1973	28.4	0.77	0.70	3.3
1977	18.3	0.68	0.60	2.5
1983	–	0.66	0.61	2.5
1987	–	0.75	0.51	2.0
1991	16.6	0.79	0.71	3.5
1995	23.0	0.83	0.77	4.3
1999	22.6	0.84	0.79	4.8
2002	43.9	0.81	0.46	1.9
2007	17.3	0.72	0.56	3.6

Source: Özbudun (2000): 77. The entries for the 1999, 2002, and 2007 elections are calculations by the author using the same methods described by Özbudun.

ANAP stayed in government until the 1991 general elections. In the meantime, the former members of the CHP had established the Social Democratic People's Party (SHP), and Demirel had established the True Path Party (DYP), while former leader and prime minister Ecevit had split from the rest of the CHP elite and established the Democratic Left Party (DSP).[15] Özal's promise of decreasing the inflation rate and stabilizing the economy never materialized. In 1991, the DYP and SHP established a coalition and stayed in power until 1995. However, they also failed in their promise of stabilizing the economy, and worse, failed to preserve hard-earned political stability, which rapidly deteriorated due to the increased effectiveness of the terror campaigns of the Kurdish nationalist PKK, in the aftermath of the Gulf War of 1990–91. The Turkish voters went through a major realignment in 1995, rapidly deserted the center of the left–right spectrum, and moved to further right. The post-Cold War international politics provided the Islamic revivalists with new political opportunities.

The post-Cold War international order and Islamic revival

In the 1995 general elections, the most important party of political Islam in Turkey at the time received the plurality of the vote with 21.4 percent of the valid national vote (see Table 10.1). The Turkish party system had been plagued with fragmentation and volatility for a long time.[16] However, when the Cold War ended in 1991, the fragmentation and volatility of the Turkish party system experienced another increase (see Tables 10.1 and 10.2). A close examination of Tables 10.1 and 10.2 would indicate that the 1990s constituted a period of sudden increases in the popularity of some parties, while others

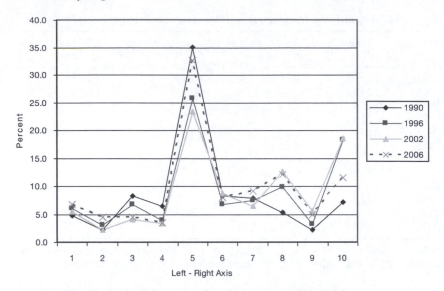

Figure 10.1 The ideological spectrum of Turkish voters (1990–2006)
Source: Kalaycioglu (2005) Turkish Dynamics: 139. The data for 2006 are from the Ali
Carkoglu–Ersin Kalaycioglu field survey on socio-political attitudes and political choices
in Turkey.

lost valuable ground. Obviously, wild swings in the vote eventually increased
to an unprecedented rate of 43.9 percent of volatility in the 2002 elections.
The old parties, which had been powerhouses of Turkish politics, never recov-
ered from the ban imposed upon them by the military government of 1980–83.
Eventually, a realignment of the Turkish voters occurred in the 1990s as the
former parties vacated the center of the left–right spectrum of ideologies and
moved to the right (see Figure 10.1). Such an ideological move to the right
enabled the parties of the far right, such as the Welfare, Virtue, and eventually
the Justice and Development Party (AKP) to obtain the plurality of the vote
and capture the prime minister's seat in the Turkish parliamentary regime.

Turkish politics, as explained in the preceding pages of this chapter, has
always been operating under the influence of deep cultural rifts that divided
up the country into clashing *kulturkampfs*. The oldest and the most established of these cultural fault lines that divide the voters into two major *kulturkampfs* is the divide between the positivist–secular versus the Islamic
revivalist blocs. However, in the 1990s, Turkey began to experience the
increasing presence and impact of another cultural division between the
Kurdish and Turkish ethnic nationalisms. Voting behavior studies in the 1990s
indicated that religion and ethnicity emerged as the two most important
determinants of party preference in Turkey.[18] When the Turkish voters overwhelmingly identified with the right-wing ideologies of Islamic revivalism and
Turkish ethnic nationalism, the Islamic revivalist and Turkish nationalist

parties benefited from the critical voter realignment of 1995. In fact, first the Islamist RP in 1995, and then the conservative AKP[19] with Islamist leaders in the 2002 and 2007 general elections obtained the plurality of the votes (see Table 10.1). The Turkish secular democratic regime began to experience another challenge from Islamism in its recent history.

The most important exogenous factor, which influenced voter realignment toward the radical right, seems to be the post-Cold War developments in the international system.[20] The new international order undermined the former Helsinki Accord of 1975, to which Turkey was a party, and it had incorporated the principle of the inviolability of borders in Europe. The territories of the former Eastern and Central European countries were now deemed as artificially imposed upon them by the Soviet Union at the end of World War II and could now change. Hence, Czechs and Slovaks, Slovenes, Croats, Bosnians, Kosovars, and eventually Macedonians and Montenegrins legitimately split from their previous federal states of Czechoslovakia and Yugoslavia, and established independent states. Borders in Europe seemed to be negotiable, which created new fears among the Turkish nationalists that a new design for redrawing the borders of Turkey was imminent. The decomposition of Yugoslavia fueled security concerns and helped new impressions of "Christian Europe" versus "Muslim Turks" to emerge in Turkey, which in turn precipitated a new surge in religious and nationalist feelings in the country.

In 1990, Iraqi forces invaded its southern neighbor Kuwait. Turkey immediately called for international action against the belligerence of Iraq, participated in the US-led coalition, and imposed an embargo on Iraq as early as the summer of 1990. The coalition eventually declared war on Iraq, defeated, and pushed that country out of Kuwait in 1991. However, the end of the Gulf War brought little respite for Turkey. The Iraqi government of Saddam Hussein moved swiftly to punish the Kurds in the north of that country for their support of the US-led coalition forces. The Kurds of northern Iraq began to take refuge in Iran and Turkey in staggering numbers. Such a sudden movement of half a million refugees into Turkey was more than the Turkish Red Crescent and government could deal with. To make matters worse, the Kurdish Maoist nationalists (PKK) had taken refuge in northern Iraq and had been operating from their bases there to attack the Turkish army and the Kurdish settlements in Turkey. They exploited the refugee movement and, under its cover, the PKK began to infiltrate southeastern Turkey. When the Turkish security forces began to take measures to stop the PKK infiltration, a chorus of European non-governmental organizations (NGOs), European governments, and the EU began to severely criticize the Turkish government for the ill-treatment of the "Kurds." In the meantime, the PKK terror campaign reached new heights, and the death toll of Turkish troops, which included soldiers of all ethnic backgrounds, increased rapidly. Turkish trade with Iraq also began to suffer as the economy of eastern Turkey began to experience a sudden and severe downturn due to the Turkish embargo imposed on Iraq. The economic downturn in the east of Turkey also increased a sense of alienation and rebelliousness among the inhabitants, Kurds included. Turkish voters had the impression that Turkey emerged as one of the biggest losers from the Gulf War. A "never again" attitude was solidly carved into the minds of the Turkish population, on the one hand, and the fears of "EU designs" to redraw the borders of Turkey were further ignited, on the other.

Islamic revival versus secularism

It was the Welfare Party (RP) activists who seemed to be most organized to benefit from the mayhem of the early 1990s. In the 1991 elections, the extreme right-wing Nationalist Work (MÇP), Welfare (RP), and the Reformist Democracy Parties (IDP) joined forces under the banner of the RP and entered the elections on a single ticket. The extreme right wing of the Turkish ideological spectrum was able to take 16.7 percent of the national vote and gained representation in the TBMM once again. In the same elections, the social democrats (SHP) had provided an opportunity for the Kurdish nationalists to join their ranks and get elected on the SHP ticket as well. The stipulation of the election law that a party needed to get 10 percent of the national vote to qualify for seats in the TBMM, which had been erected to keep parties of political Islam, ethnic nationalist Kurdism, and Turkism out of the TBMM, failed dismally.

In the 1995 elections, this time even without the MÇP and IDP joining ranks, the RP was able to take 21.4 percent of the national vote, and emerged as the party with the most votes and seats in the TBMM. The RP could be kept out of the government for a brief period, and in early 1996, President Demirel appointed the leader of the RP, Erbakan, as the prime minister of a coalition government with the DYP. It looked as if Turkish political Islam was about to attempt to make deep running changes in the secular system of Turkey. However, the RP–DYP coalition began to run into serious trouble as a car accident in Susurluk, Balikesir unearthed odious relations between politicians, bureaucrats, and the underground (*mafia*), which implicated the DYP. The government played down the importance of this matter, which precipitated opposition toward its callousness to corruption.[21] Middle-class women, the Alevi community, civil society groups, big business, most trade unions, and those who identified closely with secularism began to organize and react to the insensitivity of the RP-led coalition government toward corruption. It was under these circumstances that the anti-secular activities of the RP local organizations emerged in the media and the press. One such activity was a theatrical performance by RP activists, which propagated resistance to the Turkish army. It did not take long for the military establishment to side with the above-mentioned groups and pressure the coalition government. At a meeting of the National Security Council on February 28, 1997, the prime minister and several ministers were seriously criticized by the military and asked to adopt measures to cope with the rising tide of Islamism in the country. Prime Minister Erbakan and his council of ministers undersigned the measures, yet they only stayed in power until June 18, 1997. When the prime minister resigned, President Demirel appointed the leader of the second largest parliamentary party in the TBMM, and that was ANAP's leader Mr. Mesut Yilmaz. Yilmaz was able to establish a coalition government with the DSP, which the leader of the DYP, Ms. Çiller, considered as a coup manufactured by President Demirel to outmaneuver her from becoming prime minister again. The international media loved the phrase and have been referring to the incident as the "semi-coup" of February 28, 1997 ever since. The impression given was that secularism was saved by the action of the military. Obviously, it was an oversimplification and some misrepresentation of reality, but secularism vs. Islamic revivalism resurfaced as the most important cultural cleavage dividing Turkish society and fueling conflict, tension, and stress in Turkish politics once again.

It did not take long for the RP deputies in the TBMM to start a crusade against the very measures their party in government had undersigned and adopted at the National Security Council on February 28, 1997. Most of those measures had to do with the growing population of students in the IHLs. Mandatory elementary school education was extended from five to eight years, and thus led to the closure of the middle schools connected to the IHLs. The RP and other Islamic revivalists reacted sharply, yet in vain. In the meantime, the Public Prosecutor's Office pressed charges against the RP, and the constitutional court decided to ban it for its anti-secular activities in contravention of the constitution. The RP and some members of its front bench were banned from politics. In its place, the Virtue Party (FP) was established. In the 1999 elections, the FP received 15 percent of the national vote, which was surpassed by the Democratic Left Party (DSP) of Mr. Bülent Ecevit and the Nationalist Action Party (MHP) (see Table 10.1). Ecevit was able to establish a coalition government with the MHP and ANAP, and the FP was once again relegated to being the main opposition party in the country. Dramatically, the CHP was not able to gain 10 percent of the national vote and was kept out of legislative politics in the country. The very election laws that were designed to keep the secular and moderate parties of the regime in the TBMM started to function to keep them out, while the anti-system parties gained the upper hand and formed coalition and party governments.

The DSP-led coalition government ran into severe difficulties almost immediately after it was established in 1999. The first challenge that the coalition government met was the earthquakes of 1999. In August and November 1999, 450 km of the northern Anatolian fault line erupted with quakes of 7.4 and 7.2 magnitude (on the Richter scale), killing about 20,000 people and turning 10,000 buildings into rubble. The lack of coordination and effectiveness of the government's rescue efforts highlighted by media scrutiny caused a public uproar. The efforts at rebuilding the cities also heaped corruption allegations on various ministers and ministries in the government. Just as the public was getting over the ill-effects of the quakes, the government managed to create a new financial crisis. A declaration by Prime Minister Ecevit that

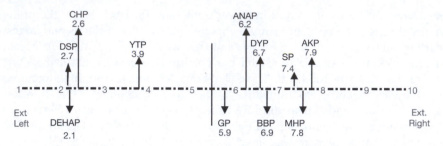

Figure 10.2 Political Parties in the eyes of voters (October 2002, May 2006)

the Turkish political system was in grave crisis, in the aftermath of a meeting of the National Security Council, over some friction between the prime minister and the president of the country, precipitated a new rush away from the Turkish lira and toward the hard currencies, on the one hand, and the stock market crash of February 2001, on the other. Nineteen of the eighty-nine banks in the country went bankrupt, and a total of 40 billion dollars, (or about 20 percent of the Turkish gross national product (GNP)) was lost almost overnight.

The tragic events of September 11, 2001 caught Turkey at a very delicate time. Jihadist extremism and violence was nothing alien or new to Turkey. Such organizations as the IBDA-C and Turkish Hizbullah had been involved in terrorizing the Turkish public since the 1990s. Sectarian violence had claimed the lives of thirty-seven Alevi poets, singers, and intellectuals in the city of Sivas in East Central Anatolia as recently as July 1993. There were calls for bloody uprisings against the lay establishment by the spokesmen of various religious associations in and out of Turkey, as well as the leader of the Welfare Party and later prime minister, Erbakan. When the US government declared the jihadist terror of Al Qaeda as a major threat to the US and declared war on terror, the Turkish government of Ecevit participated in the war efforts in Afghanistan, with almost no public reaction in Turkey in 2001.

The DSP government had decided to take a stand against the jihadists under difficult socio-economic circumstances. It looked as if the government was gearing up to meet a third challenge of jihadist terror at home and war abroad, as the drive for EU membership was leading to deeper relations with the EU. It was under these circumstances that Prime Minister Ecevit started to experience health problems. A group of ministers from his DSP decided to split and form a new party, called the New Turkey Party (YTP), and go for early elections. However, what they had not calculated was that they would neither get the kind of popular support their aging leader Ecevit had received earlier, on the one hand, nor would they be able to keep their ranks closed and not fall further apart, on the other. This gave an outstanding opportunity for the newly established AKP[22] to emerge as a party of the downtrodden, marginalized, and victimized masses, with a young and "supposedly clean" leadership.

Table 10.3 Religiosity in Turkey (2006)
a) Frequency of Prayer

Respondent's Prayer Habits	Frequency	Percent
None	177	9,6
Once a year or less	33	1,8
On Religious holidays	76	4,1
Month of Ramadan	248	13,4
Once a month	64	3,5
Every week (on Fridays)	424	23,0
More than once a week	710	38,5
Missing	114	6,2
Total	1846	100,0

b) Belief in Religion

Believes in	Frequency	Percent
God	1798	97.4
Life after Death	1716	93.0
Existence of Devil	1845	92.6
Existence of Spirit	1716	93.0
Apocalypse	1758	95.2
Heaven/Hell	1757	95.2
Sin	1766	95.7
Believes in all of the Above	**1653**	**89.5**

c) Religious Conservatism

Statement	Agrees (Frequency)	Agrees (Percent)
Restaurants should be closed during the Fast in Ramadan	1061	57,5
Would not approve daughter marry a non-Muslim	1250	67,7
Enrolling son or daughter in Imam – Hatip High School	969	52,5
Disapproves of co-educational High Schools	701	38,0
Agrees with all of the above	**469**	**25,4**

The leader of the AKP, Mr. Recep Tayyip Erdoğan, and his close associates have all come from the ranks of the National Outlook (*Milli Görüş*, MG) movement, and had served as associates of Erbakan in the capacity of mayors of metropolitan cities, ministers, deputies in the TBMM, and the like in the ranks of the RP and FP. Their political careers have all been solidly rooted in Islamic revivalism and even radical political Islamist movements in Turkey. In a field survey of political attitudes and behavior conducted in October 2002, i.e., immediately before the November 3, 2002 elections, when potential voters were asked to place the parties on a ten-point left–right scale, the AKP received an average of 7.9 points, where a full 10 indicated far right and 1 far left.

There was no other party that received a higher score from the voters to the right of the AKP (see Figure 10.2).

On November 2, 2002, the AKP not only won the plurality of the vote with 34.4 percent of the national vote, but with the CHP it emerged as one of the two parties that had enough votes to go over the 10 percent national threshold. Under the circumstances, it was able to obtain two-thirds of the seats in the TBMM and form a party government for the first time since 1991. The AKP also had enough seats in the TBMM to amend the constitution alone. With immaculate Islamic revivalist credentials, and with its front bench having long careers in radical political Islamic movements in Turkey, such a development was no less than a return to 1996 and a new confrontation between Islamic revivalists and secularists in Turkey, with the Islamic revivalists at the helm of government. Is it possible to declare the Turkish odyssey of secularism as a transient phenomenon, which has now come to the end of the rope? Or, is Turkey back to the state of politics and society at the end of the nineteenth century, under the rule of Abdulhamid II, a form of *neo-Hamidianism*, where certain religious orders participate in ruling the country, and precipitate widespread opposition, tension, and stress? Was Turkey to be embroiled in a political struggle or even a fight between the secular and Islamic revivalist camps, as had last been experienced in the 1990s?

Religion and politics in Turkey

The Turkish republic was established in the agrarian society of the 1920s, which started to rapidly change to an industrial one in the latter half of the twentieth century. In spite of the fact that two-thirds of Turkish society reside in the urban centers of the country, an overwhelming majority of the urbanites have their roots solidly established in the nomadic–agrarian culture of the villages and small towns in which they were born and raised. Such a socio-cultural mix has produced a tradition-bound majority in Turkey, which possesses a strong attachment to traditional value systems with family and religion at their core. The clash of

Table 10.4 Would you prefer to live under a theocratic state based upon "*Şeriat*"?

	1995	1996	1998	2000	2002	2003	2006
	%	%	%	%	%	%	%
Yes	19.9	26.7	19.8	21.2	16.4	15.4	9.1
No	61.8	58.1	59.9	67.9	74.1	75.6	76.5
Do not know/ no response	18.4	15.2	20.2	11.1	9.5	9.0	14.4

Sources: Ersin Kalaycioglu (2005) "The Mystery of the Türban: Participation or Revolt?" Turkish Studies 6(2), June: 233–51. The results for 2006 are from the field survey by Ersin Kalaycioglu and Ali Carkoglu on socio-political attitudes and political choices in Turkey.

the *kulturkampfs* would not have played such a central role in the democratic politics of the country if a large segment of the voters in Turkey failed to be attracted to the call of Islamic revivalism. Indeed, survey research in Turkey has recently unearthed that Turkish society is solidly religious[23] (also see Table 10.3).

Indeed, if the results of a recent survey reported in Table 10.3 are closely examined, one notices that a relatively large majority of the Turkish adult population are pious believers in Sunni Islam. It is also clear from Table 10.3 that not only do people feel religious but they also seem to practice it. In the survey, the results of which are reported in Table 10.3, we asked the respondents to rate their level of self-acclaimed religiosity on an eleven-point scale where a score of "0" indicated "not religious at all" and a score of "10" indicated "very religious." The responses indicated that 70 percent of the voting-age public in Turkey scored 6 or more on that scale, while a very similar question had elicited 86 percent of the respondents in a nationally representative sample declaring being religious in 1999.[24] The findings of the two studies indicate that religiosity has dropped from 86 to 70 percent in Turkey in recent years. However, those who reported that they were very religious in the former study accounted for only 6.1 percent in 1999, while in 2006, those who reported that they were very religious (i.e., those who scored 10 out of 10) amounted to 12 percent.

When probed further about their religious activities, such as frequenting the mosques to pray, about 31.5 percent of males and 50.6 percent of females indicated that they go to mosques more than once a week to pray in the 2006 study. So far as the Friday noon prayer ritual, which men consider the most significant public sign of being Muslim, is concerned, another 41.2 percent of the male respondents stated that they attended mosque prayers every Friday in 2006. In the Carkoglu and Toprak study of 2000, 84 percent of the respondents indicated that they attended Friday noon prayers, whereas in the survey on socio-political preferences in Turkey conducted by Carkoglu and Kalaycioglu in 2006, 61.5 percent indicated that they visited mosques more than once a day per week and attended Friday prayers (see Table 10.3). Again, a substantial fall seems to have taken place in mosque attendance between 1999 and 2006, although both figures indicate the existence of a very religious society in Turkey.

There is also evidence that religiosity does not necessarily connote any increase in protest potential, sympathy for political violence, any marked disenchantment from democratic government, and the like. There is some evidence that religiosity seems to dampen down protest potential in Turkey.[25] The political consequences of such a high level of religiosity do not seem to indicate a yearning for a *Şeriat* state and the end to the secular principles of the republic either. Indeed, when confronted with the question of whether people would like Turkey to be a *Şeriat* state, the responses not only vary but also tend to indicate a decline in any yearning for a *Şeriat* state in Turkey (see Table 10.4). In interpreting the findings reported in Figure 10.6, what we should take into account is the fact that earlier studies conducted in the 1970s

Table 10.5 Religious pressure and the "türban"

Can people properly worship in Turkey?

Yes	No	
%	%	
63,3	33,8	(2002)
68,5	27,1	(2003)
74,2	22,5	(2006)

Are religious people under pressure in Turkey? (Asked only to those who responded to the previous question as "No")

Yes	No	
%	%	
40,0	55,6	(2002)
33,7	62,5	(2003)
25,7	69,9	(2006)

Types of Pressure Mentioned

	2002	2003	2006
	%	%	%
"Türban"	67,7	74,4	68,8
Lack of freedom of worship	7,3	16,0	1,7
Praying in Governmental Offices	n.m	n.m	5,3
Status of the "İmam-Hatip High Schools"	4,6	2,6	1,7
Banning of the Kur'an Courses	n.m	n.m	3,6

Note: n.m., not mentioned.
Sources: Kalaycıoglu (2005) "The Mystery of the Türban" op. cit.: 238. The results for 2006 are from Carkoglu and Kalaycioglu's study of socio-political attitudes and political choices in Turkey.

had unearthed much less enthusiasm for a theocratic state in Turkey. Carkoglu and Toprak reported that, in the 1970s, about 7 percent of the respondents tended to lend support to the idea of a theocratic state on average.[26]

What Turkey seems to have experienced is a rightward shift of opinion in the mid-1990s, and with it emerged a yearning for theocratic rule among some voters in the country. However, public opinion seems to be receding to its former middle of the road position, and with it public demands for religious rule seem to be rapidly losing ground. We should hasten to add that, when Toprak and Carkoglu asked a battery of questions about what people meant by theocracy and *Şeriat*-based rule in Turkey, they discovered that people did not know what religious law necessitated for the status of women, inheritance, the criminal code, etc., nor did they seem to suggest that they would welcome polygamy, a smaller share of the inheritance for daughters, amputation of the hands of thieves, or re-instatement of the death penalty.[27] All the people seemed to mean by a style of rule based upon religion was vague[28] and probably no more than clean government, fairness, and justice. They seemed to be registering a desire to end what they considered to be the unjust and even immoral practices of the lay governments that fueled political corruption in the country.

In the light of the preceding findings, it is difficult to suggest that Turkey is about to become a theocratic state. However, the brandishing of religious symbols and behavior in the public space continue to influence the political agenda of the country. One such agenda item is the way women dress for work and study. A certain style of donning the headscarf, recently called *"turban,"* and covering up called *"tesettür"* in Turkish[29] have come to impose themselves on the political agenda of the country for the last three decades (see Table 10.5). Pious Sunni Muslims consider the policies of the state against those women who cover up for work and study as an infringement of the traditional image of women and the religious rights of those women, and react against those political parties and figures that support such policies. What is striking in Table 10.5 is that one out of every five voting-age Turkish citizens considers that the conditions in Turkey restrict freedom of worship, and a mere 5 percent of the population seems to consider that pious Muslims are under pressure in Turkey in 2006.

What complicates the matter further is the situation of the AKP leaders and their wives. Almost all the AKP leaders have their wives donning the *turban*, and the Turkish foreign minister, Mr. Ali Babacan, has recently, implying the *türban* issue, declared in Europe that Muslims (implying the Sunni Muslim majority) in Turkey are under pressure.[30] The courts have systematically decided that donning the *türban* constitutes an act of violation of the secular principles of the constitution, which conservative voters and political elites alike have declared to be unjust and in contradiction to their religious beliefs and rights. However, the Turkish Constitutional Court, other High Courts, and the European Court of Human Rights (ECHR) have systematically decided that donning the *türban* does not constitute a religious right.

The former speaker of the TBMM (2002–2007), who is a prominent member of the AKP, had suggested that the definition of *laïcité* in Turkey should be reconsidered.[31] Prime Minister Erdogan agreed with the speaker in public, and when criticisms mounted against the AKP on this issue, Erdogan backtracked, although the more ideological speaker, Mr. Arinc, continued to argue that the constitution does not have a definition of *laïcité*, and a definition should be inserted into its text. The overall aim seems to be to adopt such a definition of *laïcité* that would make the donning of the *türban* and covering up (*tesettür*) legal, and render the previous court decisions null and void. Such a move would lead to serious reactions from the positivist–secular camp and risks the precipitation of a severe conflict, rather than merely an amendment of the constitution, which would lead to the end of laicist policies as Turkey has known them since 1924.

In the meantime, Turkey held a general election on July 22, 2007, and the new Turkish Grand National Assembly (TGNA) elected the former prime minister and the Minister of Foreign Affairs, Mr. Abdullah Gül, as the new president of the country. Mrs. Gül not only wears the *türban*, but she has also sued the Republic of Turkey in the ECHR for not recognizing her religious rights to enroll in college with her *türban*, and thus violating her right to higher education as well.[32] Under the circumstances, the symbolism of the clash between the *kulturkampfs* has just been elevated to the level of the office of the president, and the AKP leadership seems to experience more pressure to do something about the *türban* issue.

In the aftermath of the July 22, 2007 elections during a tour of European states, in Spain, Prime Minister Erdogan suggested that even if the *türban* were a political symbol, no political symbol could be banned in university campuses. Soon after this comment, the opposition MHP tabled a motion to amend Articles 10 and 42 of the 1982 Constitution and render discrimination in the university campuses on the basis of students' attire unconstitutional. It was presumed that such a change in the 1982 Constitution would make it possible for the *turban*-wearing students to participate in all activities in university campuses unhindered. The amendment was adopted by the National Assembly by 440 deputies (out of 550), but vehemently resisted by the main opposition party CHP, which appealed the amendments with the constitutional court. In a controversial milestone decision, the court declared the amendments unconstitutional and decided that they breached Article 2 (principles of the republic including secularism) of the constitution. The moves of the right-wing political parties to provide more freedom for the *turban*-wearing university students was once more frustrated by the judiciary.

In the meantime, the public prosecutor also drew up an indictment to request a political ban of the AKP and its seventy-one members from the constitutional court on the grounds that it had begun to act as a focal point for anti-secular activities in the country, which is a violation of the constitution and the Political Parties Act. The court decided that the AKP had indeed become a focal point of anti-laicist activities in contravention of the constitution and the Political Parties Act, although did not go far enough in its decision to ban the AKP from politics. The constitutional court decided to impose a financial sanction upon the party, and withhold half of the financial aid the AKP is set to receive from the current year's state budget. The AKP seemed to be saved from a ban, yet it has received a severe warning from the constitutional court, which means that, if it were to continue its cultural policies unhindered, it is only a matter of time before it is closed down for good by the constitutional court. It seems as if the valence (religious) issue of the *türban* seems to be emerging again to threaten the very existence of the governing conservative Islamist AKP in Turkey.

However, there are still two options that may be available for the AKP and other right-wing parties that try to challenge the lay political regime (constitution) of the country. Now that Mr. Gül has become the president of the country and enjoys the power to appoint new and preferably pious Sunni or conservative judges to the bench of the constitutional court, his new appointments to the bench could act to strike down the earlier decisions of

Table 10.6 Problems facing Turkey

What is the most important problem facing Turkey?

		Years Surveys Were Conducted			
		(2002) %	*(2003) %*	*(2003) %*	*(2006)%*
1	Inflation	20,9	18,3	19,3	9,6
2	Unemployment	29,4	29,8	30,7	29,6
3	Economic Instability	33,7	30,1	30,6	8,4
4	Corruption / Bribery	1,8	1,2	1,1	2,8
5	Health / Social Welfare	0,8	0,6	0,2	3,9
6	Education	2,0	1,6	2,6	8,7
7	Terror / Security	–	–	–	14,9
8	Political Instability	6,0	1,8	1,6	3,2
9	Iraq / War	–	14,1	9,2	–
10	Türban	0,4	0,4	0,4	–
11	Crime	–	–	–	2,4
	Sample Size (n)	(2028)	(954)	(1047)	(1846)

Sources: Ersin Kalaycioglu (2005) "The Mystery of the Türban: Participation or Revolt?" Turkish Studies 6(2), June: 238. The 2006 results are from the Carkoglu and Kalaycioglu's study of socio-political attitudes and political choices in Turkey.

the High Courts on the *türban*. Alternatively, public bureaucracy, and the autonomous institutions of the state, such as the university administrations, may be pressured to turn a blind eye to the women in *türban* and *tesettür* at a later time when the Islamist revivalists regain enough self-confidence. Room may then be made for the *turban*-wearing women to enroll in higher educational programs through the services of the new conservative administration of the Higher Educational Council and the new conservative university rectors, who have been appointed by President Gül. However, no one knows whether such steps will precipitate any new tensions and conflict in the Turkish political system, or simply usher in a new round of confrontations between the positivist–secular and Islamic revivalist *kulturkampfs* in the country.

It is small wonder then that the presidential elections in the Grand National Assembly (TBMM) became very tense and conflict ridden in 2007 and precipitated a major confrontation between the two *kulturkampfs*. Large crowds turned out to protest the AKP's insistence on Gül's name as their candidate for the presidency. The military also declared that his past record indicated that Gül would be partisan and anti-laicist, and thus not fit for the job. The opposition also argued that the AKP did not have the votes to elect Gül as president in the TBMM. The main opposition party, the CHP, also appealed to the constitutional court, and the court decided that, in the first two rounds of balloting in the presidential election in the TGNA, there should be two-thirds of the deputies (367/550) present, which the AKP could not muster. Again, the controversial view of the opposition on the issue was upheld by the constitutional court.

Interestingly enough, the AKP leadership, instead of seeking compromise as to who the next president should be, preferred to confront the *laïque* (*laik*) pressure groups and the parliamentary opposition in Turkey, but tabled new constitutional amendments. These amendments proposed to submit Gül's election to popular vote instead. Popularly elected, Gül would serve for five years but could be re-elected for an additional term. The previous president, Sezer, referred this bill to a popular referendum, which took place on October 21, 2007, and about 70 percent of the valid votes cast were in support of the idea of election of the president by popular vote. However, in the meantime, Abdullah Gül had been elected to the National Assembly with the support of the MHP deputies, for a non-renewable single term of seven years. It seems as if the amended version of the constitution will come into effect after his tenure. In the meantime, the *türban* as the symbol of Sunni Islamic revivalism seems to continue to raise emotions and help to draw battle lines between the positivist–secular and Islamic revivalist *kulturkampfs* in Turkey.

If we continue to examine Table 10.5, we observe that those who consider the policies of the state vis-à-vis the "*türban*" as "pressure on the pious Muslims by the secular state" dropped steadily from 27.1 percent of the voters in 2003 to 17.7 percent in 2006. *Türban* seemed to become a less popular issue before the confrontations in 2007 flared up between the government and the secular opposition. Nevertheless, the prominent members of the AKP leadership are also part of that minority who consider *türban* as a form of pressure upon pious voters who support them. At the same time, there seems to be some evidence that the majority of voters believe that those donning the "*türban*" ought to be permitted to work as state employees.[33] In the eyes of the majority, "*türban* and *tesettür*" seem to constitute a matter of "religious liberty," but not a stealth attack on the laicist principles of the republic. The status of the graduates of the IHLs similarly attracts increasingly less attention in Turkey. The findings presented in Table 10.5 indicate that only 0.4 percent of the voting-age population mentioned the status of the IHL students as a problem. Instead, 3.6 percent seem to consider the status of the Qur'an instruction courses, where teenagers are instructed in Sunni Islam, as a greater problem than the status of the IHLs.

Finally, when we examine the perceptions of the problems facing Turkey in the eyes of the voting-age population, it becomes apparent that religious issues are of no primary concern, except for a very marginal minority of the population in Turkey (see Table 10.6). "*Türban*" was mentioned by six respondents, a mere 0.003 percent of the sample, as the most important issue facing the country, and another two respondents also mentioned "lack of religious freedom" as the most important problem for the country in our 2006 survey. About half the voting-age population systematically argues that the most important problem facing the country is of an economic nature. Turkish voters seem to believe that, among the economic problems facing the country, unemployment is the most pressing single issue. Concerns over security, terror, and political instability emerge as the second most important issue in the eyes of Turkish voters. Finally, such social welfare issues as education and health care emerge as a third issue most mentioned by Turkish voters in our surveys since the early 2000s (see Table 10.6).

However, these findings do not mean that either *türban–tesettür* or the IHLs and education are minor issues or can be safely ignored by the Turkish political elite. On the contrary, these issues will continue to occupy a major part of the political agenda for the foreseeable future. As valence issues, they are difficult to settle, for there seems to be no middle ground between those who support and those who oppose such valence issues. Any step taken to liberalize the *türban* and the IHLs will ignite strong reactions and touch sensitive nerves in Turkish society, and is most likely to violate earlier court decisions as well. They are symbols of religiosity,[34] which define the role of religion in Turkish education and socio-political life, thus deeply influencing the political interface between the major parties of the positivist–secular and the Islamic revivalist *kulturkampfs*. No electoral victory will be enough to halt the positivists or the revivalists from promoting their claims. Under the circumstances, it is not realistic to assume that the role of religion will drop out of the political, social, and economic agendas of Turkey in the foreseeable future. However, the overarching concerns of the Turkish voters seem to be quite secular and even mundane, pertaining to the worries of those who live in a rapidly industrializing, urbanizing society, which creates economic and political instabilities, and social welfare concerns over health care and education for the mass public.

Secularism and democracy: at risk or setting roots?

The Islamic revival has been a major development in Turkish society and politics since the closing phases of the Cold War. The events that led to the downfall of the Soviet Union, which rendered socialism and social democracy as obsolete or irrelevant ideologies in Turkey, and the previous and successful liquidation of the left by the military coup of 1980 coincided to create a vacuum in the urban sprawl of the big cities. Three major ideological currents and their organizations began to fill that vacuum, and they were the Islamic revivalists, ethnic Turkish nationalists, and ethnic Kurdish nationalists. Islamic revivalists had the upper hand in this struggle for the hearts, support, and votes of the lumpenproletariat, lower classes, and lower middle classes among the rural migrants in the urban centers, their rural relatives, and neighbors. Those who found themselves squeezed between the Kurdish and Turkish nationalists seemed to have turned to the non-nationalist call of the Islamic revivalists. Especially, the Kurds who fled the fight between the Maoist terrorists of the PKK and the Turkish security forces have been traditional minded, pious Muslims, who considered the call of the Islamic revivalists as a call of peace and solidarity with which they felt considerable affinity. With the socialists out of the picture, they had no other non-nationalist position to orient themselves with.

The Islamic revivalists also discovered that, with the support of the estab-lishment (which had been lavishly provided to them between 1973 and 1991), and using the services provided by the legal infrastructure of local and national government, they can accomplish a lot. Hence, they organized the fight for the support of voters at the polls. Their networks, extremely deep pockets, dedicated campaign workers, and strong communal ties provided them with an advantage over the newly established center, left, and right parties and their incoherent, individualistic, and amateurish organizations. As the parties of the moderate left and right failed to deliver what they promised at the polls (such as a curb on consumer price inflation, redistribution of national income, and fight against corruption), the voters started to shift their choices to the farther right. Increasing religiosity of the masses, which had even been encouraged by the military government of the 1980s and successfully continued by the ANAP governments, also contributed to this sharp shift to a more conservative and religious right-wing position of the voters.

It was with the AKP government that economic liberalism in its most pristine form of *laissez-faire* liberalism resurfaced as a pillar of the policies followed by that otherwise socially and even religiously conservative political party, just as ANAP had done earlier. The AKP governments began to draw up a picture of an economically liberal, socially conservative and traditional, and politically reformist party in action.[35] The AKP governments engaged in one of the most comprehensive privatization attempts in the country, and ministers of finance and state in charge of the economy system-atically argued that the unhindered rule of the market constituted the goal of their economic policies. However, such a policy created unevenness in the distribution of income, poverty, and unemployment. The AKP's approach to these issues reverted back to traditional–conservative styles and methods of handouts (alms giving) to the poor in the form of soup kitchens (*aşevi*), temporary locations (popularly known as Ramadan tents) functioning as restaurants, staple food distribution to potential voters, and increasingly affordable health care provision. In the meantime, the AKP amended the constitution in an effort to accommodate and acculturate Turkey to the Copenhagen criteria of the European Union. Such efforts at democratization also enabled the AKP to diminish the role of the military establishment in civilian politics.

It looked as if the most successful Islamic revivalist politicians in Turkey were able to establish political organizations that could appeal to large swaths of the traditional-minded majority in Turkey. The ANAP and AKP are the most successful examples of such organizations in recent times. Both parties turned into mass or even catch-all parties eventually, which is what AKP had become as of July 22, 2007. In the July 22, 2007 elections, the AKP fielded candidates from all types of backgrounds, including those formerly from the CHP front bench, agnostics, atheists, secular feminists, and the like, and obtained 47 percent of the valid vote. As the AKP began to evolve into a conservative mass party, the Islamic revivalists have continued to be the most important faction, in fact the faction in power within that political party. Under the circumstances, the revivalist radicalism seems to be balanced and checked by the other factions within the political party organization. However, under conditions of political and economic crisis, such a structure tends to fall apart, as the ANAP experienced in the 1990s.[36] It is too early yet to tell whether the AKP can find a way out of the challenges of such a crisis in the future.

The ideologically pristine Islamic revivalism has failed to attract much popular support, or stay in power without causing severe stress, friction, and conflict in government. The National Salvation (MSP), Welfare (RP), and Virtue (FP) Parties have fallen prey to their ideologically pure organizations, which failed to produce stable government. They failed to sustain the support of the masses at the polls and prove their credentials as democratic and secular organizations in the courts. All of them have been banned from political activity. The current revivalist Felicity Party (SP) has been eclipsed by the success of the AKP. The irony is that the front benches of both the SP and the AKP had functioned together in the above-mentioned MSP, RP, and FP. The younger members of these former parties seemed to have decided to change track, dilute their ideology, and mix it with liberal, economic, reformist politics, and EU-oriented foreign policy, which the pristine Islamic revivalists had systematically shunned in the past. Accordingly, the voters have failed to support the SP at the polls, as they received about 2 percent of the vote in both the 2002 and the 2007 general elections.

What is interesting to note is that what differentiates the AKP from the SP has been the success of the liberal economic policies of the former, over the vague economic policy suggestions of the latter. The support for the AKP at the polls comes from its image as a right-wing party, but among the right-wing political parties, it is the economic policy and its success that seem to matter for the voters who elected the AKP over the SP, MHP, and other political parties of the right and right of center in Turkey.[37] It is also interesting to note that the AKP is not perceived as a political party that threatens political stability in the country but, on the contrary, as a party that promoted economic and political stability. The business community in Turkey seems to be pleased not only with the market-oriented liberal economic policies of the AKP, but also with the stability its party government has been able to provide Turkey. One concept that appeared quite frequently in the campaign of the AKP was "stability." As opposed to the former Islamic revivalist parties, the AKP not only watered down its ideological orientation, but also drew up an image of a political party that does not threaten the stability of Turkish politics and economy, which in turn produces high rates of economic growth and attracts unprecedented amounts of foreign direct investment to the country. Thus, the perception of political and economic stability seems to contribute to the success of the AKP at the polls, and thus stability becomes a critical factor in the governmental performance of the traditional–conservative political party of the AKP.

Conclusion

Turkish democracy has been in effect since 1945. Out of the sixteen national elections Turkey has so far experienced, the 1946, 1961, and 1983 elections were either not free or not fair. Out of the remaining thirteen elections, the parties of the periphery (*taşra*), which partly or wholly represented the traditionalist and Islamic revivalist *kulturkampf*, won ten. Of the remaining three general elections, those in 1973 and 1977 resulted in CHP victories and the 1999 general elections yielded a DSP plurality of votes and seats in the TBMM. In the 1990s, the parties of the positivist–secularist *kulturkampf* in Turkey participated in the coalition governments led by either DYP or ANAP, which are parties of the periphery, although they represented conservative–traditional masses, rather than political Islam per se. Hence the positivist–secular parties were relegated to the position of constituting the main opposition in the country, and occasionally functioned as partners in coalition governments.

The development of democracy in Turkey in the aftermath of World War II seems to have paved the way for a dramatic resurfacing of the former political interface of the positivist–secular vs. the Islamic revivalist *kulturkampfs*. The latter made an eventual comeback with a vengeance. In this transition back to what seemed like a modern form of a late Ottoman political setting, the bulwark of laicism, the CHP seems also to have played a critical role. It was none other than the CHP government of the late 1940s that veered away from the earlier laicist policies, and relaxed certain practices such as legalizing visits to the tombs of Muslim dignitaries in the country.[38] The CHP elite of the 1970s played a critical role in legitimizing the most important party of political Islam, the MSP, by inviting them into a coalition in 1973! The positivist–secular camp in Turkey never enjoyed the support of the majority of the voters. Positivist–secular values are confined to the graduates of secular high schools and universities, who also enjoy professional careers. However, the average Turkish voter only has about six years of education, and the bulk of the voting-age population consists of peasants, housewives, and lower middle classes in Turkey. Such a voter profile suggests that an overwhelming majority of the voters are well embedded in the traditional, conservative periphery of the country. Thus, the positivist–secular parties have a great disadvantage to overcome in electoral contests.

The CHP managed to surmount such a difficulty in the 1970s when it successfully portrayed an image of a left-wing party of the downtrodden. Such propaganda was able to confuse the tradition-bound peasants and lower classes into supporting the CHP. However, the magic of those campaigns failed to last into the 2000s. It is a matter of fact that positivist–secular parties in Turkish politics have so far failed to live up to their promises in government. They projected an image, in local as well as national politics, of being incapable of governance and being callous to the demands of the majority of voters. Unless they could change their performance and image in the eyes of the voters and particularly those who place themselves at the center of the left–right spectrum (see Figure 10.1), there will be little chance for the parties of the positivist–secular camp to win elections in the foreseeable future.

The pristine form of laicism of the 1920s no longer exists in Turkey. The memories of the War of Liberation faded, and the Turkish socio-political reality and the international system in which it is embedded have changed dramatically since then. In the meantime, the Turkish political system failed to provide secular, science education to its masses and also enough proper jobs for those who were able to receive secular education. The disappointed sought alternative routes. Alternatively, religious networks emerged with deep pockets to provide most of those who joined their well-oiled organizations with jobs, credit, middle-class lifestyles, and fraternity, which contributed to the emergence of possibilities of upward social mobility through an alternative image of good society for those who were ready to trek the road of the religious orders (*tarikat*).

The laws and the decisions of the High Courts do not permit any party to promote Şeriat rule in Turkey. The constitutional court has banned both the Welfare and Virtue parties from politics in recent years on those very grounds. The *tarikat* organizations are also still illegal. Religious instruction can only be legally provided through institutions approved and controlled by the Ministry of National Education. Mosques in the country are still under the operation of the Directorate of Religious Affairs, and so are their personnel. IHLs and the Qur'an courses are both under the legal authority of the Ministry of National Education.[39] The current debate focuses more on the substance of the curriculum of such schools, the socialization practices of those who enroll at such institutions, and their allegiance to republican principles.

The recent successful ascent of the AKP in Turkish politics also indicates that a political party led by politicians from a background of political Islamism can successfully come to power on a liberal economic, socio-culturally conservative, and politically reformist platform. The AKP was able to sideline the thorny cultural and religious issues as well as those politicians from among its own ranks who voiced such issues, and focus on liberal market capitalism and political reforms for a while. The AKP seems to have acted with the hindsight of the experiences of the MSP, RP, and FP that confrontation with the secularist pressure groups in Turkey destabilizes the political system, contributes to the cooling of the voters, and increases the activism of the secularists and the military. Such a confrontation shortens the tenure of right-wing governments and even the life expectation of the political parties that project such an ideological image. The AKP has had a stability-conscious posture from the very beginning of its ascent to power in 2002 until 2007. It seems to place a high value on staying in power in a democratic context, rather than following an ideological program or religious mission into government. From 2002 to 2007, it had managed to convert itself into a mass or even a catch-all political party in the eyes of the right of center voters in Turkey.

However, since the presidential elections of 2007, the AKP seemed to launch a more ideological and confrontational approach toward the positivist–secular *kulturkampf*, and Turkey has re-entered a period of political tension, stress, and heightened conflict. The change of track for the AKP is hard to explain, for its previous strategy of moderation, pragmatism, and good governance had provided the AKP with increasing popular support at the polls. The post-2007 ideological, majoritarian, and confrontational style of the AKP in Turkish politics has not only undermined the political stability of the country, but also risked the very political existence of the AKP. The post-2007 style of conducting business by the AKP proves once more that the ideological style of governance of right-wing parties, which incorporate Islamic revivalist values, risks confrontation with the positivist–secular opposition, loads the Turkish political system overwhelmingly, and renders management of the democratic affairs of the country difficult, if not impossible.

The transformation of the Turkish socio-economic structure from an agrarian to an industrial society is still continuing with full force. In the long run, it is the forces of industrialization that will continue to fuel secularization in Turkish society. Currently, as a society, about two-thirds of its members declare themselves to be religious, and about one-third to half of the adult population declare that they practice religion regularly and, as a polity that is defined as *laïque* (*laik*) in Turkey will continue to experience the tensions and stresses of the mismatch between its political–legal system and its tradition- and custom-based society operating in part under the weight of Sunni Muslim values and orientations. Such conflict and tension will continue to fuel the social and political debate over the role of Sunni and Alevi Islam in modern, industrial, urban society, and the secular legal system of the polity. Islamic brotherhoods still continue to provide solidarity and organizational backbone to political organizations and parties. Overt demonstrations of religiosity, whether it is the donning of the *türban*, or religious garbs of various sorts, or pouring from the mosques on to the streets of major cities to pray every noon on Fridays, brandishing green flags with various verses from the Holy Qur'an written on them during rallies, or demonstrations after the Friday noon prayers, and the like continue to occur and foster tension, conflict, stress, and even physical violence in the country. Such public displays, when promoted or championed by political leaders and their parties, continue to be interpreted as violations of the laicist principles of the republic by the High Courts of the land. Still at issue are the depth, breadth, and effectiveness of secular and science education and the socialization of youth in Turkey, on the one hand, and providing professional jobs and middle-class lifestyles to those who have access to secular education, on the other. The socio-economic transformation of the country, the pace of such socio-economic change, the absorption capacity of the new labor by the Turkish economy, when combined, breed a mismatch in expectations and satisfaction of the youth, who often get frustrated with the current socio-economic political structure and search for alternative and even radical solutions to their frustrations.

In conclusion, religious and ethnic social and political organizations have become most successful in attracting the frustrated youth and the burgeoning middle classes to join their ranks in Turkey. Under the circumstances, Islamic revivalist parties and factions within right-wing parties still possess a good chance of becoming and staying in government, so long as they are inclined to follow practices of good governance, and refrain from developing ideological and confrontational postures threatening and conflicting with the positivist–secular forces of the country. It seems unwarranted to assume that one side of that cultural rift that defines the relations of the two *kulturkampfs* in Turkey will wither away any time soon. The cultural differences that deeply divide the society and polity will survive as the basis of political socialization and organization for the foreseeable future. Consequently, Turkish society, politics, media, and press will continue to debate various valence issues deeply rooted in the secular vs. Islamic revivalist values for many years to come. An occasional increase in religiosity and secularism need not be taken as the final victory of one *kulturkampf* over the other. It is the changes in the international relations of Turkey and the world, the domestic developments, economic and even natural disasters that will continue to foster one *kulturkampf* over the other for a while to come. However, in the longer run, it will be industrialization and the international relations of Turkey that will determine how secular/religious the country will become. It seems as if secular orientations and behavior will have strong inputs from industrialization in the country and the global economic relations of the burgeoning middle classes in Turkey. Although Turkey currently looks and feels like a country under the spell of Sunni religiosity, the days of secularism are far from being numbered. What we should expect to see is more of the same tug-of-war between the political forces associated with the secular and the revivalist *kulturkampfs* in the National Assembly, High Courts, university campuses, media, press, and the like in the near future.

Notes

* The author wishes to thank Isik and Sabanci Universities and the Open Society Institute for the financial support they provided for the 2006 national field survey.

1 The cult of Ali is a belief system affiliated with the Shi'ite sect of Islam, although the Turkish Alevi sect has been endogenous to Anatolia (Asia Minor) and enjoys myriad cultural products and characteristics peculiar to its homeland. For more on the Alevi sect, see Paul J. White and Joost Jongerden, eds (2003) *Turkey's Alevi Enigma: A Comprehensive Overview*. Leiden: E.J. Brill: passim.

2 Laicism meant " ... not just separation of the state from the institutions of Islam but also the liberation of the individual mind from the restraints imposed by the traditional Islamic concepts and practices, and modernization of all aspects of state and society that had been molded by Islamic traditions and ways" (Stanford J. Shaw and Ezel Kural Shaw (1977) *History of the Ottoman Empire and Modern Turkey: Volume II: Reform, Revolution, and Republic, The Rise of Modern Turkey 1808–1975*. Cambridge: Cambridge University Press: 384). Thus, it involved not only the control and regulation of the teachings and deeds of the clergy through an agency of the state, but also the rationalization of education, where science reigned supreme. The laicist reforms of the republic aimed at undermining the grip of the religious brotherhoods (*tarikat*), superstition, and folklore, which were incorporated

into the practice of Islam in the late Ottoman period, and had stifled the development of science and technology in the Ottoman Empire. On this point, see also Metin Heper (1986) "Atatürk'te Devlet Düşüncesi" in *Çağdaş Düşünce'nin Işığında ATATÜRK*. Istanbul: Dr. Nejat F. Eczacıbaşı Vakfı: 272–73. This formulation of laicism in Turkey is an amalgam of both the French political understanding of separation of state and church, known as the *laïcité*, and the emancipation of the society from a sense of the sacred without necessarily denying it, which is known as secularism (see Olivier Roy (2007) *Secularism Confronts Islam*, trans. by George Holoch, New York: Columbia University Press: 13–35 for an examination and analysis of the French, Turkish, and other examples of *laïcité* and secularization).

3 The French formulation of the separation of church and state was adopted only by 1905, and the Roman Catholic church came to terms with the French state only by 1924 (Olivier Roy, *Secularism Confronts Islam*, op. cit.: 18). It was very contemporary for the Turkish Republic of 1923 to observe, examine, and take the French *laïcité* as the "modern" practice of the civilized world as soon as the government abolished the Caliphate in March 1924. However, we should be cognizant of the fact that French *laïcité* emerged as a political principle and measure against the Roman Catholic church, its related orders and brotherhoods associated with it, while the Turkish *laiklik* emerged as a political principle and practice to cope with the Caliphate and Ottoman Monarchy and all those institutions, orders, and brotherhoods associated with it, which were presumed to act in treason in collusion with the forces of occupation to liquidate the nationalist resistance of the War of Liberation. It was the nationalist resistance who eventually won the War of Liberation, thus liquidated the Ottoman Empire, Caliphate, the religious institution of that empire and all the institutional and civic associations associated with them. The existential struggle and, later on, the objective of consolidation of power of the nationalist government of Turkey led to the liquidation of the religious establishment of the *ancien regime* and a ban imposed on all forms of its civil institutions, which has never taken place in France. The Turkish *laiklik* may indeed be considered as a Cesaropapist form of *laïcité* in the 1920s, which evolved into a form of Gallic practice of *laïcité* by the 1940s and beyond. (For the conceptualization of different forms and practices of *laïcité* in France, see Olivier Roy, *Secularism Confronts Islam*, op. cit.: 13–35.) Finally, we should add that Turkish *laiklik* was erected to deal with the challenges of the Hanefi/Sunni sect of Islam in Turkey, and its practice through the Ottoman administrations and the Caliphate, which was also embodied by the Ottoman Sultan. However, the other major sect of the Alevi in Turkey was totally ignored by the republican governments, for they constituted no threat to the republican political system. By default, the Alevis seemed to experience a more liberal form of *laiklik* in the hands of the same Turkish state. Ironically, some of the leaders of the Alevi community have now begun to demand representation in the regulatory religious agency (*Diyanet İşleri Başkanlığı*) of the state, come under the same regulatory practices as the Sunni communities of the country, and receive a certain stipend from the state budget in return as well. These developments clearly indicate that *laiklik* in Turkey takes different shapes in the relations of the state with different sects, which is so similar to the French example, and the separation of church and state also has an economic dimension, which is no less important than its political dimension.

4 Ersin Kalaycioglu (2005) *Turkish Dynamics: A Bridge Across Troubled Lands*. New York: Palgrave Macmillan: 48–50, 60.

5 The Republican People's Party (CHP) had been established shortly before the declaration of the republic in 1923. The CHP, established and led by none other than the hero of the War of Liberation, Mustafa Kemal Atatürk, functioned as the single party of the republic between 1923 and 1945. It emerged as the "party that established the republic" and has been closely associated with the state (center) and

anti-Ottoman heritage of the republic. The CHP functioned as the most important mobilizing political institution of the republic that promoted the values and standards of the Cultural Revolution of 1924–1937, and also identified with the positivist–secular *kulturkampf* of the country. The CHP did its best to penetrate the periphery of Turkish society, and provided various opportunities to socialize the masses into the newly established, republican, and national identity. Such an image undermined its popular appeal in the democratic era after 1945, although its special relationship with the center persisted until 1982, when the military junta banned all parties, including the CHP. It was re-established in 1995, and now functions as the second largest party group in the Turkish Grand National Assembly (TBMM).

6 For a more extensive analysis of the transition to multiparty politics at the end of World War II, see M. Asım Karaömerlioğlu (2006) "Turkey's Return to Multiparty Politics: A Social Interpretation," *Eastern European Quarterly* 40(1), Spring: 89–107.

7 Turkish sovereignty and independence had been supported by the Soviet Union as a nationalist struggle against the capitalist imperialist West. The relations between Turkey and the Soviet Union continued to be amicable in the interwar period. A friendship and non-aggression treaty had been signed between the two countries in 1921, and it was in effect until 1946.

8 Selim Deringil (1989) *The Turkish Foreign Policy during the Second World War: an Active Neutrality*. New York, New Rochelle, Melbourne, Sydney: Cambridge University Press: 180; William Hale (2000) *Turkish Foreign Policy: 1774–2000*. London, Portland, OR: Frank Cass: 112–14.

9 Kalaycioglu, *Turkish Dynamics*, op. cit.: 71–73.

10 J. Hinderink and Mübeccel Kıray (1970) *Social Stratification as an Obstacle to Development: A Study of Four Turkish Villages*. New York, London, Washington: Praeger.

11 See David Shankland (1999) *Islam and Society in Turkey*. Huntingdon, UK: The Eothen Press: 87–109 for a comprehensive account of Erbakan and political Islam's rise in Turkish politics. On the same topic, for a more comprehensive analysis, see also Binnaz Toprak (1981) *Islam and Political Development in Turkey*. Leiden, New York: E. J. Brill: passim; Ali Yaşar Sarıbay (1985) *Türkiye'de Modernleşme Din ve Parti Politikası "MSP Örnek Olayı."* Istanbul: Alan Yayıncılık: passim.

12 Kenan Evren (1990) *Kenan Evren'in Anıları 1*. Istanbul: Milliyet Yayınları: 280–555. See also Binnaz Toprak (2005) "Islam and Democracy in Turkey," *Turkish Studies* 6(2), June: 179.

13 Kenan Evren (1990) *Kenan Evren'in Anıları 3*. Istanbul: Milliyet Yayınları: 274–361; Erik J. Zürcher (2004) *Turkey: A Modern History*, 3rd edn. London, New York: I.B. Tauris: 288–90.

14 Mr. Turgut Ozal had earlier functioned as the Director of the State Planning Organization (DPT) and also as the undersecretary of the prime minister under Prime Minister Demirel right before the coup of 1980. However, Ozal had also run on the political Islamist MSP ticket in the 1977 elections, but could not be elected. He had his political career and roots in the National Outlook (*Milli Görüş*) movement of Erbakan. Ozal had impeccable credentials as a political figure with solid roots in political Islam. However, the military junta of 1980–83 had still signed him on as the "Minister of State in charge of the Economy" between 1980 and 1983, for he had also earned a reputation as a technocrat and was credited with the economic recovery of the country in the early 1980s.

15 Both Demirel and Ecevit were banned from all political activity by the junta for a period of ten years. They commissioned trusted aides, and in the case of Ecevit, his wife, Mrs. Rahşan Ecevit, to establish their new political parties in their absence. However, all those who mattered were fully cognizant of the fact that DYP stood

for "*Demirel'in Yeni Partisi*" (The New Party of Demirel), and the DSP was the new party of Ecevit. Both were pardoned after a referendum on re-establishing the political rights of the former politicians in 1986 and began to take part in the spotlight of politics since then.

16 For a review of fragmentation and volatility in the Turkish party system, see Ergun Özbudun (2000) *Contemporary Turkish Politics: Challenges to Democratic Consolidation*. Boulder, London: Lynne Rienner: 73–103.

17 The field survey of socio-political attitudes and political choices was conducted during late March, April, and early May 2006 in twenty-three out of eighty-one provinces in Turkey. Face-to-face interviews were conducted with 1,846 respondents aged 18 years and over. The sample of respondents was determined through a multistage stratified cluster sampling technique, which provided equal probability of selection per voting-age (18 years and older) citizen in Turkey. The primary sampling units were the regions of Turkey, which were grouped according to their population sizes into equal-sized strata of regions, which in turn were divided into various strata of subdistricts (*ilçe*) according to population size. From each stratum, subdistricts were selected according to their proportion to population residing in them (PPS). Of the 200 subdistricts selected, the Turkish Statistics Institute (TUİK) was requested to randomly select census tracks according to PPS, and then select households randomly per census track again according to PPS. The interviewers were then requested to randomly select a respondent per household. At the end of the sampling procedure, a total randomly selected nationally representative sample of 1,846 respondents participated in our study. Our margin of error for the sample was ±2.2 percent with 95 percent level of confidence.

18 Ustun Erguder (1980–81) "Changing Patterns of Electoral Behavior in Turkey," *Boğaziçi University Journal* 8–9: 45–81; Ersin Kalaycioglu (1994) "Elections and Party Preferences in Turkey: Changes and Continuities in the 1990s," *Comparative Political Studies* 27(3), October: 402–24; Ersin Kalaycioglu (1999) "The Shaping of Party Preferences in Turkey: Coping with the Post-Cold War Era," *New Perspectives on Turkey* 20, Spring: 47–76; Yilmaz Esmer (2002) "At the Ballot Box: Determinants of Voting Behavior," in Sabri Sayari and Yilmaz Esmer, eds, *Politics, Parties, and Elections in Turkey*. Boulder, London: Lynne Rienner: 91–114; Ayşe Gunes-Ayata and Sencer Ayata (2002) " Ethnic and Religious Bases of Voting" in Sabri Sayari and Yilmaz Esmer, eds, op. cit.: 137–55; Ali Carkogu (2005) "Political Preferences of the Turkish Electorate: Reflections of an Alevi–Sunni Cleavage," *Turkish Studies* 6(2), June: 273–92.

19 The ideology of the AKP has created considerable debate among students of Turkish politics. It has been described as Islamist, political Islamist, post-Islamist, and the like. For an analysis of the ideological stance of the AKP in Turkish politics, see Ahmet Yildiz (2008) "Problematizing the Intellectual and Political Vestiges" in Umit Cizre, ed., *Secular and Islamic Politics in Turkey: The Making of the Justice and Development Party*. London and New York: Routledge: 41–61.

20 Jenny B. White (2003) *Islamist Mobilization in Turkey: A Study in Vernacular Politics*. Seattle and London: University of Washington Press argues that " … the left had fallen victim to a double knockout punch: the post coup military crackdown and the global decline of socialism." (p. 123).

21 For a more extensive analysis of the "Susurluk Accident," see Ersin Kalaycioglu, *Turkish Dynamics*, op. cit.: 156–59.

22 The AKP emerged out of the Virtue Party (FP), which had been the party of the political Islamist, National Outlook (*Milli Görüş*) movement. The court decided that the FP had systematically breached the laicist principles of the Turkish republic and violated those articles of the constitution that pertained to laicism. Almost instantly, its octogenarian front bench and the youthful back bench split into two parties. The younger members of the FP, who had already started to act

as a faction within the FP, vied for power but lost the intra-party elections; they had already been popularly referred to as the "novelists" (*yenilikçiler*) and broke ranks with the old guard of the FP. Armed with youth and immaculate Islamist credentials, the young Turks of the FP swiftly established the AKP on August 14, 2001. However, they did not seek to establish a new doctrinaire party and invited all those who had split from all other parties and were ready to accept this new party to join their ranks. Such a move seemed to have toned down their commitment to political Islam, and enabled them to adopt a conservative (read Sunni Muslim), de-radicalized, democratic, pro-market stance on the political issues of the day.

23 Ali Carkoglu ve Binnaz Toprak (2000) *Türkiye'de Din, Toplum ve Siyaset*. Istanbul: TESEV Publications: 41–58.

24 Ali Carkoglu ve Binnaz Toprak, *Türkiye'de Din, Toplum ve Siyaset*, op. cit.: 42. *The Economist* reported that, in another survey conducted among the "German" Turks, 85 percent said they were "rather" or "strictly religious" ("Special Report: Islam, America and Europe," June 24, 2006: 30). It seems as if the Turks living in Germany are more religious than the citizens of Turkey. These results may indeed mean that, faced with post-industrial modernity, Turkish citizens tend to further identify with Islam, or take refuge in religion to preserve their identity. Again, Islam emerges as the most important determinant of identity for lower middle and lower class Turkish citizens anywhere in the world.

25 Ersin Kalaycioglu (2007) "Religiosity and Protest Behaviour: The Case of Turkey in Comparative Perspective," *Journal of Southern Europe and the Balkans* 9(3), December: 283–91. However, we should take note of the fact that some form of radical and even fanatical violence of Salafi Islam exists in Turkey. Al Qaeda were able to launch four attacks on two synagogues, the HSBC bank headquarters, and the British General Consulate building in 2003. In summer 2008, attacks on the US Consulate General building and in the Güngören district of Istanbul were linked with Al Qaeda by the political authorities in Turkey. In the last two decades, violence was used by the Turkish Hizbullah and various other groups as a means of propaganda for Islamism in Turkey. The police and gendarmerie have been battling these groups with some success in the country under the former left–right coalition governments, as well as the AKP government. We should also add that such fringe groups bent upon conducting terror in the name of Islam do not seem to receive much popular sympathy in the country. Nevertheless, some communities have treated the perpetrators of violent Salafism with sympathy on the grounds that they had exemplary lifestyles as Islamists. Some people have argued in the media that they had known the Salafist terrorists as devout Muslims, and even respected their depth of theological knowledge. It was their veneer of Islamic credentials that seem to have earned the Salafists the sympathy and even popularity among traditional–conservative communities in Istanbul, where they staged many of their acts of terror. Participation in the Afghan, Chechen, Iraqi, and other wars against the Soviets and later the US invasions seemed to have produced the Salafi groups and communities in Turkey, and they seem to possess a capability of perpetrating terror of various sorts against the secular political system of the country, which they consider to be evil per se, and connected with the imperialist, Christian West as well. Finally, we should note the fact that, although such a Salafist threat always exists, the Salafists are highly marginal to mainstream Turkish political parties and organizations in Turkey. Terror and violence have been shunned by a huge majority of even the conservative, pious, Sunni Muslim communities of the country. The pious Sunni Muslims seem to be content with gaining representation in the government party organization and beyond through conventional channels of participation, and do not seem to believe that violence and terror cater to their interests. That seems to be the main reason why we observe that, as the religiosity of the masses increases, their protest potential decreases. On the relationship between

political Islam and violence in Turkey, see also Menderes Çınar and Burhanettin Duran (2008) "The Specific Evolution of Contemporary Political Islam in Turkey and its 'Difference'" in Umit Cizre, ed., *Secular and Islamic Politics in Turkey: The Making of the Justice and Development Party.* London and New York: Routledge: 17–40.
26 Ali Carkoglu ve Binnaz Toprak, *Türkiye'de Din, Toplum ve Siyaset*, op. cit.: 17.
27 Ibid.
28 Binnaz Toprak (2005) "Islam and Democracy in Turkey," *Turkish Studies* 6(2), June: 170.
29 For an analysis of *"türban and tesettür"* in Turkish politics, see Ersin Kalaycioglu (2005) "The Mystery of the *Türban*: Participation or Revolt?" *Turkish Studies* 6(2), June: 233–51.
30 The Turkish press reported that Foreign Minister Ali Babacan argued in a speech he delivered at the European Parliament on May 28, 2008 that it is the Muslim majority who fail to live according to their religious beliefs (see *Hurriyet* daily of May 29, 2008 or http://arama.hurriyet.com.tr/arsivnews.aspx?id=9045167).
31 On April 23, 2006, the speaker of the Grand National Assembly, Mr. Bulent Arinç, argued that the republican principle of laicism be re-interpreted according to the needs and changes that have taken place in Turkish society. He further criticized that the current interpretation and implementation of laicism was non-democratic (see *Hurriyet* daily on May 24, 2006 or http://arama.hurriyet.com.tr/arsivnews. aspx?id=4302003).
32 Mrs. Hayrunnisa Gül dropped her case against Turkey about a year after her husband became the foreign minister, although not while he served briefly as the prime minister between November 2002 and March 2003. It looked as if the wife of the Turkish prime minister and eventually the foreign minister was suing the very government for violating her rights, while her husband was heading the bureaucracy that was to defend the republic at the ECHR. Eventually, she withdrew her case. The Turkish media and press reported at the time that the decision of Mrs. Gül occurred only after it became apparent to her that the ECHR was about to decide against other similar cases and uphold the decision of the Turkish constitutional court.
33 In the 2006 survey conducted by Ali Carkoglu and Ersin Kalaycioglu, 68 percent from a nationally representative sample of 1846 voting-age respondents declared that those women who don the *türban* or *tesettür* should be permitted to function as state employees.
34 Ersin Kalaycioglu (2005) "The Mystery of the *Türban*: Participation or Revolt?" *Turkish Studies* 6(2), June: 245–46.
35 For a more extensive analysis of the Justice and Development Party in Turkish politics, see Sabri Sayarı (2007) "Towards a New Turkish Party System?", *Turkish Studies* 8(2), June: 201–3; Ersin Kalaycioglu (2007) "Politics of Conservatism in Turkey," *Turkish Studies* 8(2), June: 239–41.
36 Ersin Kalaycioglu (2002) "The Motherland Party: The Challenge of Institutionalization in a Charismatic Leader Party," *Turkish Studies* 3(1), Spring: 41–61.
37 See Ali Çarkoğlu (2007) "The Nature of the Left–Right Self Placement in the Turkish Context," *Turkish Studies* 8(2), June: 256–69; Sabri Sayarı (2007) "Towards a New Turkish Party System?" op. cit.: 201–3 for additional arguments along these lines.
38 Kalaycioglu, *Turkish Dynamics* ... , op. cit.: 72–73.
39 It was under the rule of the AKP that Prime Minister Erdogan and other party spokespersons argued that no regulation for the activities of any person, group, and association was possible for instruction to learn to read and recite the Holy Qur'an in Arabic. Therefore, it was under the reign of the AKP government that Qur'an courses have become relatively non-regulated, yet the IHLs are still under the jurisdiction and regulation of the Ministry of National Education.

11 Conclusion

Nathan J. Brown and Emad El-Din Shahin

It should seem odd to devote an entire volume to something that does not exist—or that can be found at best in very limited or ephemeral forms: democracy in the Middle East. Even exploring the reasons for its weakness in the Middle East would first appear to be an odd way of phrasing the question: why is it that democracy's absence needs to be explained? While democracy has come to have positive normative connotations in a vast array of societies, we cannot ignore its historical rarity as a political form. To inquire into the lack of democracy risks confusing the exception for the rule. Regional political realities make it hard to avoid cynicism when discussing the topic. And the press of recent events in the region seems to vindicate such cynicism.

But the interest in the subject remains strong. Many, including those who were asked by the editors to contribute to this volume, continue to analyze, write, speak, and organize on the subject. The terrain is unpromising to be sure, but we are not alone in exploring it. The promised rewards of democracy in the region are so great that it is difficult to avoid exploring democratic possibilities. And indeed, that is the primary reason for this volume and the motivating force behind many of the contributions. It is not simply the difficulty of the task or the possible rewards that fascinate us (although they do); it is also the degree to which the non-existent (or at best embryonic) democratic institutions and practices have drawn the attention and the energies of so many able people and powerful forces. It is precisely because so many activists and intellectuals in the region—and so many Western policy makers—have focused on democratic possibilities in the region that we are moved to examine it.

The contributors to this volume examine the topic from a wide variety of angles. And while they hardly speak in a single voice—given the diversity in their perspectives, professions, places of origin, and focus, that would be impossible and maybe even undesirable—their essays do allow us to give some coherent answers to a series of questions concerning democracy in the region. In this section, we try to answer four of the most pressing questions that external actors and regional activists have been asking in recent years. First, is the Middle East becoming more democratic? Second, why is democratic change so difficult in the region? Third, can outside powers push the

Middle East toward greater democracy? Finally, is religion a democratizing force or an inhibiting one?

1 Is the Middle East becoming democratic?

In a word, no. But change is occurring, although authors differ on its extent and meaning.

None of the contributors to this volume offers dissent from a bleak view of current realities. But, as we suggested in the introduction, political developments in the region are far more interesting than the simple (if accurate) negative view suggests. The Middle East has been associated for two generations with political turmoil, but in fact the political systems of the region have shown more stagnation than volatility. Yet for the past few years, the solid regimes of the region have found themselves challenged by a variety of voices calling for democratic reform.

The essays contained in this volume suggest that those challenges have had some limited effects. First, and most notably, there has been steadily growing interest in democracy in the region itself. Some authors—such as Walid Kazziha—remind us that the interest is not new and has hardly been sufficient to build democratic structures; others—such as Shlomo Avineri—are not impressed by the strength of democratic currents within the region. But the fact that it is an older idea does not refute the growth of the attraction in recent years, it merely shows that democratic ideas may be more deeply rooted. And while Avineri might be right to compare much of the region unfavorably in this regard with Eastern Europe, it may also be the case that the deep interest in democracy is obscured by the popularity of some other ideas as well that outsiders are unaccustomed to associate with democracy (such as deeply conservative social values and non-secular religio-political arrangements).

Second, the authors, for all their realism, uncover some interesting pockets of liberalization. None is naïve enough to see such pockets as the equivalent of the fall of the Berlin Wall, and indeed, the authors are all very realistic about the limitations of the openings that have taken place. Nevertheless, there are clear signs that gradual, albeit slow, changes are under way. This is manifested by a more critical press; a young generation of bloggers and internet users who disseminate a new culture of reform among peers; evolving advocacy non-governmental organizations (NGOs) increasingly acquiring experience and recognition; and protest–reform groups sharing some vision of reform and attempting to make up for the inadequacy of ineffective party life. Few authors deny the interest in democracy in the region, even though most hasten to point to the difficulties for those who seek to transform democratic dreams into reality.

2 Why is democratic change so difficult in the region?

Because any attempt to replace existing regimes or move them in a democratic direction encounters so many obstacles.

Despite the attraction to democracy and the examples of limited liberal-ization, there is no dissent in this volume from the view that the existing regimes are deeply entrenched and that tentative steps toward liberalization hardly amount to a move toward democratization. What are the obstacles to taking the interest and the limited openings and transforming them into gen-uine democratic change? Here, the authors present different (though not contradictory) views. Some, such as Shadi Hamid, focus on structures; others, such as Emad El-Din Shahin, focus on political agents, and yet others, such as Bassel F. Salloukh, focus on societies. None finds culture an insuperable obstacle, although some, such as Avineri, have doubts at an ideological level. Kazziha moves to political society and the weakness of any organized force able to pursue democratic change.

While they diverge, these explanations share a common feature: they seek to locate the difficulties in a general language rather than one specific to the historical and cultural particularities of the region. In short, the contributions are implicitly comparative (and some, such as Avineri's explicitly so): they seek to present their findings in ways that invite comparisons with other regions rather than in terms accessible only to those with a deep familiarity with the region.

Let us pull some of these strands together in an attempt to synthesize the contributions. What are the obstacles to democratic change in the Arab world?

- Non-democratic incumbent elites who do not believe in the values of democracy over the pace of the democratic process.
- Weak, fragmented, and passive civil society and legalized political parties that have demonstrated a low propensity for resistance and challenging the status quo.
- Very low political participation and public apathy.
- Lack of clarity and agreement over the mechanisms for effecting a democratic transformation.
- External actors who may be part of the problem rather than part of the solution.

And it is precisely to such external actors that we will now turn.

3 Can outside powers push the Middle East toward greater democracy?

Perhaps, but only in some limited ways. And they do not have an impressive record to date.

If many of the obstacles are embedded deeply in social and political structures, ideologies, and leaderships, then they would seem to be difficult to change. And that suggests that any external role to engineer social change, fundamental political change, and ideological change from the outside is necessarily limited and clumsy, and none of the authors here suggests any easy way to do it.

But what is more remarkable is that the contributions here suggest that the outside powers who have spoken about democratization so enthusiastically are uncertain in their own commitment. Salloukh goes so far as to imply that external involvement has damaged the cause of political reform. Whether external involvement is malignant or merely bumbling, none of the authors sees it as a factor that clearly supports democratization.

This skepticism does not come simply from those schooled in a long history of unconstructive external involvement in regional political matters. It also comes from an examination of the design of the policies themselves. Both of the essays that focus primarily on external actors—Brown and Hawthorne on the United States and Youngs on Europe—find that general support for democracy has not led to a clear set of priorities and policies. When policy makers effectively ignore tensions among their various goals, the result is less a set of policies than a collection of decisions that pull in different directions. It is no wonder that those in the region question the external commitment to political reform. In short, external actors are only half-committed to the cause and do not have a clear idea of how to pursue it even when they are sincere. External efforts at democratizing the region might have some positive effects, but they are likely to be marginal and localized—and thus far have probably justly earned the cynicism they provoke in the region.

Why do external actors find themselves far more able to talk about democracy than actually encourage it? Again, let us synthesize what we have learned:

- Whereas existing regimes in Eastern Europe were communists and anti-Western, in the Middle East, many have found ways to make themselves friendly to Western security interests (in cases where they have failed to do so—in Iran, Iraq, and Palestine most notably—there has been far less hesitancy by Western powers in calling for democratic change).
- In the East European context, the opposition was ideologically democratic and pro-Western; in the Middle Eastern context, it is Islamic and unpredictable from a Western standpoint.
- Western states could claim support and pressure from various domestic constituencies in working to topple communist/atheist East European regimes, whereas they are not under the same internal or international pressure to push for democracies that can bring Islamists to power.

Two of these three factors point immediately in the direction of the Islamists, leading to our next question.

4 Is religion a democratizing force or an inhibiting one?

We need to ask less about religion as an abstraction and more about political forces that base themselves on religion. And here we should abandon the search for absolutes.

Azza Karam shows the different aspects of the democracy debate among Islamists, their attempts to contextualize democracy, and views on specific democracy-related issues. They move beyond the dichotomous debate of Islam and democracy by addressing Islamist views about democracy and human rights, explaining the reasons why people vote for Islamists, and discussing the international implications of their ascendancy to power through the ballot box. Karam shows that Islamist movements fall on a spectrum, and many of them are pursuing ideas and principles very similar to those pursued by liberals.

Other authors do not explicitly address the issue of Islamists or do so at most in passing. But the logic of the contributions of many to this volume is clear: if democracy is weak because existing regimes can do what they like and social and political forces cannot organize constituencies to stop them, then those few independent and powerful social movements must be brought into the equation. Democracy in the region will not come over the dead body of Islamists. The biggest challenge for democratic change may be how to harness the social and political power of Islamists in ways that promote healthy political competition rather than repression and violence.

Where to?

We close with some advice. What should scholars, external actors, and Middle Eastern democrats do? Scholars need to broaden their vision; policy makers need to steady their nerves; and democrats need to turn to the people.

When discussing democratic transformation in the Middle East, one is struck by the lack of a systematic comparative approach to the process of transformation in the region. Admittedly, excellent work has been done on authoritarianism, liberalization, or Islam and democracy, but focusing either on the region as a whole or case by case. But comparison among cases is still missing. Also, studies comparing the region or some of its parts with countries in other regions are lacking. The region can offer insights and contribute to the study of democratic transformations and the transition literature, particularly with regard to issues such as the role of external actors in promoting or impeding democratization; the impact of foreign aid on the persistence of authoritarianism; the interconnection between rentier economies and the democracy deficit; the prospects of democratization in states with weak civil societies, marginal political parties, and ineffective parliaments; and the difficulty of promoting democracy in non-consensual societies. Comparisons with idealized versions of Western experiences can provide some inspiration but might prove to be impractical. Democratization in the Middle East generates challenging policy choices for the external actors. Times of transitions are by nature uncertain and unstable, particularly in the short term. They also involve clear risks. The unwillingness of the external actors to undertake such risks and insist on promoting democracy while holding fast to their short-term security interests undermines their credibility. At best, they appear confusingly eclectic in both their values and their policies. Worse, they are perceived as strong backers of authoritarian, non-democratic regimes in the region. Democracy is good to promote when it is in the interests of the external actors, and can be readily undermined when it threatens such interests. It will be difficult to reconcile (at least over the short term) a declaratory position of promoting change and the practical policy of maintaining stability. Some tough choices have to be made, even if the outcome is unpredictable and the possible new players are not to the liking of Western policy makers. Ironically, this precarious choice might provide more stability in the long term.

For the internal promoters of democracy, the challenges are even greater. They seem to be caught between a constituency that might not yet consider democracy as a primary value and ruling regimes that are too entrenched and too difficult to dislodge. It is unfair to place all the blame on Arab societies for their apathy, lack of participation, and withdrawal from politics. So far, most democracy activists have been elitists, with an alienating discourse and unappealing, hesitant political stands. "Liberal" Arab intellectuals need to come up with an "Arab" or indigenous liberal model, which can be posited in terms free from specific Western historical experiences and built on existing social and political realities in their own societies and the dominant belief system of the people. While it is useful to focus on democracy as a "grand end," perhaps at this transitional juncture, it might be necessary to give more intellectual attention to the processes and mechanisms of the transition and making this "end" tenable. Activists, in particular, need to build clear links between democracy and the fulfillment of people's aspirations for development and economic growth, independence, and sovereignty. Considering the gradual, and sometimes reversible, nature of the process of democratization, the internal democracy promoters should take advantage of any existing openings, form a consensus on common aspects of reform, and build strong democratic blocs to offset the power of their respective hegemonic regimes.

Bibliography

Abdel Salam, Sidhamed and Anoush Ehteshami, eds (1996) *Islamic Fundamentalism*. Boulder, CO: Westview Press.

Abu-Nimer, Mohammed (2001) "Conflict Resolution, Culture and Religion: Towards a Training Model of Interreligious Peacebuilding," *Journal of Peace Research*, 38 (6): 685–704.

Ahmad, Eqbal (2001) *Terrorism: Theirs and Ours* (with a foreword by David Barsamian). New York: Seven Stories Press.

Ahmed, Leila (1992) *Women and Gender in Islam: Historical Roots of a Modern Debate*. New Haven and London: Yale University Press.

Alger, Chadwick (2002) "Religion as a Peace Tool," *The Global Review of Ethnopolitics* 1(4), June: 94–109.

Appleby, Scott (1999) *The Ambivalence of the Sacred: Religion, Violence and Reconciliation*. Boston: Rowan and Littlefield.

Armstrong, Karen (2001) *Holy War: The Crusades and their Impact on Today's World*. New York: Anchor Books.

Ayubi, Nazih (1991) *Political Islam: Religion and Politics in the Arab World*. London: Routledge.

Barber, Benjamin R. (1996) *Jihad vs. McWorld: How Globalism and Tribalism Are Reshaping the World*. New York: Ballantine Books.

Belling, Willard A., ed. (1998) *The Middle East: Ten Years After Camp David*. Washington, DC: The Brookings Institution.

Benavides, Gustavo and Martin W. Daly, eds (1989) *Religion and Political Power*. Albany, NY: SUNY Press.

Bergen, Peter (2002) *Holy War, Inc.: Inside the Secret World of Osama Bin Laden*. New York: Simon and Schuster.

Berger, Peter L., ed. (1999) *The Desecularization of the World: Resurgent Religion and World Politics*. Grand Rapids, MI: William B. Eerdmans Publishing Co.

Capan, Ergun, ed. (2004) *Terror and Suicide Attacks: An Islamic Perspective*. Somerset, NJ: The Light, Inc.

Choueiri, Youssef (1990) *Islamic Fundamentalism*. London: Pinter Publishers.

Danforth, John (2006) *Faith and Politics: How the "Moral Values" Debate Divides America and How to Move Forward Together*. New York: The Penguin Group.

Davis, G. Scott, ed. (1996) *Religion and Justice in the War Over Bosnia*. New York and London: Routledge.

do Ceu Pinto, Maria (1999) *Political Islam and the United States: A Study of U.S. Policy Towards Islamist Movements in the Middle East*. Reading: Garnet Publishing.

Eck, Diana L. (2001) *A New Religious America: How a "Christian Country" Has Become the World's Most Religiously Diverse Nation.* San Francisco: Harper.

Efrat, Moshe and Jacob Bercovitch, eds (1991) *Superpowers and Client States in the Middle East: The Imbalance of Influence.* London: Routledge.

Eickelman, Dale F. and James Piscatori (1996) *Muslim Politics.* Princeton: Princeton University Press.

El-Said, Sabah (1993) *Between Pragmatism and Ideology: The Muslim Brotherhood in Jordan 1989–94.* Washington, DC: The Washington Institute for Near East Policy.

Emerson, Steven (2002) *American Jihad: The Terrorists Living Among Us.* New York: The Free Press.

Esposito, John (1992) *The Islamic Threat: Myth or Reality?* Oxford: Oxford University Press.

Fox, Jonathan (2001) "Religion as an Overlooked Element in International Relations," *International Studies Review* 3(3): 53–74.

Fuller, Graham (1991) *Islamic Fundamentalism in the Northern Tier Countries.* Santa Monica, CA: Rand.

Ghanayem, Ishaq and Alden Voth (1984) *The Kissinger Legacy: American Middle East Policy.* New York: Praeger.

Ghorayeb, Amal (2000) *Hizbullah.* London: Pluto Press.

Gopin, Mark (2000) *Between Eden and Armageddon: The Future of World Religions, Violence and Peacemaking.* Oxford: Oxford University Press.

Guazzone, Laura, ed. (1995) *The Islamist Dilemma: The Political Role of Islamist Movements in the Contemporary Arab World.* Reading, UK: Ithaca Press.

Gunaratne, Rohan (2002/2003) *Inside Al Qaeda: Global Network of Terror.* New York: Berkley Books.

Hal, John, Philip Schuyler, and Sylvaine Trinh, eds (2000) *Apocalypse Observed: Religious Movements and Violence in North America, Europe, and Japan.* London: Routledge.

Halliday, Fred (1995) *Islam and the Myth of Confrontation: Religion and Politics in the Middle East.* London: I.B. Tauris.

Heikal, Mohammed (1996) *Secret Channels: The Inside Story of Arab–Israeli Peace Negotiations.* London: HarperCollins.

Hoffman, Bruce (1990) *Recent Trends and Future Prospects of Iranian Sponsored International Terrorism.* Santa Monica, CA: Rand.

Hourani, Hani, Taleb Awad, Hamed Dabbas, and Sa'eda Kilani (1993) *Islamic Action Front Party.* Amman: Al-Urden Al-Jadid Research Center.

Hunter, Shireen (1995) "The Rise of Islamist Movements and the Western Response: Clash of Civilizations or Clash of Interests?" in Laura Guazzone, ed., *The Islamist Dilemma: The Political Role of Islamist Movements in the Contemporary Arab World.* Reading, UK: Ithaca Press, pp. 316–50.

——ed. (1988) *The Politics of Islamic Revivalism: Diversity and Unity.* Bloomington, IN: Indiana University Press.

Huntington, Samuel (1993) "The Clash of Civilizations?" *Foreign Affairs* 72(3), Summer: 19–23.

Indyk, Martin (1992) "The Implications for U.S. Policy" in Yehudah Mirsky and Ellen Rice, eds, *Islam and the U.S. Challenges for the Nineties.* Washington, DC: The Washington Institute for Near East Policy, pp. 49–51.

Institute for National Strategic Studies (1995) *Strategic Assessment 1995: U.S. Security Challenges in Transition.* Washington, DC: National Defense University Press.

Johansen, Robert (1997) "Radical Islam and Nonviolence: A Case Study of Religious Empowerment and Constraint Among Pashtuns," *Journal of Conflict Resolution* 34 (1): 53–72.

Johnson, Chalmers (2000) *Blowback: The Costs and Consequences of American Empire*. New York: Henry Holt and Company.

Johnston, Douglas and Cynthia Sampson, eds (1994) *Religion: The Missing Dimension of Statecraft*. New York/Oxford: Oxford University Press.

Karam, Azza, ed. (2004) *Transnational Political Islam: Religion, Ideology and Power*. London: Pluto Press.

——(2000) "Islamisms: Globalisation, Religion and Power" in Ronaldo Munck and Purnaka L. de Silva, eds, *Postmodern Insurgencies: Political Violence, Identity Formation and Peacemaking in Comparative Perspective*. London and New York: Macmillan and St. Martin's Press.

——(1998) *Women, Islamisms and the State: Contemporary Feminisms in Egypt*. London: Macmillan.

Kramer, Martin, ed. (1997) *The Islamism Debate*. Tel Aviv: The Moshe Dayan Center for Middle Eastern and Islamic Studies.

Lebor, Adam (1997) *A Heart Turned East: Among the Muslims of Europe and America*. London: Warner Books.

Lewis, B. (2001) *What Went Wrong? Western Impact and Middle Eastern Response*. New York: Oxford University Press.

Lynch, Marc (2007) "Brothers in Arms," *Foreign Policy* September/October: 70–74.

Mirsky, Yehudah and Ellen Rice, eds (1992) *Islam and the U.S. Challenges for the Nineties*. Washington, DC: The Washington Institute for Near East Policy.

Nielsen, Jorgen (1992) *Muslims in Western Europe*. Edinburgh: Edinburgh University Press.

Norris, Pippa and Ronald Inglehart (2004) *Sacred and Secular: Religion and Politics Worldwide*. Cambridge: Cambridge University Press.

Phillips, James (1992) "Rethinking U.S. Policy in the Middle East," *The Heritage Foundation Backgrounder* 891, 10 April: 1–18.

Quandt, William B. (1998) "Domestic Influences on United States Foreign Policy in the Middle East; The View from Washington" in Willard A. Belling, ed., *The Middle East: Ten Years After Camp David*. Washington, DC: The Brookings Institution, pp. 386–412.

Rashid, Ahmed (2000) *Taliban: Militant Islam, Oil, and Fundamentalism in Central Asia*. London: I.B. Tauris.

Robertson, R. (1992) *Globalization*. London: Sage.

Roy, Olivier (1995) *Afghanistan: From Holy War to Civil War*. Princeton, NJ: Princeton University Press.

——(1994) *The Failure of Political Islam*. London: I.B. Tauris.

——(1990) *Islam and Resistance in Afghanistan*, 2nd edn. Cambridge: Cambridge University Press.

Rubenstein, Richard L., ed. (1987) *Spirit Matters: The Worldwide Impact of Religion on Contemporary Politics*. New York: Paragon House Publishers.

Rubin, Barry (1993) *Radical Middle East States and U.S. Policy*. Washington, DC: The Washington Institute for Near East Policy.

Samuel, Terrence (2002) "The Peak of Political Power" in *US News and World Report*, December 23, 2002.

Sayyid, Bobby (1997) *A Fundamental Fear: Eurocentrism and the Emergence of Islamism*. London: Zed Books.

Scahill, Jeremy (2007) *Blackwater: The Rise of the World's Most Powerful Mercenary Army*. New York: Nation Books.

Schoenbaum, David (1993) *The United States and the State of Israel*. Oxford: Oxford University Press.

Smith, Christian, ed. (1996) *Disruptive Religion: The Force of Faith in Social Movement Activism*. London and New York: Routledge.

Stork, Joe (1975) *Middle East Oil and Energy Crisis*. New York: Monthly Review Press.

Taheri, Emir (1988) *Nest of Spies: America's Journey to Disaster in Iran*. London: Hutchinson.

Telham, Shibli (1990) *Power and Leadership in International Bargaining: The Path to the Camp David Accords*. New York: Columbia University Press.

The BBC Reports: On America, Its Allies and Enemies, and the Counterattack on Terrorism (with an introduction by Harold Evans). Woodstock and New York: The Overlook Press, 2001.

Tillman, Seth (1982) *The United States in the Middle East. Interests and Obstacles*. Bloomington, IN: Indiana University Press.

Vertovec, S. and C. Peach, eds (1997) *Islam in Europe: The Politics of Islam and Community*. London: Macmillan.

Victor, Barbara (2003) *Army of Roses: Inside the World of Palestinian Women Suicide Bombers*. Emmaus, PA: Rodale Inc.

Waters, Malcolm (1995) *Globalization*. London and New York: Routledge.

Wilner, John, and Dan Bloementhal, eds (1995) *America and the Middle East: An Enduring Role in a Changing World*. Washington, DC: The Washington Institute for Near East Policy.

Newspapers and magazines

The Guardian Weekly
The New York Times
Al-Ahram (Arabic)
Al-Ahram Weekly
Al-Hayat (Arabic)
Foreign Policy
The Economist
Le Monde Diplomatique
US News and World Report

Suggested further reading

Ajami, Fouad (1998) *The Dream Palace of the Arabs: A Generation's Odyssey*. New York: Pantheon Books.

Avineri, Shlomo (1992) "The Return to History," *The Brookings Review* Spring.

Banac, Ivo, ed. (1993) *Eastern European Revolution*. New York: Macmillan.

Carothers, Thomas (2004) *Critical Mission: Essay on Democracy Promotion*. Washington, DC: Carnegie Endowment for International Peace.

Diamond, Larry and Marc E. Plattner (1994) *Nationalism, Ethnic Conflict and Democracy*. Baltimore/London: The Johns Hopkins University Press.

Fukuyama, Francis (1992) *The End of History and the Last Man*. New York: The Free Press.

Garber, Larry and Bjornlund, Eric (1996) *The New Democratic Frontiers*. Washington, DC: National Democratic Institute.

Germek, Bronislaw et al. (1998) "Peaceful Transitions to Democracy," *Cardozo Law Review* 19(6), July: 1891–1985.

Glenny, Misha (1993) *The Rebirth of History—Eastern Europe in the Age of Democracy*. London: Penguin Books.

Lewis, Bernard (2002) *What Went Wrong?* New York: Oxford University Press.

Linz, Juan and Stepan, Alfred (1996) *Problems of Democratic Transformation and Consolidation*. Baltimore: The Johns Hopkins University Press.

Matynia, Elżbieta, ed. (1996) *Grappling with Democracy*. New York and Prague: Sociologicke Nakladatelstvi.

Ottaway, Marina S. (2005) *Uncharted Journey: Promoting Democracy in the Middle East*. Washington, DC: Carnegie Endowment for International Peace.

Index